HIKE THROUGH THE BIBLE

AN IN-DEPTH EXPLORATION

COLIN S. SMITH

MOODY PUBLISHERS
CHICAGO

This material began as a series of sermons, preached at The Orchard Evangelical Free Church in 2000 and 2001. These were published by Moody in 2002 as a four-volume series, Unlocking the Bible Story. The content was then made available in a shortened form at openthebible.org with some chapters dropped and others added. After further revisions, it is now being published under the title *Hike Through the Bible*. Portions of this book that were previously published by openthebible.org are used by permission.

All emphasis in Scripture has been added.

Published in association with the literary agency of Wolgemuth & Wilson.

Edited by Pam Pugh
Interior design: Puckett Smartt
Cover design: Brittany Schrock
Photo man hiking courtesy of Oziel Gómez/Pexels. All rights reserved.

Library of Congress Cataloging-in-Publication Data

Names: Smith, Colin S., 1958- author
Title: Hike through the Bible : an in-depth exploration / Colin S. Smith.
Description: Chicago : Moody Publishers, [2025] | Includes bibliographical references. | Summary: "Gear up for some trails that will change your life. This 50-session journey helps you navigate through difficult passages of Scripture and takes you down exciting new trails where you'll encounter the Lord in a personal way. Smith leads you on paths where you'll explore the depths of God's Word"-- Provided by publisher.
Identifiers: LCCN 2025022611 (print) | LCCN 2025022612 (ebook) | ISBN 9780802432285 paperback | ISBN 9780802472816 ebook
Subjects: LCSH: Bible--Criticism, interpretation, etc. | God--Biblical teaching | Theological anthropology--Biblical teaching | BISAC: RELIGION / Biblical Studies / General | RELIGION / Biblical Commentary / General
Classification: LCC BS511.3 .S6395 2025 (print) | LCC BS511.3 (ebook) | DDC 220.6/1--dc23/eng/20250801
LC record available at https://lccn.loc.gov/2025022611
LC ebook record available at https://lccn.loc.gov/2025022612

Originally delivered by fleets of horse-drawn wagons, the affordable paperbacks from D. L. Moody's publishing house resourced the church and served everyday people. Now, after more than 125 years of publishing and ministry, Moody Publishers' mission remains the same—even if our delivery systems have changed a bit. For more information on other books (and resources) created from a biblical perspective, go to www.moodypublishers.com or write to:

Moody Publishers
820 N. LaSalle Boulevard
Chicago, IL 60610

1 3 5 7 9 10 8 6 4 2

Printed in the United States of America

For Andrew and David

I have no greater joy than . . .
that my children are walking in the truth.
(3 John 4)

CONTENTS

TRAILHEAD

SUPPOSE YOU HAVE A TICKET to a two-act play, but you arrive late and miss all of act one.

The curtain rises on act two, and the scene is set in a stable. A manger and a newborn child are center stage, with animals nearby. As the scene unfolds, you learn that this is not an ordinary child. Unlike any other character in human history, He is born of a virgin; an angel announces that He is the Son of God and that He will save His people.

In front of you, a wife nudges her husband. "He will be the One who was promised. You wait and see; it will all center around Him. He'll be the answer to the problem."

But since you have just arrived, you don't know what the problem is. And when you hear that He is the Son of God, you don't even know who God is. When you hear that He will save His people, you don't know what they need saving from. You don't know the problem and you don't know the promise, so all you see is a baby lying in a manger, surrounded by a few animals. Having missed act one, you struggle to grasp what this story is about.

Perhaps that describes you. You have more questions than answers. Or perhaps you have been a believer for many years. You know stories from the Bible, but you don't feel that you have a good grasp of the Bible as a whole.

Wherever you are, I'm inviting you to join me on a hike through the Bible story.

There is much to explore along the pathway: You will discover who God is, who you are, what the human problem is, why God sent His Son into the world, what He accomplished, what He offers, and how all of this can change your life forever.

The whole Bible is one story. It begins in a garden, ends in a city, and all the way through points to Jesus Christ. Getting to know Him will help you to make sense of everything else.

Imagine yourself at a theater for the first performance of a new play. The curtain goes up, but the stage is empty. Then the author walks out and introduces himself to the audience, telling you who he is, why he wrote the play, and what it is about. The author does not present an argument for his own existence, but simply introduces himself and begins to speak about his work.

1

LIFE

GENESIS 1–2

The Bible begins with God walking onto the stage and introducing Himself: "In the beginning, God created the heavens and the earth" (Genesis 1:1). The Author wants you to know that what you are about to see is entirely His work.

The Creator has the rights of an owner. We live in a world of trademarks and patents. If I say "Just do it," you will immediately think about Nike's iconic slogan. A slogan is owned by its creators, who always have the rights of ownership—and God owns all He has made.

If your life were an accident, only a result of indifferent natural processes, you would be a free agent, accountable to no one but yourself. But if you were created, your Creator would have full rights of ownership over your life.

One or the other of these things must be true: Either you are an accident of history and therefore completely at liberty to do whatever you please with your life, or you are a created being and your Creator has absolute rights of ownership over your life.

God introduces Himself as your Creator and therefore your owner. You are not your own. Your life is a trust given to you from God. That means you are not worthless. You are not the product of random chance. God has a purpose for you, and as you get to know God your Creator, you'll begin to discover it!

The Image of God

Then God said, "Let us make man in our image" (Genesis 1:26). "Man" is used as a generic term here; it includes male and female. We are specifically told, "God created man in his own image . . . male and female he created them" (1:27). Notice the plural "us" in 1:26. It is a fascinating hint about the nature of God to be revealed more fully later.

After five days of creation, the crowning moment has come. It is almost as if God has a conversation with Himself: "Let's do it! Let Us make man in Our image." An image is a reflection, and so God is telling us that He made us in such a way that we would be able to reflect something of His own nature and glory.

The image of God is what distinguishes people from animals. Animals were made *by* God, but none of them were made *like* God. That is why no man or woman should ever be treated like an animal or behave like an animal. Men and women who believe they are simply developed animals have missed the most fundamental thing that God says about them. We are made in the image of God!

The Kiss of Life

Men and women are made in the image of God, but we must always remember we are not God. God made the first man from the dust of the ground, so we should not be surprised if there are similarities to the animals at a biological level. But there is more to human life than chemistry or biology.

"The Lord God formed the man of dust from the ground and breathed into his nostrils the breath of life, and the man became a living creature" (Genesis 2:7). God formed a body that lay lifeless on the ground. Then God breathed His own breath into the body. He gave man the kiss of life, and the body became a living, self-conscious being.

God is always doing what He did that day: "[God] gives to all mankind life and breath and everything" (Acts 17:25). God sustains you one breath at a time, and you are absolutely dependent on Him. If you can grasp these twin truths—that you are made in God's image and that you are dependent on Him—you will discover a great dignity and, at the same time, a profound humility.

God gave Adam four special gifts that made his life wonderfully rich—a place, a purpose, a partner, and most of all, the gift of God's presence.

Taking a Walk with God

God is Spirit. That means He is invisible to the human eye. Yet right at the beginning of the Bible we read about God relating to Adam and Eve in such a way that they could see Him, hear Him, and enjoy Him. "They heard the sound of the LORD God walking in the garden in the cool of the day" (Genesis 3:8).

The Old Testament has many examples of God appearing in visible form. We call these theophanies. Later in the Bible story, we will see that God became a man, so it should not seem strange that in the Old Testament He would appear in a visible form.

These appearances show us the intense desire in the heart of God to have fellowship with us. It is almost as if the Son of God could not wait to come. He burst out of heaven, entering human time and space, and walked with the first man and woman in the garden.

What that would have been like! God was interested in what Adam had done in the day, and He was listening to whatever was on Eve's mind. That's the kind of relationship God wants you to enjoy with Him.

As we'll see in the next chapter, this fellowship between God and man was broken, and it has remained so throughout the generations of human history. But Jesus Christ came into the world to restore that broken relationship and to make it possible for us to walk with God again.

We cannot see God, but when we come to Him with faith and in the name of Jesus Christ, His presence is as real as it was when He appeared in visible form to Adam. Think about that next time you pray.

A Place Called Home

We don't know precisely where Eden was located, but the important things to grasp are that it was a real place and that God put the man and the woman there: "The LORD God planted a garden in Eden, in the east, and there he put the man whom he had formed" (Genesis 2:8).

God created a place where Adam and Eve would know and enjoy His blessing, and He does the same thing for us. He has determined the exact places for all of us to live (see Acts 17:26). Try to envision God walking with you into your home, your workplace, or your church and saying, "This is the place I have prepared for you." You are not where you are by accident. When you know, as Adam did, that God has set you where you are, you will have stability in the most difficult times.

There's Work to Be Done

God, who "called the light Day" and "the darkness . . . Night" (Genesis 1:5), invited Adam to participate in His work of naming things: "Now out of the ground the LORD God had formed every beast of the field and every bird of the heavens and brought them to the man to see what he would call them. And whatever the man called every living creature, that was its name" (Genesis 2:19).

Right from the beginning Adam was occupied with work: "The LORD God took the man and put him in the garden of Eden to work it and keep it" (2:15). Work existed before sin entered the world, and it will continue after sin has been cleared out. Sin has introduced frustration into our work, but the first thing to say about work is that it is a good gift from God.

God has work for you to do, and you will find it helpful to think about how your work reflects the work of God. God brings order out of chaos. When you clean out a closet, bring order to a home, or organize a business, you are reflecting God's work. God creates what is beautiful. If you paint, draw, or design, you are reflecting God's work. God protects, and everyone who guards the safety of others reflects His work. God provides, and all who play any part in building homes or in growing, transporting, selling, or cooking reflect God's work. Think about how your work reflects God's work, and you will find great joy in knowing that this is the work He has given you to do.

God took a personal interest in Adam's daily work by bringing the animals to him (2:19). Adam was God's fellow worker. God worked with him and through him, and it was in this way that God's purpose for the world was advanced. God is interested in your work and wants to be involved in it. That's something to consider when you're in front of the computer, on the shop floor, at school, or stirring something on the stove.

A Marriage Made in Heaven

"The LORD God said, 'It is not good that the man should be alone; I will make him a helper fit for him' . . . And the rib that the LORD God had taken from the man he made into a woman and brought her to the man" (Genesis 2:18, 22).

Once again the Lord appeared to Adam, and said, "Adam, I have someone I want you to meet." Adam's jaw must have dropped wide open. He certainly seemed pretty pleased! He said, "This at last is bone of my bones and flesh of my flesh" (2:23).

Notice, the Lord Himself brought the two together. The first wedding service was conducted by almighty God. Try to picture it in your mind: The Lord God takes her hand and puts it into his hand, and says, "Here is the partner I have made for you. Help each other, and love each other well."

We will see in the next chapter that this marriage had more than its fair share of troubles. But whatever their problems, Adam and Eve knew that they had been joined together by God.

There will be times in every marriage when a husband and wife need to come back to this. Marriage is the joining of one man and one woman by God. As the Scripture says, "Therefore a man shall leave his father and his mother and hold fast to his wife, and they shall become one flesh" (2:24).

If you are married, try to picture God taking your hand and the hand of your spouse and joining them together. As He does this, God says, "Go through life together, love each other, and forgive each other." This is what God did for Eve and Adam, and if you are married, this is what God has done for you. Knowing that God has joined you and your spouse together will help you weather the toughest storms.

If you are looking for a marriage partner, remember that God brought Eve and Adam together. The pressure of trying to find the right person can be intense, but you can trust God to bring the right person to you, or to bring you to the right person. I am not suggesting that you should be passive, but you have no need to panic. You can trust the Lord with every area of your life.

TRAIL MARKERS

God wants you to know that He is the Owner of all things. He made you in His image and you have unique dignity and worth.

At the beginning of human history, God made it possible for our first parents to know Him and enjoy Him. He brought the man and his wife together. He led them to their home and gave them their work. He provided all that they needed, and He shared in their life. What God did for them, He continues to do for us today. The only difference is that we don't see Him do it. We walk by faith and not by sight (2 Corinthians 5:7).

1. What is your reaction to the creation account — that God created you and therefore you belong to Him? Doubt? Fear? Comfort? Something else?

2. Do you think it matters whether you were intentionally created by God or the product of random chance? Why or why not?

3. What do you think the Bible means when it says that God made us "in his own image" (Genesis 1:27)?

4. Would you like to experience walking with God as Adam and Eve did in the garden of Eden? Why or why not?

5. What would it mean to you to know for sure that your home, job/school, or spouse is a gift to you from God Himself?

To memorize:

So God created man in his own image, in the image of God he created him; male and female he created them. (Genesis 1:27)

Adam enjoyed the companionship of his wife and the company of God. His work was fulfilling. His whole life was one of blessing and joy. But soon Adam found himself struggling to make a life in a very different world. The man and the woman were outside the place where God had blessed them — with no way back. They experienced pain, fear, and guilt, and they no longer saw God. Something had gone terribly wrong. Genesis 3 tells us the story.

2

CURSE

GENESIS 3

The Bible never gives us a full explanation of the origin of evil, but it does indicate that the devil was an angel who became inflated with pride and tried to usurp the position of God (Isaiah 14:12–14).

Satan's rebellion led to his being excluded from the presence of God and cast down to the earth. So right from the beginning of the human story there was an enemy bent on destroying the work of God.

This enemy, known most commonly as Satan, the devil, or "the father of lies" (John 8:44), attempted to recruit the human race into his rebellion. And his first aim was to introduce the man and the woman to the experience of evil.

Understanding Our Opponent's Strategies

A good coach will study an opponent's plays, so that he or she can plan an effective defense. Satan used his best plays in the garden, and once you learn these plays you will be able to defend against them.

The First Strategy: Confusion

Satan's first play is to pose a question: "Did God actually say, 'You shall not eat of any tree in the garden'?" (Genesis 3:1). God had given one simple instruction, and Satan's first action was to question it. By questioning what God said, Satan made it easier for the man and the woman to disregard the Lord's command.

Whenever Satan tempts you to sin, his first strategy will be to create confusion. He will try to lower your defenses by suggesting that maybe a sin you want to commit is not really forbidden by God, or at least that the Bible is not clear about the matter.

The Second Strategy: Presumption

God had made it clear that sin would result in death (2:17), but Satan suggested to the woman that the consequences of sin had been greatly exaggerated: "You will not surely die" (3:4).

Satan wanted the woman to presume on the grace of God. "After all, God loves you," he was saying, "so how could He allow anything bad to happen to you?" When Satan tempts you to sin, he will lower your defenses by suggesting that you can do this and get away with it.

The Third Strategy: Ambition

Adam and Eve were made in the image of God, but Satan suggested that they could progress further: "Your eyes will be opened, and you will be like God, knowing good and evil" (3:5).

This is one of the enemy's most subtle strategies. He loves to suggest that we should take the place of God. He appeals to our pride when he suggests that we do not need God to tell us what is good and what is evil. His message is still the same: "You can be your own god. You can decide what is right for yourself!"

The Knowledge of Evil

God's first law was, like all His commandments, a wonderful expression of His love: "You may surely eat of every tree of the garden, but of the tree of the knowledge of good and evil you shall not eat" (2:16–17).

All that Adam knew was good, and when God told Adam not to eat from "the tree of the knowledge of good *and evil*," it was for his protection. "Adam, you already know about good, but you also need to understand that there is another reality in the universe called evil. I don't want you to ever experience it, so don't eat from this tree!" But Adam and Eve felt that they would like to have this knowledge of evil, and we have all lived with it ever since.

Excluded from Paradise

Evil has no place in the presence of God, so God banished Adam and Eve and placed angels called cherubim at the entrance to the garden, barring the way to the tree of life (3:23–24).

Adam and Eve were outside the place of God's blessing. Their perfect marriage became strained, and their work became frustrating. They experienced pain, fear, and loss. And death was a terrible reality they could no longer avoid. Worst of all, they were alienated from God and alone in the world. Paradise was lost and there was no way back.

After God drove the man and the woman out, He "placed the cherubim and a flaming sword that turned every way to guard the way to the tree of life" (3:24). The flaming sword flashing back and forth speaks of the judgment of God. Getting around it was impossible. This sight must have been terrifying for Adam and Eve.

So here is the Bible's diagnosis of the human condition: We have a knowledge of evil, and we are excluded from the presence of God. We can't get free from this knowledge of evil, and we can't get back into God's paradise. That is the diagnosis, so what is the prescription?

Hope That Began with a Curse

Hope began on the day that Eve and Adam sinned, and it began with a curse! God said to the serpent, "Cursed are you" (3:14).

A curse is an "utterance of deity, consigning a person or thing to destruction."[1] So when God cursed the serpent, He was announcing that evil would not stand. Satan would not have the last word. Adam and Eve must have been overjoyed at hearing this news.

We can thank God for His curse on evil. Without the curse, we would be stuck with the knowledge of evil forever. But this curse opens the door of hope for us. If God did not consign evil to destruction, who else could? Throughout human history we have tried and failed. Our news continues to be dominated by violence and abuse. We can't get free from it. But God said to Satan, "cursed are you." And from that moment on, our enemy was consigned to ultimate destruction.

1. Concise Oxford Dictionary, 6th ed.

Then God pronounced a second curse. Turning to the man, He said, "Cursed . . ." and Adam must have held his breath. God had cursed the serpent, and now He was looking straight at Adam as He spoke that dreadful word. Adam must have thought that He was going to be utterly destroyed. But he was in for a surprise. Instead of saying to Adam, "Cursed are you," God said, "Cursed is the *ground* because of you" (3:17).

Here we discover one of the most important things that we need to know about God. He announces that He will destroy evil, but at the same time He deflects the curse so that it falls on the ground and not on the man or the woman directly, creating room for them to be reconciled to God.

God is just, and the curse must go somewhere. So at the right time, God sent His Son and directed the curse of our sin onto Him. This is why Jesus died on the cross. "Christ redeemed us from the curse of the law by becoming a curse for us" (Galatians 3:13).

One day the effect of Christ's triumph will transform the whole planet. By diverting the curse to the ground, God has subjected the creation to frustration, but He has also promised that "the creation itself will be set free from its bondage to corruption and obtain the freedom of the glory of the children of God" (Romans 8:21).

The Ongoing Battle

Then the Lord God said to the serpent, "I will put enmity between you and the woman, and between your offspring and her offspring; he shall bruise your head, and you shall bruise his heel" (Genesis 3:15).

"Enmity" sums up the relentless battle against evil that has gone on through the generations of human history. We are always trying to get rid of evil, but we simply can't get beyond frustration, pain, disease, and death. We are stuck with the knowledge of evil. But God promises that a deliverer will come and engage in a great struggle against the evil one. He will inflict a fatal blow by stamping on the head of the enemy, and in the process, the enemy will bite the heel that crushed him.

Say you're standing on the head of a venomous snake. It bites you and inflicts a wound, but then your wounded foot bears down on the snake and brings its destruction. In the same way, through His death, Jesus inflicted a deadly wound on the enemy and opened the way for men and women to be delivered from his power (see Colossians 2:15).

Christ came from heaven, not only to overcome the power of evil, but also to open a way back into paradise for us. Picture yourself standing outside the paradise of God, looking back at the cherubim and the flaming sword of judgment. As you look, someone comes out of the presence of God and stands with you. Then He turns and advances toward the flaming sword. You cringe as you watch. The flaming sword is flashing back and forth, and you can see what will happen to Him when He gets there. But He keeps walking forward, steadily, relentlessly.

The sword strikes Him and kills Him. It breaks His body, but in breaking His body, the sword itself is broken and lies shattered on the ground. That's what happened when Jesus died. The judgment that keeps us out of God's presence struck Him. It was spent and exhausted on Him. The sword of God's judgment broke itself on Him, and so the way back into God's blessing is wide open for all who will come.[2]

TRAIL MARKERS

We can only begin to make sense of our world when we understand that we live with the knowledge of evil and are excluded from the paradise of God. But God has not abandoned us. He sent His Son into our ongoing battle with evil. Through His death on the cross, He broke the power of the enemy and opened a new and living way into the presence and blessing of God.

1. If everything God created was good, what is the Bible's explanation of why the world is as it is today?

2. Where have you seen one of Satan's strategies (confusion, presumption, or ambition) at work in your own life?

---

2. I owe this imagery to a sermon by Martyn Lloyd-Jones, published in *The Gospel in Genesis: From Fig Leaves to Faith* (Crossway, 2009).

3. Think about one of the curses God pronounced on the day Adam and Eve sinned. What does this tell you about God?

4. How do you see people battling against evil around you? What do you believe about how a person can fight against evil?

5. What has God done to open a way for us to come back into His presence and blessing?

To memorize:

"I will put enmity between you and the woman, and between your
offspring and her offspring;
he shall bruise your head, and you shall bruise his heel." (Genesis 3:15)

In the last chapter, we saw how the knowledge of evil changed everything. Paradise was lost. The man and the woman experienced difficulty in their work and dysfunction in their marriage. They were dislocated from their home, and they were at a distance from God. The knowledge of evil spread. But God would not allow it to prevail.

3

SALVATION

GENESIS 6

Everything you need to know for life flows from two convictions: You need to know who God is, and who you are. Get these right, and you will have a firm foundation for life. Get them wrong, and you will soon be adrift.

These truths are foundational to a biblical worldview. A worldview is a set of core beliefs that will determine how we think and how we live. People choose very different lifestyles because they operate on different core convictions about who God is and who they are.

If you believe that your life is an accident, that it belongs to you, and that good gifts come by chance, your life will revolve around discovering and being true to yourself. But if you believe that God created you, and that every good gift comes from His hand, your deepest joy will be to know Him and to obey Him.

If you believe that when you die you will simply cease to exist, it will be natural for you to feel that your purpose on earth is to find fulfillment. But if you come to believe that after your short life in this world you will meet the God who made you, your first priority will be to prepare for that day.

These are two entirely different worldviews, and they cannot both be right. Your convictions are like a rudder on a boat that will control the direction you take in life, and convictions formed in your heart today will determine where you will be tomorrow.

Same Start, Different Directions

From the beginning, the human family has been divided in its response to God. Adam and Eve had two children, and the world's first brothers chose different paths. Abel sought God, but Cain resisted God and his anger spilled over onto his brother. In the end, Cain killed Abel and became the world's first murderer.

Cain's actions isolated him from God and from his family, but God showed him great kindness. Cain's achievements were impressive. He built a city, and his offspring made significant contributions to music, art, and culture. But without God there was a continued restlessness in his life.

After the death of Abel, God gave another son to Adam and Eve. His name was Seth, and the focus of the Bible story is on his line.

Amazing Grace

All the way through the Bible we find God reaching out to save people by grace, through faith, and in Christ. The pattern is established right at the beginning in the story of Noah: "Noah found favor [or grace] in the eyes of the LORD" (Genesis 6:8).

God showed kindness to Noah, first, by warning him that judgment was coming, and second, by telling him what he needed to do in order to be saved from it: "Make yourself an ark of gopher wood" (6:14).

The warnings of judgment in the Bible are not the angry outbursts of a vindictive God; they are the gracious call of a loving God, who is saying, "I must destroy evil, and I will. But I don't want to destroy you, and here is how you can escape."

Faith in Action

God told Noah to prepare for an unprecedented flood. In the same way, God tells us to prepare for something that has not happened yet. Jesus Christ will come to judge the living and the dead.

Faith believes what God has said and shows itself in action. The evidence of Noah's faith was that he built an ark. He believed what God told him, and he acted on it. "Faith apart from works is dead" (James 2:26). True faith is a living tree bursting with the fruit of obedience.

Jesus used the story of Noah to draw a comparison in Matthew 24:37–39:

> "For as were the days of Noah, so will be the coming of the Son of Man. For as in those days before the flood they were eating and drinking, marrying and giving in marriage, until the day when Noah entered the ark, and they were unaware until the flood came and swept them all away, so will be the coming of the Son of Man."

Eating, drinking, and marrying are all good gifts from God, but if we enjoy these things and give no thought to the coming judgment, our joy will be short-lived. Noah's great priority was to be ready for the day of judgment. And the only way to be ready was to believe what God had said and to do what He had commanded.

God told Noah to get into the ark a full seven days before the rain began (Genesis 7:1–7). Loading the ark when there was not a drop of rain falling was an act of faith. There was no obvious reason for getting in there except for the word of God. Noah must have felt rather foolish.

But then the rain came, and along with it, springs of water came up from the earth (7:11). The ship built in the desert rose, and Noah and his family were lifted up by the water and saved from the judgment of God.

Christ, the Ark

The flood was a judgment that will never be repeated (see Genesis 9:8–16). But God warns us about another more terrible judgment to come. Just as God provided the ark for Noah, He has provided a way for us to be saved from the final judgment through Jesus Christ.

All who were inside the ark were safe. All who were outside the ark were destroyed. God has provided an ark for us, and Jesus Christ is that ark!

God spoke through Noah's preaching, telling the people of his day that there was an ark they could come into and be saved (2 Peter 2:5). In the same way, God points us to Christ and tells us that we can be saved if we will come to Him.

The apostle Paul describes Christians as being "in Christ" (e.g., Romans 8:1). Just as Noah was in the ark, so you can be in Christ. When the day of judgment comes, those who are in Christ will be carried safely through the judgment of God and brought into a glorious new world.

This ark is open to all who will come. Jesus said, "Whoever comes to me I will never cast out" (John 6:37). The people of Noah's time had an open door of opportunity. An ark was built, and the whole community could have been saved. But outside of Noah's family, there was not a single person who believed his warning.

Get Out of the Rain

One day, some years ago, I was sitting in my study in London writing a sermon for the coming Sunday. The rain was pouring down outside—a real London soaker! A couple was walking up the street. The rain had obviously caught them by surprise, because neither of them had a raincoat or an umbrella. They stood under a tree that was at the edge of our property. It was winter, and the tree was absolutely bare, so it gave them no shelter whatsoever.

I grabbed a coat and went out to them. "You'll get soaked out here," I said. "Why don't you come into the house?" They looked at me, and in true polite English style said, "No, thank you very much, we are quite all right out here."

"But you are getting soaked!" I said. "You can come in and be dry."

Nothing I said could persuade them, and in the meantime I was getting soaked myself. I left the door to the house open and told them that if they wanted to come in, they were more than welcome. But they remained outside.

That sudden rainstorm is a good picture of the judgment of God. If you stand outside, the rain will fall on you directly, and you will be overwhelmed by it. But if you are in the house, the downpour will fall on the roof, and because you are inside, it will not touch you.

Jesus Christ is the house God has provided for you—the ark that shelters you from the storm of God's judgment. When Jesus died on the cross, the judgment of God for sin fell on Him, and God invites us to come to Him as our shelter. If you are in Christ, God's judgment will not fall on you, because it has already fallen on Him: "There is therefore now no condemnation for those who are in Christ Jesus" (Romans 8:1).

Here's the question: Are you in Christ? Have you put your trust in Him as your Savior and Lord? Why would you stand outside when the door is open for you to come in?

TRAIL MARKERS

Grace, faith, and salvation in Christ are not new ideas that emerge in the New Testament. The Bible is one story. God is gracious. He always has been and always will be. The ark helps us to understand what it means to be in Christ. Just as Noah and his family were brought safely through the judgment of God because they were in the ark, so we will be brought safely through the final judgment if we are in Christ.

Pause for Prayer

Father, I believe You are the Creator and that You have absolute rights over my life. I recognize that I have a knowledge of evil and that I am excluded from paradise. I believe Your Word about judgment to come, and I recognize that apart from You I have no other hope.

Thank You that in Your grace You sent the Lord Jesus Christ. I believe in Him today. I put my whole trust in Him. I call upon Him to be my Savior. Save me through Jesus Christ. Amen.

1. On a scale of 1 (not at all) to 10 (perfectly), how well do you think you know God? How well do you think you know yourself?

2. How did God show grace/kindness to Noah? What is your reaction when you hear God's warning of a coming judgment? How much thought have you given to it?

3. How did Noah demonstrate faith? How do you demonstrate faith?

4. How is Jesus like the ark? Why do you think so many people fail to come in?

5. In your own words, describe what you think it means to be *in* Christ?

To memorize:

I am not ashamed of the gospel, for it is the power of God for salvation to everyone who believes, to the Jew first and also to the Greek. (Romans 1:16)

The early chapters of Genesis chart the growing power of sin in the world. This knowledge of evil that seemed so attractive at the beginning turned out to be a destroying power and a bitter enemy. Adam and Eve's sin attached itself to them, and when Cain, the world's first baby, was born, it was already attached to him.

4

JUDGMENT

GENESIS 11

Just one more push and he was out. And a moment later the noise began as the world's first baby announced his arrival on the scene. His mother had no midwife. She only had her husband to help her, and he didn't have the faintest idea of what to do. Neither did she; but somehow in the mercy of God, they both got through. And now she could hold their little son, Cain, in her arms.

Eve must have seen the blessing of God in the birth of her child. After all, God said that it would be through the offspring of the woman that the head of the serpent would be bruised. Perhaps as she looked into her son's eyes she pondered how he might reverse the tide of evil and restore them to paradise.

If those were her thoughts, she must have been very disappointed, because the baby into whose seemingly innocent eyes she stared turned out to be the world's first murderer. Far from being the one who would deliver the family from evil, Cain was the one who introduced new depths of evil to the world and new depths of pain to his parents' hearts.

Genesis 4 describes how Cain became an angry young man. An impulse to fight against God was already inside him, and seeing his brother enjoy the blessing of God made his anger even worse. Cain told his brother, "Let's go out to the field." The two of them went out, and while they were there alone, "Cain rose up against his brother Abel and killed him" (Genesis 4:8). Evil had reached a new depth, and violence erupted for the first time.

It's natural for us to think that if we provide a loving environment for our children, give them a good education, and bring them to church, the result will be godly kids. But, as the world's first parents discovered, it's not always like that. When Adam and Eve finally grasped that evil was a growing power, they began to call on the name of the Lord (4:26). That was the first prayer. Maybe you will discover the reality of prayer in your pain also.

In the generations that followed, sin became rampant. Man's wickedness on earth became great, and "every intention of the thoughts of his heart was only evil continually" (Genesis 6:5). The world "was filled with violence" (6:11). In a short time we fell from one act of disobedience in the garden to a tide of violence that swept across the earth. Far from telling us that human nature gets better (as our culture likes to believe), the Bible tells us that we become worse as we move away from God.

God Cuts Back Sin

God sent a flood to restrain the pervasive power of evil. This flood was a devastating judgment in which God cut the entire human population back to just one family of eight people who were saved through the ark (Genesis 7:23).

Noah had a wonderful opportunity as he emerged from the ark into a new beginning, in a new environment, with no old scores to settle and no enemies to fight. But Noah carried the seeds of sin into the new world with him. Before long, he was drunk, and the seeds of cynicism were growing in one of his children (9:20–23).

When Karen and I lived in London, we spent sixteen years battling bindweed, a fast-growing, vinelike weed that wound its way round our roses. The bindweed was deeply rooted in the clay soil of our garden and, having attached itself to the roots of our plants, it was impossible to remove. The best we could do was to cut it back and try to keep it under control.

Sin is like that. When you choose to violate one of God's commands, you plant a living seed and it will grow. The devil tells you that experience will broaden your horizons, but the reality is that sin will set up terrible battles in your soul.

God tells us to flee from evil (Psalm 37:27). Get as far from it as you possibly can because it is a growing power. Don't set yourself up for wounds, scars, and battles that may be with you for years.

Maybe you're thinking, "I wish I had thought about that years ago, because I've done some things that have formed habits in my life and now they're battles within my soul." That's a great response. You are being honest about the weeds you've allowed to grow, and you don't want them to take over your life. Now is the time for you to fight back, and you can do that through the strength that God gives you (Philippians 4:13).

God will not allow the bindweed to take over His garden, so He cuts it back. If God did not exercise judgment in this way, sin would destroy everything good. So God keeps cutting it back. Adam and Eve disobeyed God, so God checked the progress of their sin by excluding them from the garden. Cain became the first murderer, so God separated him from his family. In the time of Noah, evil multiplied, so God cut it back through the flood. But sin kept growing, and it was not long before a community of people at Babel found a new way to express their defiance toward God.

Confusion on the Twenty-Second Floor

In the course of time, a new technology was developed that opened up a world of possibilities. Bricks paved the way for a magnificent project: "Come, let us build ourselves a city and a tower with its top in the heavens, and let us make a name for ourselves, lest we be dispersed over the face of the whole earth" (Genesis 11:4).

The problem with this building was not its height but its purpose, which was to proclaim human greatness. Men wanted to make a name for themselves and to provide for their own security. Once again, we were grasping at the throne of God.

God watched the building of man's city and allowed it to proceed to a certain point, but then He cut it back. The Lord said, "Behold, they are one people, and they have all one language, and this is only the beginning of what they will do. And nothing that they propose to do will now be impossible for them. Come, let us go down and there confuse their language, so that they may not understand one another's speech" (11:6–7).

Imagine that for the last two months you have been working alongside the same man on the twenty-second floor of the tower of Babel. One day when you arrive and greet him, he responds with incomprehensible sounds. *What is wrong with this guy*? You soon discover that the rest of the crew seem to be talking gibberish as well, and you wonder if this is some kind of joke.

Eventually, to your relief, you find someone else on the building site who speaks just like you. So you say to him, "The rest of these folks are mad. Let's get out of here." The two of you find others who talk like you, and together you move off to start a new community where everyone will speak the same language.

God cut man's rebellion back by confusing human language, and in this way, "the LORD dispersed them over the face of all the earth" (11:9). Babel was abandoned by little groups of families going off in every direction with the seeds of future conflict already sown in their hearts. Ironically, the fragmentation men tried to avoid was the very thing God caused to happen, and He did it in order to restrain the advance of evil.

Room for God's Grace

When God cuts back sin, He always creates room for His grace. Adam and Eve were excluded from the garden, but God promised a deliverer. Cain murdered his brother, but God gave another son, Seth, who began a new line of hope. The flood destroyed all human life, but God saved Noah and his family in the ark. So when God brought His judgment at the tower of Babel, we are left wondering how His grace will take the initiative.

Later in the Bible story, we read about the day of Pentecost when God reversed Babel (Acts 2). God's Spirit was poured out on those who believed in Jesus, and they found themselves speaking spontaneously in languages they had never learned, so that people from all over the world could hear and understand the good news of Jesus in their own language (Acts 2:5–8, 11).

Do you see the contrast? At Babel, the tongues were a judgment from God leading to confusion and people being scattered. At Pentecost, the tongues were a blessing from God leading to understanding and people being gathered together.

The story of God gathering His people culminates in the last book of the Bible, where we find a vast crowd of people from every tribe and nation and language (Revelation 7:9) united as one, as they worship Christ who redeemed them and brought them together: "Salvation belongs to our God who sits on the throne, and to the Lamb" (7:10).

TRAIL MARKERS

God divided mankind into different linguistic groups in order to put a brake on man's growing rebellion. The brake has been remarkably effective. Throughout human history there have been multiple attempts to bring the nations together, though success has been limited and short-lived.

But God is bringing people from all nations together through Jesus Christ. In heaven all the barriers that have divided people throughout history—race, class, and language—will be completely removed, and God calls His people to begin expressing that unity now in His church.

1. What do you think about the common sentiment in our culture today that people are generally good? How does this square with the early chapters of Genesis?

2. Where have you seen the reality of the power of sin in your own life?

3. Can you think of a time when you may have personally experienced God cutting back sin in your life?

4. React to this: "When God cuts back sin, He always creates room for His grace."

5. Have you ever thought about why we have multiple languages in the world today?

To memorize:

Making known to us the mystery of his will, according to his purpose, which he set forth in Christ as a plan for the fullness of time, to unite all things in him, things in heaven and things on earth. (Ephesians 1:9–10)

From the beginning, the Bible is a story of hope. When sin entered the world, God promised that it would not stand. God would send a deliverer, an offspring of the woman who would bruise the head of the serpent. The story of how God fulfilled His promise begins in Genesis 12.

5

PROMISE

GENESIS 12

God appeared to Abraham, just as He had appeared to Adam and Eve in the garden (Acts 7:2). He said, "I will bless you and make your name great, so that you will be a blessing. . . . In you all the families of the earth shall be blessed" (Genesis 12:2–3). So the promise to Abraham is a promise for us. This is why, from Genesis 12 on, the Bible story follows the line and family of Abraham.

God's Promise Is a Gift of Grace

God promised that Abraham's descendants would be a blessed people: "I will make of you a great nation, and I will bless you" (12:2), and that through them God's blessing would come to all people: "In you all the families of the earth shall be blessed" (12:3).

That's the Bible story in a nutshell. It's all about how God steps into this fallen world, to gather a blessed people and to make them a blessing to others. That's why at the end of the story we see the joy of a great company of people from every tribe and nation gathered in the presence of God (Revelation 7:9).

But there was a problem: Abraham had no children. He was seventy-five years old, and Sarah was just ten years behind him, so both of them were eligible for social security and well past the hope of having children. Only God could bring the promise about. The promised blessing came from God and depended on God. It was a gift of grace.

God's Promise Is Received by Faith

Years passed without any sign of a baby arriving. But Abraham "believed the LORD, and he counted it to him as righteousness (Genesis 15:6). This is one of the most important verses in the Old Testament because it tells us how we can come into a right relationship with God.

The Bible does not say that God counted Abraham righteous because he obeyed or because he prayed. Abraham was counted righteous because he believed. So what did Abraham believe that led to God counting him as righteous?

The Bible is one story given to us by God, and what is hard to understand in one place is often explained in another. We interpret Scripture in the light of Scripture.

Roll the Bible story forward to the time of Jesus, and you find our Lord in a conversation about Abraham: "Your father Abraham rejoiced that he would see my day. He saw it and was glad" (John 8:56).

Two thousand years before Jesus was born, Abraham was given a glimpse of Jesus Christ. He understood that God would give him a descendant through whom God's promise to bless the world would be fulfilled. This descendant is Jesus, the Son of God, who came into the world through Mary, an offspring of Abraham.

The first book of the Bible tells us how we can be right with God, and it tells us that it is by faith. Abraham was saved in the same way as we are, by believing in the Lord Jesus Christ. He saw the day of Christ from a distance, and he believed.

Though he did not know the name of Jesus or the details of the cross, Abraham looked forward to the coming of Jesus, just as we look back to Him in faith. It is by believing in the Lord Jesus Christ that we are made right with God.

The key question is not simply "Do you have faith?" but "Do you believe in the Lord Jesus Christ?" Do you believe as Abraham did?

How does faith in Jesus make us right with God? Suppose you have a bank account that is in deficit, and a friend decides to help you. He asks you how much you owe. "It's ten thousand dollars," you say.

Your friend agrees to help you, and when his money is deposited into your account, your debt is paid. Your gain is his loss. What is counted to you is counted against him. That's the language here. Abraham "believed the LORD, and he counted it to him as righteousness" (Genesis 15:6).

If Christ is to credit righteousness to us, He must assume a massive debt, and He did this at the cross. All our debt was loaded onto Jesus, and when you believe in Him, the Father will credit the righteousness of Jesus to you.

God's Promise Comes at Unimaginable Cost

"After these things God tested Abraham and said to him, 'Abraham!' And he said, 'Here I am.' He said, 'Take your son, your only son Isaac, whom you love, and go to the land of Moriah, and offer him there as a burnt offering on one of the mountains of which I shall tell you'" (Genesis 22:1–2). You read these verses and you wonder, *What in the world is this all about? Why would God ask Abraham to do this?*

God had promised that His blessing would come to the world through Abraham's offspring, but there was no offspring. Then in a miracle of grace, God gave the offspring. And now God says that the blessed offspring must be given up!

It was through Isaac and his line of descendants, that the deliverer would come into the world. So Isaac had to live; he had to marry and have children. How could the promise possibly be fulfilled if Isaac was sacrificed?

Abraham did not question the need for a sacrifice. This is striking because when God told Abraham about the judgment on Sodom, Abraham stood before the Lord and pleaded for the city to be spared (Genesis 18:22–23). But when God said that there must be a sacrifice, Abraham raised no objection.

Abraham seemed to understand that if God's blessing was to flow to the world, a sacrifice would have to be made. Maybe his conscience told him that. God had said, "walk before me, and be blameless" (Genesis 17:1). Abraham was far from blameless. At one point he had lied about his wife, and at another he had laughed at God's promise. At best, Abraham had only obeyed God in part. He could not hold up his head and say, "I have done all that God told me to do." He was *not* blameless, and neither are we.

So how could God's promise of blessing to the world be fulfilled if Abraham had not fulfilled its conditions? There had to be a sacrifice, and Abraham knew it.

God Provides the Sacrifice

As Abraham climbed the mountain with his son, Isaac said to his father Abraham, "'My father!' And he said, 'Here I am, my son.' He said, 'Behold, the fire and the wood, but where is the lamb for a burnt offering?' Abraham said, 'God will provide for himself the lamb for a burnt offering, my son'" (Genesis 22:7–8).

When they arrived at the top of the mountain, it appeared that Isaac would be the sacrifice. Abraham bound his son and laid him on the altar. Isaac would have been a young man at the time, so forget any artistic impression you may have seen of a young child lying helpless on the altar. Isaac carried the wood on his shoulders (22:6). He was in the prime of life and could easily have overpowered Abraham, who was over a hundred years old, if he had wanted to.

But Isaac didn't do that. He was willing to lay down his life. So what you have here is a father who is willing to give up his son, and a son who is willing to give himself. And they are of one mind in what they are doing in order to bring blessing to the world.

Then at the critical moment, the angel of the Lord called out from heaven: "Do not lay your hand on the boy or do anything to him" (22:12).

Then God provided the sacrifice: "Abraham lifted up his eyes and looked, and behold, behind him was a ram, caught in a thicket by his horns. And Abraham went and took the ram and offered it up as a burnt offering instead of his son" (22:13).

How do you respond to this story? I hope you will recoil in horror. You are meant to read this story and say, "What kind of unimaginable cost is this?!" Then, I hope you will gaze with wonder at the reality to which this story points. God never intended that Abraham should sacrifice Isaac. But this harrowing story of a father ready to give up his son and of a son ready to lay his life down is here to show us what it cost for the promise of God to be fulfilled and for His blessing to come to the world.

God did what Abraham and Isaac could only illustrate. God the Father gave up His Son. God the Son gave Himself freely for us. As Isaac carried the wood on his back, Jesus carried the cross on His shoulders. He became the sacrifice. He took our place in the fire of the judgment of God.

God the Father and God the Son were one in self-giving for you and for me. Which is harder, to lay down your own life or to give up the one you love? God experienced both agonies at the same time. The Father did not spare his own Son but freely gave Him up for us all (Romans 8:32). The Son of God "loved me and gave himself for me" (Galatians 2:20). God's promised blessing came at an unimaginable cost that God Himself bore for us.

TRAIL MARKERS

God's promise to bless the world through Abraham's descendant is fulfilled in Jesus Christ. God the Father was pleased to send His Son into the world, where He carried our sins on the cross and laid down His life as a sacrifice, so that His righteousness might be credited to all who come to Him in faith.

1. Why does the Bible follow the story of Abraham and his line?

2. Abraham "believed the Lord, and he counted it to him as righteousness" (Genesis 15:6). What does this verse tell us?

3. Do you believe as Abraham did? How is your faith similar? How is it different?

4. How does faith make a person right with God?

5. React to this statement: "God has provided the sacrifice for your sins."

To memorize:

"I will bless you and make your name great, so that you will be a blessing . . . and in you all the families of the earth shall be blessed." (Genesis 12:2, 3)

The family God had promised to bless grew. Abraham's son Isaac fathered Jacob, and Jacob had twelve sons, who became the fathers of the twelve tribes of Israel. God's people moved to Egypt because of a famine, and over the next four hundred years they grew from an extended family of seventy to around two million people. As they grew, they were oppressed, but God heard their cry for help and delivered them.

6

BLOOD

EXODUS 12

Racial oppression has been one of the greatest evils of human history, and one of the earliest examples involved God's people. Pharaoh subjected them to forced labor and decreed that all their male babies be thrown into the Nile River (Exodus 1:22).

So when Moses was born, his mother hid him in a basket on the Nile to preserve his life. Pharaoh's daughter found him and, in God's wonderful providence, appointed Moses' mother to nurse him.

Moses grew up in the palace, but when he saw the reality of life in Egypt, he was outraged over the way his people were treated. Taking matters into his own hands, he killed an Egyptian who was abusing one of God's people. When word of this got out, Moses had to run for his life. He ended up in the remote land of Midian, where he married Zipporah and settled down to make a living as a shepherd. Having begun his life in a palace, Moses was now living in obscurity.

God Breaks His Silence

Like any student in a university today, Moses would have grappled with beliefs and philosophies that were very different from the teaching he had received from his mother about the God of Abraham, Isaac, and Jacob. In the palace he would have learned about the Egyptian pantheon—Osiris, Heqet, Apis, Ra, and other gods of Egypt.

It would have been easy for Moses to assume that the God of the Bible was one of many possible options, and that the god you worship is only a reflection of the culture in which you are raised. Five hundred years had passed since God appeared to Abraham, so the great question for Moses was "Who is God?" The story of how he discovered the answer is found in Exodus 3.

The Self-Sustaining Fire

"And the angel of the LORD appeared to him in a flame of fire out of the midst of a bush. He looked, and behold, the bush was burning, yet it was not consumed" (Exodus 3:2). Moses saw a fire resting on a bush, but it did not burn the bush on which it rested. The fire was self-sustaining. Fires go out when they have exhausted the fuel that sustains them. A candle only burns until the wax is gone, and then the flame goes out. But this flame was unlike any other. It sustained its own life. Moses had never seen anything like it.

As Moses drew closer, God spoke to him out of the fire: "I am the God of your father, the God of Abraham, the God of Isaac, and the God of Jacob" (3:6). Then God revealed the name by which He wanted to be known: "I AM WHO I AM" (3:14).

God had revealed Himself to Abraham, Isaac, and Jacob, but He was not dependent on them for His existence. Businesses depend on customers, schools depend on students, and churches depend on members. But God does not depend on believers. God is. He exists by the power of His own being. And because He is, He always will be, whether we believe in Him or not.

The Personal Insult of Reshaping God

God is who He is. He is not whoever we want Him to be. When people say that they don't believe in a God who will judge, or that they can't believe in a God who saves people only through Jesus, what they are really saying is that they do not like the God of the Bible and they have chosen to invent another god more to their liking.

To get a sense of how offensive this is, imagine a man editing a digital picture of his wife, making changes to all the features he dislikes. She is carrying a few extra pounds, so he edits her image. Then, when he has the picture as he wants it, he says to his wife, "This is what I want you to look like!"

That's really offensive! The man's wife might well look him straight in the eye and say, with defiance, "I am who I am. I am not whoever you want me to be." In the same way, it is deeply insulting to God for us to open the Bible, see things about Him that we do not like, and reshape Him into an image more pleasing to us. God is not whoever you want Him to be. He is who He is!

The Point of the Plagues

It is all very well for the God of the Bible to say, "I AM," but how do we know that He is and that the other gods are not? That is the point of the plagues (Exodus 7–12). Pharaoh refused to obey God's command to let God's people go. He did not recognize the authority of God in his life. Perhaps he took the view that he had his own gods and that there was no reason for him to obey the God who had spoken to Moses.

As long as Pharaoh continued to believe that he could worship his own gods, he would never submit to the authority of the one true God. So the living God gave proof of who He is by bringing down the powers behind the gods of Egypt. God said, "On all the gods of Egypt I will execute judgments: I am the LORD" (Genesis 12:12).

Pharaoh worshiped many gods, including Osiris (the god of the Nile), Heqet (the goddess of birth), and Ra (the sun god). The common wisdom was that each of these gods brought particular blessings to Egypt.

Much more was at stake in the plagues than simply a conflict between Moses and Pharaoh. God was essentially saying to Pharaoh, "You worship Osiris, saying that the Nile sustains you, but I will turn the Nile into a lifeless swamp. You worship Heqet, the goddess of birth who is depicted as a frog, but I will give birth to so many frogs that you will wish you had never known her. You worship Ra, saying that the sun will shine on you, but I will turn the sun to darkness. What you have put in My place will become like a plague to you."

The great question at the beginning of the book of Exodus was whether God could rescue His suffering people—and if He could, would He care enough to act? We still ask the same questions when we see suffering around us in the world today. God has answered these questions: "I have surely seen the affliction of my people who are in Egypt and have heard their cry because of their taskmasters. I know their sufferings, and I have come down to deliver them" (Exodus 3:7–8).

Defying the Living God

God commanded Pharaoh to let His people go, but Pharoah refused. So God sent the first plague. More plagues followed, and each time Pharaoh resisted, the cost of his defiance became higher.

Many in our culture feel free to defy God because they do not believe that He will bring judgment. But the plagues demonstrate that God will destroy evil, and when you grasp this, you will begin to see why we need a savior.

A Blood Sacrifice in Egypt

When the final plague came on Egypt, God made a way for His people to be kept safe. Every family was to choose a lamb. They were to keep it for four days and then kill it. The lamb's blood was to be painted on the doorframe of every house. God said, "When I see the blood, I will pass over you" (12:13).

Moses had heard the voice of God. He knew that God had provided one way in which families could be kept safe through this night of terror. The way of deliverance was by the blood of a sacrificed animal.

Picture Moses going from house to house asking, "Are you covered by the blood of the lamb? Is it over your door? The day of judgment is coming, and God has said, 'When I see the blood, I will pass over you.' Take God at His word and obey His command. Paint the blood on the doorframe of your house. Why haven't you done this?"

Notice that God did not say, "If you offer a certain number of prayers, I will pass over you." He did not say, "If you are sincere, I will pass over you." He said, "When I see the blood, I will pass over you."

I expect that when the final plague came, some of the people would have looked up at their doors and wondered: *What will happen? Will that blood really protect us?* All they had to go on was the word of God. Two million people believed and obeyed, and every one of them was kept safe through the judgment of God.

The Lamb of God

The theme of blood runs throughout the Bible story. When Adam and Eve sinned in the garden, "the LORD God made for Adam and for his wife garments of skins" (Genesis 3:21). That means that God killed an animal on the day the first sin was committed.

God told Adam that disobedience would lead to death, and there was a death in the garden that day. Adam's life was spared. An animal died instead. We find the same pattern in the story of Abraham and Isaac. God provided an animal that was killed in Isaac's place. Now, a lamb would be killed for every family in Egypt.

God was teaching the same message to a new generation. He was saying, "You will be saved from judgment through the death of another, and this will involve the shedding of blood. It was like that for Adam and for Abraham, and this is how it will be for you." As we're told in Hebrews 9:22, "without the shedding of blood there is no forgiveness of sins."

Animal sacrifices in the Old Testament pointed forward to the coming of Jesus. When John the Baptist saw Jesus, he said, "Behold, the Lamb of God, who takes away the sin of the world!" (John 1:29). Jesus is the Lamb provided by God so that we will be kept safe through the final judgment when God will destroy all evil.

Fifteen hundred years after the exodus from Egypt, Jesus celebrated the Passover with His disciples. During the meal, He took the cup and said, "This cup that is poured out for you is the new covenant in my blood" (Luke 22:20). Jesus was telling His disciples that just as the blood of the lamb delivered God's people in Egypt, so His own blood would deliver them from the judgment of God.

At the end of the Bible story, we see a great crowd of people standing in the presence of God, filled with joy. Who are these people? They are those who have "washed their robes and made them white in the blood of the Lamb" (Revelation 7:14).

TRAIL MARKERS

Through the animal sacrifices in the Old Testament, God was preparing His people to understand the need for, and the significance of, the sacrifice of Jesus Christ.

"Christ, our Passover lamb, has been sacrificed" (1 Corinthians 5:7). He bore the judgment of God so that it will not fall on us. But as in the Passover, the blood must not only be shed, it must also be applied. There had to be an act of faith and obedience in which God's people applied the blood to the doorframes of their houses, and in the same way it is through faith that the saving power of the blood of Jesus is applied to you.

1. Where do you encounter teachings or philosophies that are different from the teaching of the Bible? How do these teachings impact you?

2. Have you ever wondered if the stories you've heard about God are simply traditions?

3. Have there been times in your life when you've avoided thinking seriously about God?

4. Why did God's judgment "pass over" some houses on the night of the Passover? What was involved in being obedient to God on that day?

5. Why did Jesus die on the cross? How does the blood of Christ get applied to a person's life today?

To memorize:

Without the shedding of blood there is no forgiveness of sins. (Hebrews 9:22)

It must have been a strange feeling for Moses to return to the place where God had spoken to him out of the burning bush. On his first visit, he was surrounded by a flock of sheep. Now he was surrounded by two million people. God had been faithful, and in one of the greatest miracles in the Old Testament, He delivered His people from Egypt and brought them to Mount Sinai, where He gave the Ten Commandments.

7

LAW

EXODUS 19–20

The law of God was never a ladder for unsaved people to climb up to heaven. It was always a pattern of life for God's people who had been saved from judgment by the blood of the Lamb. That's why the Ten Commandments begin with God reminding His people, "I am the LORD your God, who brought you out of the land of Egypt, out of the house of slavery" (Exodus 20:2).

God was not saying, "I'm giving you these commandments so that by keeping them you may become My people." He was saying, "I am giving you these commandments because you already are My people." The commandments are not telling you what you must do to be saved. They are mapping out the life to which God calls you when He saves you by grace, through faith in the Lord Jesus Christ.

A Glimpse of the Glory of God

The Ten Commandments are not an arbitrary set of rules. They are a direct reflection of the character of God.

In the New Testament, sin is defined as falling short of the glory of God and as breaking the law (Romans 3:23; 1 John 3:4). Putting these two together, we may reasonably conclude that the law is an expression of God's glory.

Why should you not commit adultery? Because God is faithful. Why should you not steal? Because God can be trusted. Why should you not lie? Because God speaks the truth. Why should you not covet? Because God is at peace and content in Himself.

When God says, "You shall have no other gods before me" (Exodus 20:3), it is because He is the only God. There is no one else like Him. And when God commands that we rest on one day of the week, it is because He rested from His work on the seventh day.

God's commands were given to His own redeemed people. If you belong to Him, they are for you. God says to you, "You are mine, so model your life on who I am."

A Mirror Reflecting the Love of God

God is love, and the Ten Commandments spell out what a life of love looks like. Our Lord Jesus was asked on one occasion, "Which is the great commandment in the Law?" (Matthew 22:36). Instead of picking one, Jesus wrapped them all together and said, "You shall love the Lord your God with all your heart and with all your soul and with all your mind. This is the greatest and first commandment. And a second is like it: You shall love your neighbor as yourself" (22:37–39).

What does a life of love look like in practice? The Ten Commandments give the answer. The first four commandments tell us what it means to love God.

If you love God,

1. You will have no other gods before Him.
2. You won't make an image of Him. You will love God as He is, not as you would like or imagine Him to be.
3. You will honor God's name, and never use it in vain.
4. You will give God time—time to worship, time to serve, and time to remember that ahead of you is a vast eternity for which you must prepare.

The last six commandments tell us what it means to love your neighbor as yourself.

If you love your neighbor,

5. You will honor your father and mother, the first people God puts in your life.
6. You will revere human life as a sacred gift from God.
7. You will be faithful to your spouse.
8. You will not take advantage of the weakness and vulnerability of others.
9. You will be true to your word.

10. You will rejoice in what God has given to others, rather than coveting these gifts for yourself.

The Ten Commandments are a mirror reflecting the glory of God. God is love, and He calls us to reflect who He is. What that looks like is spelled out in the Ten Commandments.

An X-Ray of the Soul

I remember a visit to the dentist that I'd been putting off for a long time, mainly because I had no pain. The experience was not encouraging.

My dentist took some X-rays and then held them up to the light. "Mmm . . . Oh dear! . . . Nasty. There's a lot of decay underneath these fillings," he said.

"But I have no pain," I insisted. He didn't seem impressed. "You're going to need some pretty major work," he said, "and the sooner, the better."

Many people go through life with no sense of pain over their spiritual condition. They make the false assumption that things are well with them and that, having lived generally respectable lives, they are in good spiritual shape. But God's law is like an X-ray of the soul. It shows us that we are people who find it difficult to let God be God, and that it is natural for us to love ourselves more than other people.

The first reason you need Jesus Christ is not that you'll have a richer, fuller, and more satisfying life. It is that you are a sinner by nature and by practice. The X-ray of God's law shows it.

The law is a good thing, just as X-rays are good, even if they bring us bad news. I didn't like the news at the dentist, but I was grateful to know about the problem before it got worse. If you don't know there's a problem, you won't pursue the remedy.

Jesus made it clear that the commandments go deeper than our actions. They search out the thoughts and intentions of our hearts. "You have heard that it was said, 'You shall not commit adultery.' But I say to you that everyone who looks at a woman with lustful intent has already committed adultery with her in his heart" (Matthew 5:27–28).

A proper understanding of the Ten Commandments will lead you to faith in Jesus Christ (Galatians 3:24). If the law has not yet brought you to Christ, you have missed its greatest purpose. That was the point of Jesus' statement to the

Pharisees: "You search the Scriptures . . . yet you refuse to come to me" (John 5:39–40). They were busy studying the law, but they missed the whole point, which was to show them their need of a Savior.

Laying Track for the Train

The Old Testament story makes it clear that God's people were not able to keep His law. The law tells us what to do, but it doesn't give us the power to do it.

Later in the Bible story, God promised a new covenant in which He would not only tell us what to do but also give us the power to move in that direction: "I will put my Spirit within you, and cause you to walk in my statutes and be careful to obey my rules" (Ezekiel 36:27).

God's law is like track for the train. The track gives direction, but the train won't move forward unless there is power in the engine. And it is the special work of the Holy Spirit to give God's people power to move in the direction that is laid out for us in God's law.

Turning Commands into Promises

There's a great story about a man serving time in prison because he was a thief. Stealing was his way of life, until the long arm of the law caught up with him. During his time in prison, he heard the good news of Jesus Christ and was wonderfully converted.

When the time came for his release, the man knew that he would face a great struggle. Most of his old friends were thieves, and it would not be easy for him to break the pattern of his former way of life.

On the first Sunday of his new freedom, he slipped into a church building. The Ten Commandments were inscribed on a plaque at the front, and his eyes were immediately drawn to the words of the command that seemed to condemn him: "You shall not steal."

That's the last thing that I need, he thought. *I know my weakness. I know my failure, and I know the battle I'm going to have.*

As the service progressed, he kept looking at the plaque. And as he reread the words, they seemed to take on a new meaning. Previously he had read these words in the tone of a condemning command: "You shall not steal!" But now it seemed that God was speaking these same words to him as a liberating promise: "You shall not steal!" The man was a new creation in Christ, and God was promising that the Holy Spirit would make it possible for him to overcome his old way of life.

When you believe in the Lord Jesus Christ, God will give you His Holy Spirit so that you can live a life that is pleasing to Him. His power will make the difference between a struggle in which you are destined for defeat and a battle in which you will have ultimate victory. The law tells you how God wants you to live. Jesus Christ makes this life possible.

TRAIL MARKERS

The law is a mirror that exposes the hidden sins of our lives. Properly understood, it will convict us of our need for a savior and bring us to Christ. And when the Holy Spirit lives in us, the law is no longer a list of impossible demands but a description of new possibilities.

1. How do the Ten Commandments begin? Why were they given? What is the message of the law to us today?

2. Are the Ten Commandments time-bound? Do we need new commandments for today? Why or why not?

3. How might the Ten Commandments challenge a person who is living a generally respectable life?

4. How would a person know if he or she has missed the purpose of God's law?

5. How is the law like a path through a forest? What else does the law need in order to accomplish the work God that intends for it to do in a person's life?

To memorize:

"I will put my Spirit within you, and cause you to walk in my statutes and be careful to obey my rules." (Ezekiel 36:27)

What would it be like to experience an earthquake, a wildfire, and lightning—all at the same time? Absolutely terrifying! That's how it was when God came down to Mount Sinai (Exodus 19:16–20). Moses had gathered the people to meet with God. But feeling the terror of His awesome presence, the people begged Moses, "You speak to us, and we will listen; but do not let God speak to us, lest we die" (20:19).

8

ATONEMENT

EXODUS 32

Moses went up the mountain to meet with God and was gone forty days and forty nights (Exodus 24:18), and by the end of that time, the people were tired of waiting. They gathered around Aaron, the brother of Moses, and said, "Make us gods who shall go before us. As for this Moses . . . we do not know what has become of him" (32:1).

Aaron seemed like the natural choice to be Moses' successor. He already had a recognized ministry, and when God's people approached him, they found him ready to step up and lead.

Aaron's first move was to raise funds for the launch of his new ministry. People donated their jewelry, and from these gifts he shaped a golden calf. Aaron became the sad father of those whose ministry is driven primarily by the question "What do people want?"

Of course, Aaron wanted to claim that what he was doing was well within the bounds of orthodoxy, and so he said, "Tomorrow shall be a feast to the Lord" (32:5). But Aaron's festival was nothing more than an indulgent vehicle of self-expression.

The next day "the people sat down to eat and drink and rose up to play" (32:6). In other words, out came the drinks and off came the clothes. It was a big celebration, but it was worshiping the wrong god.

It is worth pausing to ask what a contemporary news reporter might make of this. After all, the golden calf would make a great subject for a journalist reporting on world religion: "Out here in the Sinai Desert, a remarkable new religious movement has been born," our reporter would begin. "These people have adopted an innovative style of worship marked by creativity and self-expression." Then there would be a couple of interviews with exuberant dancers, who would say that the festival of the golden calf was deeply meaningful to them.

Breaking Up the Party

The people may have thought it was meaningful, but God thought it was abominable. God's people had corrupted themselves by breaking His first commandment. This happened so quickly and so flagrantly that God was ready to wipe these people out and begin again with Moses: "Now therefore let me alone, that my wrath may burn hot against them and I may consume them, in order that I may make a great nation of you" (32:10).

Moses' first task on returning to the people was to confront Aaron: "What did this people do to you that you have brought such a great sin upon them?" (32:21). Had the people subjected Aaron to some horrible torture? In fact, all it took to persuade him to disobey the law of God was public demand. He led them into sin because he was unable to resist the demands of the people.

Aaron attempted to deflect responsibility. He had shaped the gold into an idol "with a graving tool" (32:4), but when Moses challenged his brother, Aaron gave a sanitized version of the story: "I said to them, 'Let any who have gold take it off.' So they gave it to me, and I threw it into the fire, and out came this calf" (32:24). It just happened!

After confronting his brother, Moses called the people to make a decision: "Who is on the LORD's side? Come to me" (32:26). Everyone was given the opportunity to repent, and the overwhelming majority did.[3]

3. Given that there were around two million people in the camp, we may assume that 1,997,000 responded to Moses' appeal and took their stand with him. We know this because there were 3,000 people who refused the invitation, and that day was the last day of their lives (Exodus 32:28).

The Meaning of Atonement

The next day Moses said to the people, "You have sinned a great sin" (32:30). Talk about preaching to the choir! These people already knew they had sinned, and they had repented! So why did Moses get up the next day and say, "You have committed a great sin"? Whatever happened to forgiveness?

Why didn't Moses draw a line under it? Wasn't it his duty to tell them that they were forgiven? These people were sorry. What more did Moses want from them? And isn't it God's duty to forgive us? No. Something else must happen before sins can be forgiven.

At this point in the story, we discover the biblical word *atonement*. Moses told the people, "I will go up to the LORD; perhaps I can make atonement for your sin" (32:30). Atonement is what it takes to put right something that is wrong. Wherever there is an offense, we face the question of atonement. What will it take to put things right?

Being Sorry Won't Do It

Once while I was playing a soccer match in college, the other team made a breakthrough on goal, and I was the last defender. In a desperate lunge, I managed to clear the ball from the goal line.

Unfortunately, the ball sailed toward the college president's study and smashed his window. The president was remarkably kind about it—but he did require that I replace the window and clean up the mess. That was what it took to make it right.

The first thing to grasp about an atonement is that its requirements are always determined by the injured party. Standing there in my muddy shorts beside the broken window, I didn't feel I had a lot of bargaining power! "I'm very sorry," I said. That was good, but it wasn't good enough. Damage had been done, and it had to be repaired. I wanted to say, "I won't do it again," but that wouldn't have helped much either.

"Here is what you need to do," the president said. "Clean up the mess and replace the window." That was the atonement, the price that had to be paid to make things right.

What will it take to right our wrongs against God? Some people think it all boils down to being sorry. They feel that if we are truly repentant and genuinely try to change, things will be right with God. But being sorry for what we have done will not remove the guilt of our sin. We need an atonement.

A Great Leader Can't Do It

Perhaps making atonement was something Moses could do. He knew from the death of the lamb at the Passover that God was prepared to accept a substitute in order to spare the lives of the people. What if Moses could be the substitute?

Moses said to the people, "I will go up to the Lord; perhaps I can make atonement for your sin" (32:30). So there was a volunteer! The greatest spiritual leader in the Old Testament stepped up and said to God, "This people has sinned a great sin. . . . But now, if you will forgive their sin—but if not, please blot me out of your book that you have written" (32:31–32). Moses was ready to lay down his life for the people. And if he had to enter hell to make atonement for them, he was ready to do it.

But God did not accept the offer. Moses had sins of his own, and a man with his own sins is in no position to atone for the sins of others.

Life would go on for these people, but without an atonement, they would forfeit the presence of God (33:3). When the people heard this, they mourned (33:4). What would it take to bring back the presence of God? If being sorry wouldn't do it, and if Moses couldn't do it, what would atone for their sins?

Painstaking Obedience Won't Do It

Perhaps a serious commitment to obeying God's commands would bring back the presence of God. In Exodus 25–30 God gave precise commands for building the tabernacle, and Exodus 36–39 records that God's people obeyed these commands in meticulous detail. God's people did exactly what He told them to do: "The people of Israel did according to all that the Lord had commanded Moses" (39:32).

So a woman is embroidering the curtains for the tabernacle. As she follows God's detailed instructions, she thinks, *If I'm obedient, perhaps God will come back to us.* Over there, a carpenter wishes that he had not grieved the Lord. He wonders, *If my hands can do what God has commanded, perhaps He will bless us again.*

God's people gave themselves to meticulous obedience, but at the end of it all there was still no sign of God's presence returning. They must have wondered what it would take to make things right with God.

A Worthy Sacrifice Will Do It

After several months in which the people had been longing for the presence of God to return, Moses told them how it could happen: "This is the thing that the LORD commanded you to do, that the glory of the LORD may appear to you" (Leviticus 9:6). There must have been a stunned silence as the people waited to hear what he would say next.

Moses then turned to Aaron and said, "Draw near to the altar and offer your sin offering and your burnt offering and make atonement for yourself and for the people" (9:7). God's presence and blessing could only return when atonement was made.

Aaron did as God commanded. The people must have held their breath as they waited to see what would happen: "Moses and Aaron went into the tent of meeting, and when they came out they blessed the people, *and the glory of the LORD appeared to all the people*" (9:23). God was back! "And when all the people saw it, they shouted and fell on their faces" (9:24).

Imagine a couple sitting in their tent, talking about what they just witnessed: "I've never seen anything quite like it," he says. "Who would have figured that shedding the blood of an animal would bring back the presence of God?"

"Yes, it's incredible" she says. "But I don't understand why the sacrifice did it when all those months of being truly sorry, and all those months of painstaking obedience, and even Moses' offer to lay down his life for us made no difference whatsoever. There must be something very powerful about a sacrifice that involves the shedding of blood."

Even at this early stage in the story of the Bible, God was preparing for the coming of Jesus. The whole purpose of the sacrifices in the Old Testament was to shape our thinking so that we would understand why the Son of God had to come into the world. In His death on the cross, Jesus accomplished what the Old Testament sacrifices could only anticipate. Christ made atonement for our sins. He brings back the presence and the blessing of God for all who trust in Him.

TRAIL MARKERS

Maybe you feel that if you are sufficiently sorry for your sins, you will be right with God. Or maybe you feel that if you are obedient to God by attending church and saying your prayers, you can atone for your sins. These things are good, but they are not good enough. It's the sacrifice of Jesus and the shedding of His blood that makes atonement with God. "He is the atoning sacrifice for our sins, and not only for ours but also for the sins of the whole world" (1 John 2:2 NIV).

1. If you had been there when God gave the Ten Commandments, would you have wanted Moses to speak to you rather than hear God's voice directly? Why or why not?

2. Is it God's duty to forgive people?

3. Have you ever thought that being sorry or being obedient would be enough to make things right with God?

4. What is an "atonement"?

5. What is the difference between the animal sacrifices in the Old Testament and Jesus' sacrifice on the cross?

To memorize:

But when Christ had offered for all time a single sacrifice for sins, he sat down at the right hand of God, waiting from that time until his enemies should be made a footstool for his feet. (Hebrews 10:12–13)

God's people discovered that the God who loves them is holy. As sinners, it is not possible for us to get near Him and survive. There must be an atonement, which is what it takes to put right something that is wrong. Atonement for sin is made through a sacrifice, a substitute, a life laid down. In this session, we are going to see how the atonement was accomplished and how it gets applied to us.

9

PRIEST

LEVITICUS 16

If you ever find yourself in a court of law, you will probably want to hire an attorney to present your case. Law courts are intimidating places, and they operate under some complex rules. So you need an attorney to speak on your behalf.

In the Old Testament, the priests did something similar. They represented the people before God and spoke on their behalf. They served in a mobile worship center called the tabernacle. It was separated into different areas by a series of curtains and contained various pieces of symbolic furniture.

At the center of the tabernacle was the Most Holy Place, which was screened off from view by a heavy curtain. Inside was the ark of the covenant, a wooden chest carried on poles, with a lid on top. Rising from the lid were two golden figures of cherubim—angels representing the judgment of God. Between these two figures was an area known as the atonement cover or the mercy seat.

A Five-Act Drama

Once every year on the Day of Atonement, the high priest would go behind the curtain into the Most Holy Place. God Himself would come down, just as He had done on Mount Sinai. He did not make Himself visible, but He appeared in a cloud over the mercy seat and met with the high priest (Leviticus 16:2).

God often teaches us through pictures, and what happened on the Day of Atonement was like a great drama in five acts, each pointing forward to Jesus Christ and helping us understand the significance of His death on the cross.

Act 1: The Priest Appears

If you saw the high priest, you would immediately have known that he was one of the most important people in the land. His magnificent robes displayed the dignity of his office.

But on the Day of Atonement, the high priest discarded his robes and appeared in the streets wearing a simple white cloth, the kind of clothing the lowest servant would wear. People would line the route to view the spectacle of the high priest dressed as a common slave as he made his way toward the tabernacle like a boxer entering the ring.

Act 2: The Priest Prepares

Before the high priest could enter the presence of God to offer a sacrifice for the sins of the people, his first priority was to deal with his own sins. He took the blood of a slaughtered bull into the Most Holy Place and sprinkled it on the mercy seat.

This must have made a powerful impression on the people. The high priest, holding one of the most dignified positions in the land, was saying, "I stand in need of a sacrifice myself." The high priest was recognizing, as every other priest, pastor, or religious leader would always have to admit, "I have sins of my own, and therefore I am in no position to deal with yours."

Act 3: Atonement Is Made

A goat was brought forward and slaughtered. Then the high priest took its blood behind the curtain and sprinkled it on the mercy seat between the two golden figures of the cherubim, which represented God's judgment. Justice was satisfied, and mercy was released when the sacrifice was made.

Just as in the garden God had diverted the curse away from Adam and onto the ground, so now, God allowed the death sentence to be passed on an animal instead of the sinner.

Act 4: Sin Is Confessed

What happened next was the most dramatic part of the whole Day of Atonement.

A second goat was brought forward. God had instructed the high priest to "lay both his hands on the head of the live goat, and confess over it all the iniquities of the people of Israel, and all their transgressions, all their sins" (Leviticus 16:21).

In churches today, during a service of dedication or baptism for an infant, the pastor or priest will hold the child as he says a prayer. This can cause some problems with children, thrust into the hands of a stranger, who understandably do not want to be separated from their parents.

I have often struggled to offer a coherent prayer as a wriggling infant tried desperately to escape my clutches. But such problems are nothing compared to what the high priest had to do here. He had to confess all the sins of Israel while holding on to a live goat!

The high priest identified specific sins in his prayer, and if you were in the crowd, you might have heard a prayer similar to this: "Almighty God, we confess our idolatry. We have loved Your gifts more than we have loved You. We confess our envy. We have seen what You have given to others and have coveted it for ourselves. We also confess our anger. We have been short-tempered and resentful toward others . . ."

Since the high priest had to confess all the sins of the people, this would have been a long prayer. But he prayed in such a way that the people would recognize the sins he confessed as their own. If you had been standing in the crowd, eventually you would have thought, *Yes, that sin is one of mine.*

When the high priest confessed the sins of the people with his hands laid on the head of the goat, an act of transfer took place in which God moved the guilt of these sins onto the goat. "Aaron shall lay both his hands on the head of the live goat, and confess over it all the iniquities of the people of Israel, and all their transgressions, all their sins. And he shall put them on the head of the goat" (16:21). So now you have one guilty goat!

Act 5: Guilt Is Removed

What happened next is a marvelous picture of how God deals with our sins when they have been confessed and their guilt has been transferred. God told the high priest to send the goat away "into the wilderness" (16:21).

Imagine the scene as the goat is led away, between the tents and then outside the camp and into the desert. You watch until the man and the goat are only a dot on the horizon, and then you cannot see them at all.

I cannot envisage a more powerful visual presentation of the gospel. This five-act drama was like a preview showing us what God would do when Jesus Christ came into the world.

From the Preview to the Main Event

Run forward through fifteen hundred years of history and you arrive at the main event, featuring Jesus Christ in the role of the high priest who came to make atonement for our sins. The Old Testament tells us what this would take; the New Testament tells us how this was done.

Act 1: Christ Appears

Jesus Christ is our great High Priest! He is the Son of God, and His glory is far greater than the splendid clothes worn by any other priest. He shared the glory of the Father before the world began. But just as the high priest discarded his magnificent clothing on the Day of Atonement, so Christ laid aside His glory and took the form of a servant. He was wrapped in strips of cloth and laid in a manger.

Act 2: Christ Prepares

Jesus Christ lived a life that is different than any other life that has ever been lived. He did the will of the Father and fulfilled all the work the Father had given him to do. "He committed no sin" (1 Peter 2:22), and so He needed no sacrifice for Himself. Having lived the perfect life Jesus was qualified to achieve what all the other priests could only illustrate.

Act 3: Christ Makes Atonement

After three years of His public ministry, Jesus was arrested and sentenced to be crucified. On the cross, He became the sacrifice for our sins. When His blood was shed, God's justice was satisfied, and God's mercy was released. Our great High Priest made atonement for us and opened a new and living way into the presence of God.

Act 4: We Confess Our Sins

There were two goats on the Day of Atonement. One was sacrificed, and the other was led into the wilderness. Both of these animals help us understand what Christ does for His people. He is the one who sacrificed His life as the atonement for our sins, and He is also the one who takes our guilt away.

This is where you have a part to play in the drama. Just as the high priest laid both hands on the head of the live goat and confessed the sins of the people, God invites you to "lay hold" of Jesus Christ in an act of faith and confess your sins to Him. When you do, your guilt will be taken away.

Act 5: Our Sins Are Removed

When your sins have been laid on Jesus, God promises that He will take them as far from you "as the east is from the west" (Psalm 103:12).

Consider a person who has been struggling with a troubled conscience. Let's call her Sarah. She has made a foolish choice and wonders if God can ever forgive her.

Sarah is in the crowd watching the great drama of the Day of Atonement, but she is struggling with her conscience when a friend comes to talk with her.

"Sarah, think about what you have just seen. What happened when the high priest grabbed that goat by the head?"

"He confessed our sins."

"And did he confess your sin, Sarah?"

"Yes, he did, and I felt so ashamed."

"What happened, Sarah, to the sins he confessed?"

"They were laid on the goat's head."

"And what happened to the goat?" Sarah's friend asks.

"It was taken away."

"How far was it taken, Sarah?"

"Farther than my eyes could see."

Take that picture and apply it to your life. Can you envision your sin being taken so far from you that you can no longer see it, and it can never come back? God is telling you that through Christ's finished work your sin is forgiven and your guilt is removed.

TRAIL MARKERS

The Day of Atonement illustrates how Jesus dealt with sin. When His blood was shed, mercy was released for sinners. The atonement is applied to our sins in particular when by faith we lay hold of Christ, believing in Him and confessing our sins to Him. God will remove the guilt of your sin as you lay hold of Jesus by faith. And when God removes your guilt, you can look up to Him with the joy and freedom of someone who is truly forgiven.

Pause for Prayer

Gracious Father,

Thank You that the Lord Jesus Christ has come into the world to be my High Priest. Thank You that He was willing to lay aside His glory and to be born in a manger. Thank You for His perfect life that qualified Him to make atonement. Thank You that He did this by laying down His life and shedding His blood.

I confess my sins to You . . . [Take time to confess your sins to the Lord.]

Thank You that Christ died for my sins. Help me now enjoy the peace of knowing that You have taken them as far from me as the east is from the west, through Jesus Christ my Lord. Amen.

1. What was the role of the priests in the Old Testament?

2. What did the Day of Atonement point to? What does it help us understand?

3. Why is no priest, pastor, or religious leader in a position to deal with your sins?

4. How was guilt transferred and removed on the Day of Atonement?

5. What is our part to play in the drama?

To memorize:

Aaron shall lay both his hands on the head of the live goat, and confess over it all the iniquities of the people of Israel, and all their transgressions, all their sins. And he shall put them on the head of the goat and send it away into the wilderness. (Leviticus 16:21)

God led His people through the wilderness, going ahead of them in a pillar of cloud and of fire. He provided for them by sending food that they gathered each morning. But when they came close to the land God had promised to give them, they were gripped with fear. Would they exercise faith?

10

COURAGE

NUMBERS 13

Sooner or later you will come to a place where obedience to God seems costly. For the Israelites it was sooner. God told Moses to take a census of all the men in Israel twenty years old or more who were able to serve in the army (Numbers 1:2–3). That tells us what the book of Numbers is about—God was leading His people into warfare. He was preparing them for a military campaign in which they would take possession of the promised land. Costly battles lay before them.

The Lord said to Moses, "Send men to spy out the land of Canaan, which I am giving to the people of Israel" (Numbers 13:1–2). Moses sent out the spies, and they traveled through the land for forty days gathering information. But when they got back, things went terribly wrong. The majority took the view that the land couldn't be conquered, and as their pessimism spread, the people lost heart.

Numbers is the story of an unnecessary detour. God's people were faced with an open door of opportunity, but they held back when they should have pressed forward. The story warns us about the long-term consequences of cowardly choices, and if we can understand where these people went wrong, it will help us to avoid repeating their mistakes.

Complaining People

Instead of pressing forward in obedience to God's command, the people complained about their hardships, their food, and their leaders (see Numbers 11:1, 4–6; 12:1). God determined that the grumblers and complainers would not enter the land (Numbers 14:22–23). So they spent the next thirty-eight years in the desert until that whole generation died and their children took their place.

Complaining is always dangerous. The tragedy of this story is that when great things lay ahead, the people God had blessed became dissatisfied with what He had given. It is hard to make good decisions when you have a bad attitude. If you are dissatisfied with what God has given to you, be careful! That's where God's people were when they made the mistake of a lifetime.

A critical spirit drained strength from their spiritual convictions. It sapped the passion of their commitment to the Lord and left them spiritually limp, so that when the moment of decision came, they moved in the wrong direction. Critical, complaining people usually end up choosing the wrong path. Behind a bad decision you will usually find a bad attitude.

Complacent Leaders

Moses sent out twelve leaders (Numbers 13:3) to gather information that would help him form a plan to accomplish the will of God. But after their forty-day trip behind enemy lines, they returned to tell Moses that the will of God was not practical! "We are not able to go up against the people, for they are stronger than we are" (13:31). The spies were saying, "We can't do it. The land is already occupied. This project is beyond us."

Notice that they made no reference to God in their report. These leaders had stopped asking "What does God want us to do?" and focused instead on what seemed manageable. If leaders make that shift, it will be costly for the people of God. And if we lose focus on what God is calling us to do, we will soon find ourselves wandering aimlessly in the desert.

Two of the spies, Joshua and Caleb, presented a minority report focusing on the fact that God was with them. But by the time they were given the opportunity to speak, the people had already made up their minds.

Moses allowed the situation to get out of control. First, the research team reported to the wrong audience. The spies were commissioned by Moses, but they went public with their report. Second, they exceeded their authority. Moses asked for information, but the spies made a recommendation. The result was that the people ended up making a bad decision over an issue that should never have been brought before them in the first place. The question to be decided was not *if* they should go into Canaan, but *how* they should go into Canaan. Complacency and mismanagement brought the whole community to the verge of disaster.

There are some important lessons for us here. If God's people are to advance His purpose, they must be thankful and their leaders must be faithful. They must see beyond the data and trust in God. Here are two critical tests of the health of any church: Is there a grateful and unified spirit among the people? Is there faith among the leaders?

Casting Your Vote for Costly Obedience

It is easy for us to be certain that we would have voted for entering the land of Canaan. But if you knew that following God's command would expose husbands and fathers to the risk of being killed, and women and children to the risk of being taken captive, would you really have been so quick to vote for entering the land (see Deuteronomy 1:39)?

The great irony is that if the parents had chosen the path of costly obedience to the Lord, their children would have grown up in "a land flowing with milk and honey" (Leviticus 20:24). But because the parents prioritized the safety of their children over obedience to God's word, they spent decades wandering in the desert. Obedience always has a cost, but these parents did themselves and their children a great disservice.

God was faithful to His people even in the desert. He provided food for them every day, and He never left them. But this generation of people who had experienced the abundant grace of God contributed nothing to advancing His purpose. Once we see this danger, the great question is "How are we going to avoid being like that?"

Understand Your Calling

First, we must grasp that our calling is to a life of unconditional obedience. The will of God for Israel in the book of Numbers was for the people to enter the land of Canaan. The will of God for us today includes the Great Commandment—"Love the Lord with all your heart . . . [and] love your neighbor as yourself" (Mark 12:29–31)—and the Great Commission of Matthew 28:19: "Go and make disciples of all nations."

It takes courage to love people who may not love you, and it takes courage to share the hope of the gospel with people who may not want to hear. But this is what God calls us to do.

The more God blesses you, the harder it is to live a courageous life. It is easy to get the idea that our comfort is the thing that matters most. But God has not called us to a life of convenience. Christ died for us that we should no longer live for ourselves, and He sends us out as the means by which His will gets done in the world.

Counting the Cost

Second, we must count the cost of an obedient life. When God delivered His people from Egypt, He shielded them from the full cost of their calling by leading them by the way of the wilderness, rather than the direct route that would have taken them through enemy territory. For God said, "Lest the people change their minds when they see war and return to Egypt" (Exodus 13:17). But as time went on, God brought them to a place where obedience was more costly.

When my father took me to an auction, he told me, "If you're going to bid, make sure you know your upper price limit." That's great advice for anyone going to an auction, but it would be a lousy approach to the Christian life.

Jesus won't allow us to set an upper price limit. He said, "If anyone would come after me, let him deny himself and take up his cross and follow me" (Mark 8:34). He doesn't tell us what our cross will be, only that we must be ready to take it up.

As followers of Jesus, we must be willing to say, "My money is Christ's, my time is Christ's, my life is Christ's. There is no upper price limit."

Keep Your Eyes on the Prize

Third, we must look beyond the cost to the great reward that is promised to all who follow Jesus. "Whoever would save his life will lose it, but whoever loses his life for my sake and the gospel's will save it" (Mark 8:35). Following Jesus is always worth it, no matter what it costs.

One day a rich man came to Jesus and asked Him what he had to do to inherit eternal life. Jesus knew that money was strangling the man's spiritual life and that the only way he would ever be free was if he gave his money away. Mark tells us that Jesus, "looking at him, loved him," and said, "Go, sell all that you have and give to the poor . . . and come, follow me" (Mark 10:21). Like God's people on the verge of Canaan, this man struggled with the cost. And he "went away sorrowful" (10:22).

The life of Jesus had a very different outcome. His calling involved extreme suffering and loss (Luke 9:22), but He was ready to pay the price. And the book of Hebrews tells us how He did it: Jesus endured the cross "for the joy that was set before him" (Hebrews 12:2). In other words, when Jesus faced the cross, He looked through it to the joy that was on the other side. He focused on the outcome, and Isaiah tells us that "out of the anguish of his soul he shall see and be satisfied" (Isaiah 53:11).

So here are two stories about different choices and outcomes. One story ends with a man who is sorrowful; the other ends with a man who is satisfied. The difference is in their readiness to obey the will of God without regard for the cost. Sorrowful or satisfied—which of these two words will describe what you feel when you look back on your life?

TRAIL MARKERS

Some generations contribute more to advancing the purpose of God than others. The book of Numbers leads us to expect this. Not all generations serve willingly. Unity among God's people and courage among their leaders will save us from aimless wandering and position us to advance God's purpose in the world.

1. Are you dissatisfied with something God has given (or not given) to you? If you're not sure, think about what you have been complaining about recently.

2. React to the statement: "God calls you to a life of unconditional obedience."

3. Where are you most likely to set an upper price limit with God? Your money? Your time? Your life? Other?

4. What is the prize of the Christian life? How would you know if you had begun to lose sight of it?

5. What do you most need to change if you are to look back on your life and be satisfied rather than sorrowful?

To memorize:

> "If anyone would come after me, let him deny himself and take up his cross and follow me. For whoever would save his life will lose it, but whoever loses his life for my sake and the gospel's will save it." (Mark 8:34–35)

After forty years of wandering in the desert, Moses died and God raised up Joshua as his successor. Joshua was a strong and courageous leader, and he led God's people into the promised land. The book of Judges takes up the story of God's people after they had conquered the land of Canaan.

11

DELIVERER

JUDGES 2

After the generation that had conquered the land of Canaan died, there arose another generation "who did not know the LORD or the work that he had done for Israel" (Judges 2:10). This is one of the saddest verses in the Bible, and it sets the scene for the book of Judges, which tells us what happens when a generation grows up not knowing God.

How could this have happened in one generation? Perhaps it was simply that the parents were busy in a prosperous land. These people had seen God do wonderful things in their own lives, but they clearly neglected the systematic teaching of their children. And within a generation the knowledge of God was lost.

So here in Judges we have a generation that was born in prosperity, fascinated with the search for spiritual meaning, but not knowing the Lord or what He has done.

This crisis in Israel reminds us of our priorities. We are to teach our children who God is and what He has done. These are the essentials, and without this knowledge faith is impossible.

As the apostle Paul puts it, "How are they to believe in him of whom they have never heard?" (Romans 10:14). It only took one generation for the knowledge of God to be lost. But what can be lost in one generation can be restored in another.

Going Around in Circles

The book of Judges records a cycle of events that was repeated many times over a period of several hundred years.

First, people forsook or abandoned the Lord and turned to idols: "The people of Israel did what was evil in the sight of the LORD and served the Baals. And they abandoned the LORD. . . . They went after other gods, from among the gods of the peoples who were around them, and bowed down to them" (Judges 2:11–12).

Second, God became angry and gave His people into the hands of their enemies: "They provoked the LORD to anger. . . . So the anger of the LORD was kindled against Israel, and he gave them over to plunderers, who plundered them" (2:12–14).

Third, the people cried to God for help, and God raised up a military leader, or "judge," to deliver them: "Then the LORD raised up judges, who saved them out of the hand of those who plundered them" (2:16).

Fourth, when the judge died, the people abandoned God and the whole cycle started over again. God's people were going around in circles—idolatry, judgment, crying out to God, deliverance, and then back to idolatry again (2:18–19).

The Attraction of Idols

As you read through the Old Testament, you will keep coming across the theme of idolatry. It may seem rather remote, but the fact that it comes up so often shows that it is important.

Idolatry is attractive because it puts you in a position of control. Suppose you invent a fictional character and call him "Dwayne Bieber," a sort of mixture of Dwayne "The Rock" Johnson and Justin Bieber. You decide that Dwayne will be a pioneer, and you sit down at the computer and begin to write about him. *Dwayne is rugged and muscular. He has a black mustache . . . No, wait!* You press the delete key. *He has a brown mustache.*

You describe Dwayne's encounter with a bear in the Rocky Mountains. But then you need a bit of romance in the story, so you give Dwayne a sensitive side. *Underneath that rough exterior, all his life Dwayne has been looking for true love.*

As you build the story, you are absolutely in control. Dwayne is under your power. You can make him whoever you want him to be, and he will do whatever you want him to do. This is the attraction of idolatry. Instead of worshiping the living God, many people prefer to create a god that suits their own spiritual needs.

Inventing a character is all very well in writing a novel, but try doing this with a real person and you will find yourself in court for libel or defamation of character! Idolatry is powerfully attractive, but it is also deeply offensive.

God responds to our idolatry by saying, "I am who I am. You cannot redefine Me, and if you try to, I will take away My protection and deliver you into the hands of your enemies." If we pursue idols, God will allow us to live with the consequences of our own choices. But thank God that is not the end of the story.

The God Who Delivers

Idols may be attractive because we are the ones who shape them, but they are powerless because they are nothing more than projections of our own imagination. That's why when God's people were overrun by their enemies, they turned back to God and called out to Him for help. God raised up judges. The Spirit of the Lord came upon Othniel, Ehud, Shamgar, Deborah, Barak, Gideon, and Samson, enabling them to deliver God's people.

When the going gets tough, the question becomes very simple: "Is there a God who is able to help you?" When that is the question, the idols are no longer attractive. Redefining God may be convenient, but when you are in a crisis, calling on a figment of your own imagination will be of no help to you.

As you read through the book of Judges, it is clear that while these military leaders achieved remarkable things, they also had significant limitations.

Most of them were seriously lacking in character. Ehud seems like a cowardly assassin (Judges 3:12–23). Gideon was so lacking in faith that he needed multiple confirmations of what God was telling him to do (6:36–40). Jephthah made a disastrous choice that involved sacrificing his daughter (11:30–40). Samson's moral failures are legendary (Judges 14–16). There is no one in this book that you can truly admire. Reading through the book of Judges will leave you thinking, "We need a better deliverer."

The contrast between Jesus and the judges is striking. The judges made their mark by taking the lives of others; Jesus came to give His life for us. The judges addressed the external circumstances of God's people; Jesus focused on the heart.

The achievements of the judges were short-lived; the deliverance Jesus brings lasts forever.

Defining God as you would like Him to be will only lead to your life going around in circles, just as the book of Judges. Jesus came to break that cycle. He is the great deliverer, and He is able to save you from a futile journey in which you never make progress, by bringing you to know who God is and what He has done.

TRAIL MARKERS

Idolatry is redefining God. Across the centuries people have repeatedly chosen to invent their own gods rather than bow before the living God. The gods we create are attractive because we can control them, but they only exist in our minds and are powerless to deliver us from sin, death, and hell. Only God can deliver us, and this is why He sent His Son into the world.

1. What is idolatry?

2. What makes idolatry attractive to some people?

3. How does God respond to idolatry?

4. When do idols tend to lose their appeal?

5. How has Jesus helped you to break a cycle of sin in your life?

To memorize:

> He has delivered us from the domain of darkness and transferred us to the kingdom of his beloved Son, in whom we have redemption, the forgiveness of sins. (Colossians 1:13–14)

The obvious weakness with the judges was that they lacked continuity. Other nations had kings and standing armies and when a king died, his successor was immediately crowned. But God only raised up judges in times of crisis when His people called out to Him, and this meant that the people were dependent on God all the time. Why couldn't Israel have stability and continuity like everyone else?

12

KING

1 SAMUEL 8

If you asked a four-star general to analyze the battles fought by the Israelite army, he would be baffled. God gave His people victory, even when they were hopelessly ill-equipped and outnumbered. Their battles made no military sense at all.

For example, on arriving at the well-fortified city of Jericho, God told Joshua to march around the city seven times blowing trumpets. When God's people did this, the walls of the city fell down—surely one of the most unusual victories in the annals of military history!

Then in the book of Judges, God tells us about Gideon, who raised an army of 32,000 people to fight the Midianites. God said that was too many, and so Gideon reduced the number to three hundred. They entered the camp of the enemy armed only with torches, pitchers, and trumpets, and God caused confusion among the Midianites, who ran off in panic.

Israel's victories were not by might or by power, but by the intervention of the Spirit of God. The Lord repeatedly made it clear that He was the one who led them to victory. But God's people were not satisfied.

The Frustrations of Living by Faith

God was Israel's king. He did everything that a king would do for his people and much more. But God's people did not want to depend on Him alone, or to wait on Him to raise up their leaders. They wanted a system of succession, a flesh-and-blood person to lead them.

Eventually the elders of the community came to Samuel, a judge and a prophet, and asked him to appoint a king (1 Samuel 8:5). This request was not pleasing to God. The Lord said to Samuel, "They have not rejected you, but they have rejected me from being king over them" (8:7). By asking for a king like other nations had, they were turning away from a life of faith in which they depended on the Lord alone. But God let them have their way.

The Significance of Choices

God's people made a poor choice. They knew that their desire for a king was displeasing to God, and Samuel warned them of the consequences: A king would send their sons off to war. He would require them to serve in his fields and in his household. He would call on their daughters to serve in his kitchens. He would seize their land. He would tax their crops and their flocks. "You will cry out because of your king, whom you have chosen for yourselves, but the LORD will not answer you in that day" (8:18).

Samuel could not have given a stronger warning, but God's people were not listening. They said, "No! But there shall be a king over us, that we also may be like all the nations" (18:19–20). Their minds were made up, and so God gave them what they asked for.

Poor choices always lead to painful consequences. But God is sovereign, and that means that no choice, however poor, can put us beyond His grace. We all make bad decisions at some points in our lives, and sometimes we live with ongoing regret. That may be your experience—a frustrating career, a disappointing marriage, or an impulsive decision that leaves you looking back saying, "If only . . ."

The good news is that God can redeem bad decisions. There is no sin that puts you beyond the grace of God and no decision that puts you beyond the help of God.

Leadership Qualifications

God knew that His people would ask for a king and, back in the book of Deuteronomy, He had already given a profile of the person who should lead His people.

First, **the king must be anointed by God**. "You may indeed set a king over you whom the LORD your God will choose" (Deuteronomy 17:15). The New Testament parallel to this is in Acts 6, where the first deacons are appointed, and the church is told to choose men who are filled with the Holy Spirit (Acts 6:3). Christian leaders must have the mark of God's presence in their lives. This is the primary qualification.

Second, **the king must belong to God's people**. "One from among your brothers you shall set as king over you. You may not put a foreigner over you, who is not your brother" (Deuteronomy 17:15). Again in Acts 6, the apostles told the believers to choose leaders from their own number (6:3). God's people should look for leaders who have proved themselves in the local church.

Third, **the king must exercise faith**. "Only he must not acquire many horses for himself or cause the people to return to Egypt in order to acquire many horses" (Deuteronomy 17:16). The king was to model faith. Other nations trusted in chariots and horses, but God's people were to trust in the name of the Lord their God (Psalm 20:7). Again we see this mirrored in the New Testament. When the church appointed the first deacons, they chose Stephen because he was "a man full of faith" (Acts 6:5). Leadership among God's people must always be in the hands of those who trust in the living God.

Fourth, **the king must be loyal**. "He shall not acquire many wives for himself, lest his heart turn away" (Deuteronomy 17:17). The same principle is reflected in the New Testament: the elder must be "the husband of one wife" (1 Timothy 3:2). A Christian leader's loyalty to God will be expressed in his loyalty to his wife.

Fifth, **the king must not be greedy**. "Nor shall he acquire for himself excessive silver and gold" (Deuteronomy 17:17). The leader among God's people must not use his position to feather his own nest. He is the servant of God and of the people. In the New Testament, Peter wrote to pastors and elders, instructing them not to be greedy for money, but eager to serve, not domineering over the flock (1 Peter 5:2–3).

Sixth, **the king must be a student of Scripture**. "When he sits on the throne of his kingdom, he shall write for himself in a book a copy of this law. . . . And it shall be with him, and he shall read in it all the days of his life, that he may learn to fear the LORD his God by keeping all the words of this law and these statutes, and doing them" (Deuteronomy 17:18–19). This meant that the first duty of the king was to write out his own copy of the entire book of Deuteronomy, and then to read it every day! In the same way, deacons must "hold the mystery of the faith with a clear conscience" (1 Timothy 3:9). Leaders among God's people are to study, revere, and obey the Word of God.

Seventh, **the king must be humble**. The king's "heart may not be lifted up above his brothers" (Deuteronomy 17:20). Similarly, pastors and elders are to serve, "not domineering over those in [their] charge, but being examples to the flock" of God (1 Peter 5:3).

This profile for leaders is crucial for pastors, elders, lay leaders, and all who participate in appointing them. It is a profile for students preparing for ministry and for everyone who wants to see God's will get done.

If you want to be used by God, seek the anointing of His Spirit. Be committed to God's people and learn to trust God in all things. Cultivate loyalty in all your commitments—especially in your marriage. Place the pursuit of money on the altar, and determine to receive whatever God gives you gladly. Be crystal clear in your convictions regarding the central truths of the gospel, and feed on the Word of God daily as you walk humbly with your God.

Who Fits the Profile?

Would it surprise you to know that none of the Old Testament kings measured up to God's profile?

Saul, the first king, was self-willed and disobedient. Solomon, the third king, had seven hundred wives. And when he became old, his wives turned his heart toward other gods (1 Kings 11:4). Even David, who is described as "a man after his [God's] own heart" (1 Samuel 13:14), was guilty of adultery and murder! None of Israel's kings came close to fulfilling God's mandate.

God's people waited a thousand years for the king who would get His will done, and then God answered their longing for a flesh-and-blood leader who would deliver them from their enemies. A king was born, and wise men followed a star to worship the "king of the Jews" (Matthew 2:2).

Jesus completely fulfilled God's profile for the king.

1. **He was anointed by God.** At His baptism God announced, "This is my beloved Son, with whom I am well pleased" (Matthew 3:17).

2. **He belonged to God's people,** being born into the line of David.
3. **He exercised faith.** In the garden of Gethsemane Jesus said, "Your will be done" (Matthew 26:42), and in His suffering He entrusted Himself to the Father "who judges justly" (1 Peter 2:23).
4. **He was loyal.** When Satan tempted Him, Jesus refused any alliance with the enemy (Matthew 4:1–11).
5. **He was not greedy.** Jesus told His disciples that He "came not to be served but to serve, and to give his life as a ransom for many" (Mark 10:45).
6. **He was a student of Scripture.** The Word of God filled the mind of Jesus, and people who heard Him were amazed at His understanding.
7. **He was humble.** "Being found in human form, he humbled himself by becoming obedient to the point of death, even death on the cross" (Philippians 2:8).

Jesus fulfilled God's profile for the king, but He was not the king that the people wanted.

The Mocked and Humble King

When Jesus was brought to trial, Pilate asked him: "Are you the King of the Jews?" Jesus replied simply, "You have said so" (Matthew 27:11). Pilate then handed Jesus over to be crucified, and he said to the people, "Behold your King!" (John 19:14).

The Roman soldiers "stripped him and put a scarlet robe on him, and twisting together a crown of thorns, they put it on his head and put a reed in his right hand. And kneeling before him, they mocked him, saying, 'Hail, King of the Jews!'" (Matthew 27:28–29).

The will of God was finally done through this bruised, disfigured, and crucified King. God raised Him to life and gave Him the name that is above every name (Philippians 2:9). Jesus is the "King of kings and Lord of lords" (Revelation 19:16).

If your trust has been broken by a leader who failed you, there is a king you can trust, and His name is Jesus. Christian faith is not about trusting Christian leaders. It is about trusting in the Lord Jesus Christ, and those who trust in Him will never be disappointed (Isaiah 49:23 NIV).

TRAIL MARKERS

Jesus is the King who fulfills all that God requires of any leader. It is through our King that the will of God will be accomplished in our lives and in the world. God calls all who aspire to leadership to submit themselves to Christ the King and follow His example.

1. Why did God's people want a king? Why do you think it was displeasing to God?

2. Have you made a poor choice/bad decision and you sometimes wonder if it has put you beyond the grace/help of God?

3. As you look at the qualifications for leadership among God's people, which one would you need to grow in, in order to be more effective in serving the Lord?

4. Why do you think the people of Jesus' time rejected Him as their leader?

5. Is there an area of your life that needs to be more fully submitted to Christ the King?

To memorize:

Some trust in chariots and some in horses, but we trust in the name of the Lord our God. (Psalm 20:7)

Israel's first king, Saul, achieved great things, but he was not godly and what he achieved did not last. God raised up David, an unknown shepherd, to succeed him. When David defeated Goliath, everyone knew who he was. Saul was jealous of David, and he spent the last years of his life trying to destroy the future. But God's hand was on David, and when Saul died, the way was open to crown the king with a heart for God.

13

THRONE

2 SAMUEL 7

There was immediate resistance to the new king. Some of Saul's loyalists fought to defend their turf, but during the next two years the house of David grew stronger while the house of Saul grew weaker (2 Samuel 3:1) until eventually everyone accepted David as king (5:1–5).

Under David's leadership God's people captured Jerusalem, and when the city was taken, David built his palace and established his center of government there. Then David brought the ark of the covenant, the place where God met with His people, to Jerusalem. The presence of God was at the center of national life.

The nation was united, God's people prospered, and there was peace. David had been more successful than he had ever dreamed, and he felt that it was time to give something back. David was a godly man with a good heart and a great idea.

A King's Plan to Honor God

David didn't feel right about living in a lavish palace while the ark of God was housed in a tent. He had it in mind to build a temple for God, so he called his friend Nathan, who said, "Go, do all that is in your heart, for the LORD is with you" (7:3). But that night God revealed to Nathan that, rather than David building a house for God, God would be the one to build a house for David.

Have you ever been in a situation when you wanted to do something good and God closed the door? You pursued some initiative, but it didn't work out. Or you had a great idea, and someone else ran with it. When God closes the door, you will face the ultimate test of humility.

C. S. Lewis described humility as "a state of mind in which [a person] could design the best cathedral in the world, and know it to be the best, and rejoice in the fact, without being any more (or less) or otherwise glad at having done it than he would be if it had been done by another."[4] True humility means you are more concerned that God is glorified and less concerned about whose name gets on it.

To David's credit, he learned humility. It would not have been surprising if David had lost interest in the temple after God told him that he would not be the one to build it. But David's humility is shown by the fact that he drew up the plans, gathered the materials, and then trusted the task of building the temple to his son (1 Chronicles 28:11–20).

Disappointment and the Door of Promise

When David faced the disappointment of a closed door, God gave him a wonderful promise: "The Lord will make you a house" (2 Samuel 7:11). Then God explained that He was not talking about putting up brick and mortar. He was making a promise about one of David's descendants: "When your days are fulfilled and you lie down with your fathers"—that is, when you are dead—"I will raise up your offspring after you, who shall come from your body, and I will establish his kingdom" (7:12).

God promised that He would raise up a descendant of David. And of this offspring God said, "He shall build a house for my name, and I will establish the throne of his kingdom forever. I will be to him a father, and he shall be to me a son" (7:13–14).

Which son of David would fulfill these promises? How could any king's reign last forever? How could a son of David possibly be the Son of God?

A Promise Deferred

God allowed David's son Solomon to fulfill his dream of building the temple. And when it was dedicated, the cloud of God's glory came down, filling the building

---

4. C. S. Lewis, *The Screwtape Letters* (Macmillan, 1942), 73.

with His presence. But a few hundred years after his death, Solomon's temple was destroyed.

From the time of David onward, the Bible story revolves around the search for a son of David who would build a temple, whose throne would last forever, and who would be the Son of God. The first verse of the New Testament introduces us to Jesus as this promised son: "The book of the genealogy of Jesus Christ, the son of David" (Matthew 1:1).

Luke records the angel's announcement to Mary that God's promise would be fulfilled: "You will conceive in your womb and bear a son, and you shall call his name Jesus. . . . And the Lord God will give to him the throne of his father David" (Luke 1:31–32).

When Jesus began His ministry and people saw His miracles, they were so astonished that they said, "Can this be the Son of David?" (Matthew 12:23). And when, three years later, He entered Jerusalem, they were waving palm branches and shouting, "Hosanna to the Son of David!" (Matthew 21:9).

The Throne That Will Last Forever

When the angel Gabriel announced the birth of Jesus, he said, "The Lord God will give to him the throne of his father David, and he will reign over the house of Jacob forever, and of his kingdom there will be no end" (Luke 1:32–33). But how can any kingdom last forever?

Jesus rose from the dead and He ascended into heaven. Death no longer has power over Him. As King of kings, Jesus is seated at the right hand of the Father, where "he must reign until he has put all his enemies under his feet" (1 Corinthians 15:25).

Jesus Christ will reign forever (Revelation 11:15). And He has promised that His disciples will share in His reign. "The one who conquers," Jesus said, "I will grant him to sit with me on my throne, as I also conquered and sat down with my Father on his throne" (Revelation 3:21).

God had promised that a son of David would build a temple and reign forever, and we have seen how Jesus identified Himself with these great promises. But the most remarkable part of God's promise was that God Himself would be a Father to David's son. How could any son of David be described as the Son of God?

Jesus Christ, the Son of God

God's promise that David's son would be His own Son points us to the greatest miracle in the Bible. Jesus was born to Mary, who was engaged to Joseph, a descendant of David (Matthew 1:16). But Jesus was not born as a result of intercourse between Mary and Joseph (1:25). He was conceived in the womb of the virgin by a creative miracle of God: "The Holy Spirit will come upon you, and the power of the Most High will overshadow you; therefore the child to be born will be called holy—the Son of God" (Luke 1:35). Jesus, the son of David, is the Son of God!

When we think of a son, we usually think of someone who is born twenty or thirty years after his father. But when the Bible tells us that Jesus is the Son of God, it is telling us that He shares the nature of His Father, and it is the nature of God to have no beginning. There never was a time when the Son of God was not with the Father: "In the beginning was the Word, and the Word was with God, and the Word was God" (John 1:1).

How God became a man in Jesus is a mystery, and yet once this truth is grasped, it begins to make sense of everything else. God became a man. The eternal Son took flesh. The One who has always been beside the Father became a son of David, bringing God and us together.

Children of God

God the Father will adopt you into His family when you come to faith in His Son, Jesus: "To all who did receive him, who believed in his name, he gave the right to become children of God" (John 1:12).

If you are struggling with self-worth and significance, let the truth of who Christ is and what He does for His people seep into your heart and mind. Jesus is the Son of God. Faith joins you to Jesus, and through Him are you adopted into the family of God. Your body is now a temple of the Holy Spirit, who lives in you. You are a son or daughter of God, and your destiny is to enjoy Him forever. Take that into your most ordinary day or into your darkest hour. See the honor that God has bestowed upon you and let this lift you up.

TRAIL MARKERS

God's people can be confident about the future because Jesus Christ is on the throne. Through Him we are reconciled to the Father and become members of His family. Christ has many enemies, but they will all be put under His feet (Psalm 110:1). And the destiny of God's people is to enjoy the blessing of His reign and rule forever.

1. Have you ever been in a situation where you wanted to do something good for God, but then it felt like He closed the door? What happened?

2. When God closed the door on your good plans, what did it show you about yourself (especially your humility, or lack of it)?

3. How was God's promise to David fulfilled? What do we learn from this about how God fulfills His promises?

4. In your own words, what does it mean that Jesus is the Son of God?

5. How could you have a more confident assurance that you are a child of God?

To memorize:

He shall build a house for my name, and I will establish the throne of his kingdom forever. I will be to him a father, and he shall be to me a son. (2 Samuel 7:13–14)

Have you ever wished that God would speak to you in an audible voice? That's what God did at Mount Sinai, and when He spoke, His people trembled. They said to Moses, "You speak to us, and we will listen; but do not let God speak to us, lest we die" (Exodus 20:19). So God spoke to Moses, and Moses spoke the words of God to the people. This was the ministry of the Old Testament prophets.

14

PROPHET

2 SAMUEL 12

People who are given positions of power often begin to feel that they are somehow beyond the rules that apply to others. That's how it was for David. One day the king saw a married woman named Bathsheba. David had the power to get what he wanted, so he ignored God's law and took the woman.

David loved the Lord, but even a heart that loves God can harbor some strange affections. David's feelings for Bathsheba were utterly offensive to God, but they were also very powerful and he gave way to them.

When David found that Bathsheba was pregnant, he scrambled to cover his tracks. David ordered that the woman's husband, Uriah, be sent home from the battlefield under the guise of bringing news from the army. If Uriah spent a few nights at home with his wife, he would be identified as the father of the child.

But it didn't work. Uriah was a conscientious soldier, and he did not feel that he should be at home with his wife while others were risking their lives on the field of battle. So David had to resort to more desperate measures. He ordered that Uriah be put on the front lines, making his death inevitable (2 Samuel 11:5–17).

A short time later, David took the recently widowed Bathsheba to be his wife. There was no public scandal, but God saw what was done, and He did not remain silent. What David had done "displeased the LORD" (11:27).

Speaking the Word of God

God sent Nathan the prophet to expose David's sin. Using a clever parable, Nathan told David about a rich man who stole a poor man's lamb. As David listened to the story, he was filled with anger at what this man had done. He wanted to know who the man was so that he could bring him to justice.

Notice that what angered David was a reflection of his own sin. The rich man took what belonged to, and was dearly loved by, another person. This was what David had done. And when he saw his sin in someone else, he hated it and condemned it.

When someone else's sin makes you angry, ask God to show you where you might be guilty of the same thing. What makes you most angry about others may be hiding in your own heart.

God opened David's eyes to his hidden sin through Nathan the prophet. When David asked who stole the poor man's lamb, Nathan said, "You are the man!" (2 Samuel 12:7). David's defenses were ripped wide open. But this was God's grace in action. David had moved into the darkness, and God sent a prophet to bring him back into the light.

Standing in a Prophet's Shoes

What was it like for a prophet to receive the Word of God? The apostle Peter tells us about this in the New Testament: "No prophecy of Scripture comes from someone's own interpretation. For no prophecy was ever produced by the will of man, but men spoke from God as they were carried along by the Holy Spirit" (2 Peter 1:20–21).

The best way to grasp what Peter is saying here is through a story in the book of Acts. Paul was under arrest, and he was being taken by ship as a prisoner to Rome. Luke records: "A tempestuous wind, called the northeaster, struck down from the land. And when the ship was caught and could not face the wind, we gave way to it and were driven along" (Acts 27:14–15).

The word Luke used for the ship being "driven along" by the wind is the same word Peter used for the prophets being "carried along" by the Holy Spirit. How much control do you have when you are in a ship being carried along in a storm? Not much. The direction of the boat is controlled by the wind. In the same way, the message of the prophets was controlled by the Spirit.

The words of the prophets came from God. These men "spoke from God" (2 Peter 1:21). They did not control the message; the message controlled them. It came to them from God like a mighty wind, and they were carried along so that what they wrote was exactly what God wanted them to say.

How do we know who God is? How do we know what truth is? If God had not spoken, all we would have is the sum of human experience, much of which is immensely painful. But God has spoken. The prophets were given the unique privilege of standing in the presence of God and hearing the voice of God, so that they could speak the words of God to the people.

This is how the prophets could speak about things that otherwise could not have been known. Isaiah spoke about a virgin who would conceive and give birth to a son (Isaiah 7:14). Zechariah spoke about a king who would come to Jerusalem riding on a donkey (Zechariah 9:9). Prophets knew these things because God revealed them.

How did Nathan know about David's adultery? God told him!

Responding to the Word of God

When God confronted David through Nathan, the king said, "I have sinned against the LORD" (2 Samuel 12:13). David could have said, "Nathan, you don't understand. My marriage has been dead for years." That may have been true. Or David might have said, "Nathan, I know that I've done wrong, but other leaders have done the same thing or worse." That also would have been true. But David made no excuses. He said, "I have sinned against the LORD." Would you have said that? How you respond to the Word of God when your sin is revealed will say a great deal about you.

David found that honest confession led to forgiveness from God. The pain of his suppressed conscience was released, and the joy of his salvation was restored.

> For when I kept silent, my bones wasted away
>   through my groaning all day long.
> For day and night your hand was heavy upon me;
>   my strength was dried up as by the heat of summer.

> I acknowledged my sin to you,
> and I did not cover my iniquity;
> I said, "I will confess my transgressions to the Lord,"
> and you forgave the iniquity of my sin. (Psalm 32:3–5)

A thousand years later, God confronted another king, Herod, through a prophet whose name was John. Herod was very interested in spiritual things, and he liked listening to John the Baptist's preaching.

One day God gave John words to speak to Herod about his illicit relationship with his brother's wife. The king didn't want to hear it, and in the end, he ordered that the head of John the Baptist be brought to him on a plate.

Despite this atrocity, Herod was interested in meeting Jesus. And when he had the opportunity, he plied him with many questions, but Jesus refused to answer (Luke 23:9). Herod had refused God's word to him through John the Baptist. He had hardened his heart, and now the Savior had nothing more to say to him.

David made a better choice than Herod. He listened to the Word of God even when it exposed him, and he responded with faith and repentance. God restored David, and He did it through His Word.

Jesus Is the Word of God

Down through the centuries, God spoke His Word through the prophets. But in the fullness of time, God spoke through His Son. The words Jesus spoke were given to Him by the Father: "I have not spoken on my own authority, but the Father who sent me has himself given me a commandment—what to say and what to speak. . . . What I say, therefore, I say as the Father has told me" (John 12:49–50).

But Jesus is more than a prophet. He claimed what no other prophet would ever dare to say: "I and the Father are one" and "Whoever has seen me has seen the Father" (John 10:30; 14:9). And Jesus is more than a prophet because of who He is and what He does:

> Long ago, at many times and in many ways, God spoke to our fathers by the prophets, but in these last days he has spoken to us by his Son, whom he

> appointed the heir of all things, through whom also he created the world. He is the radiance of the glory of God and the exact imprint of his nature, and he upholds the universe by the word of his power. (Hebrews 1:1–3)

TRAIL MARKERS

If you have ever wished that God would speak to you, you need to know that He does. God speaks to us by His Son. And all that we know of His Son comes to us through His Word.

As you study the Bible and hear it proclaimed, you will find that God says some things that can be hard to take. Hearing the truth about your sins will make you uncomfortable. But whenever God speaks, it is a sign of His grace. His purpose is always to restore and to bless.

1. Have you ever tried to cover up something you did, and then later on, God made it known? What happened?

2. In your own words, how would you describe what it was like for a prophet to receive a word from God?

3. Why is Jesus more than a prophet? And why does it matter?

4. How does God speak to us today?

5. How are you responding to the Word of God? Are there places where the Word makes you feel uncomfortable?

***To memorize*:**

> Long ago, at many times and in many ways, God spoke to our fathers by the prophets, but in these last days he has spoken to us by his Son, whom he appointed the heir of all things, through whom also he created the world. He is the radiance of the glory of God and the exact imprint of his nature, and he upholds the universe by the word of his power. (Hebrews 1:1–3)

The Bible story is about how men and women can live in the presence of God. God's presence was lost through man's choice of sin and disobedience, and His presence is restored by God's initiatives of grace. These initiatives included the appearances of God to Abraham and Moses, His presence on Mount Sinai where He gave the law, and over the ark of the covenant where God promised to come down and meet with the high priest.

15

TEMPLE

1 KINGS 8

God said that when His people came into the promised land, He would choose a place where He would meet with them (Deuteronomy 12:5). David discerned that Jerusalem was the place, and he wanted to honor God by building a temple that would house the ark of the covenant. But God said to David, "[Your son] shall build a house for my name" (2 Samuel 7:13), and the privilege of building the temple fell to Solomon.

Time for the Temple

Normally, building sites echo with the sounds of cutting, hammering, and shouting, but the temple was put up in total silence. Every stone was cut and dressed in the quarry and then brought to the building site ready for assembly.

When all the materials were prepared, the command to build was given, and the temple went up in silence: "Neither hammer nor axe nor any tool of iron was heard in the house while it was being built" (1 Kings 6:7).

This picture is taken up in the New Testament, where God's people are described as "living stones" (1 Peter 2:5). Everything that God is doing in your life is shaping you for your eternal destiny. Your pain and suffering are like the hammer and chisel, shaping you to be a living stone in God's temple. When Jesus Christ returns, the preparation will be complete, and God's people will be a glorious temple in which His presence dwells.

God's Stonecutters

Some years ago, Karen and I had the opportunity of welcoming Romanian pastor Joseph Ton into our home for several days. He had been imprisoned for his faith during the Communist years, and we listened intently as he talked about the cost of his commitment to Christ.

He described how the prisoners hated the guards because of their cruelty, but Joseph prayed for them and for their families. When one of the guards asked him, "Why are you not filled with bitterness toward me?"

Joseph answered, "Because to me, you are God's stonecutter."

Who are God's stonecutters in your life? They may have brought you pain, but God will use that pain to shape you into the likeness of Christ. God can also use difficult circumstances with your health, family, job, or finances to shape you for His purpose. The process is always painful, but when Christ returns you will be all that He calls you to be. And you will take your place in heaven where you will know and enjoy God's presence forever.

A Service of Dedication

Once the building was complete, the people gathered for a service of dedication that proved to be one of the greatest occasions in the history of God's people. When the priests brought the ark of the covenant into the Most Holy Place at the center of the temple, God's presence came down: "A cloud filled the house of the LORD, so that the priests could not stand to minister because of the cloud" (1 Kings 8:10–11).

These people had never experienced the immediate presence of God. The last time God's glory had shown itself like this was in the desert, more than four hundred years earlier. So Solomon had to explain to the people what was happening: "The LORD has said that he would dwell in thick darkness" (8:12).

The Most Holy Place at the center of the temple was a darkened room built to house the ark of the covenant. On the lid of the ark were golden figures of cherubim, representing the judgment of God. So when God's presence came down, He broke through the separation represented by these figures and came among His people.

Responding with Worship

Solomon's first response to the presence of God was to worship! "Blessed be the LORD, the God of Israel, who with his hand has fulfilled what he promised with his mouth to David my father" (8:15).

But Solomon knew that no building could ever contain God, and that the cloud of God's presence could leave as quickly as it came. He longed for more than an occasional experience of God's presence. He wanted the temple to be the place where God's presence could always be found, so he made this request: "[May] your eyes . . . be open night and day toward this house, the place of which you have said, 'My name shall be there'" (v. 29).

Solomon also asked that God would hear the prayers of people living many miles from Jerusalem: "Listen to the plea of your servant and of your people Israel, when they pray toward this place. And listen in heaven your dwelling place, and when you hear, forgive" (8:30).

Joy filled Solomon's heart as he anticipated a future blessed with the presence of God: "Blessed be the LORD who has given rest to his people. . . . The LORD our God be with us, as he was with our fathers. May he not leave us or forsake us" (vv. 56–57).

The Sad Story of the Temple

But the joy did not last. After the time of Solomon, there was a long line of kings who led God's people into idolatry. Idols were set up in God's temple, and this was so offensive to God that after four centuries of forbearance He gave His people into the hands of their enemies.

The Babylonian army laid siege to Jerusalem, the city fell, and the temple was destroyed.

Jerusalem was reduced to a pile of rubble. The ark of the covenant was lost, and it has never been found. This fact is of huge significance. Without the ark, the temple could no longer be the place where God meets with His people.

The temple was rebuilt, but it was only a shadow of the one built by Solomon. People gathered for worship, but the cloud of God's presence never came down.

The Temple with Us

Describing the birth of Jesus, John said, "The Word became flesh and dwelt among us" (John 1:14). "Dwelt" literally means "tabernacled," or "pitched his tent," so John is telling us that when Jesus was born the presence of God came down among His people.

Early in His ministry, Jesus came to the temple, and said, "Destroy this temple, and in three days I will raise it up" (John 2:19). Those who heard Him thought he was referring to the building, but Jesus was referring to His own body, indicating that He Himself is the place where we meet with God: "If you want to meet with God," He was saying, "come to Me."

The place where men and women can meet with God is not a building in Jerusalem or anywhere else. The place where you can meet with God is through Jesus Christ. Solomon asked that God would listen to the prayers that were directed toward the temple, but Jesus promises that God will hear prayers that are offered in His name: "Whatever you ask of the Father in my name, he will give it you" (John 16:23).

The Spirit in Us

When the disciples were with Jesus, they had open access to the presence of God. He was with them in the person of Jesus, so when Jesus began to speak about leaving, the disciples were troubled.

But Jesus said, "I will ask the Father, and he will give you another Helper, to be with you forever, even the Spirit of truth . . . for he dwells with you and will be in you. I will not leave you as orphans; I will come to you" (John 14:16–18). The disciples had known the presence of God *with* them in Jesus, but now they would know the presence of God *in* them by the Holy Spirit.

The gift of the Holy Spirit in the life of the believer is so astonishing that Paul asks, "Do you not know that your body is a temple of the Holy Spirit within you?" (1 Corinthians 6:19). Try to take this in: Your body is a temple of the Holy Spirit. Just as God's glorious presence came down to Solomon's temple when it was dedicated, so God's presence fills the lives of those who are dedicated to Him. That is why Paul prays that believers will "know the love of Christ that surpasses knowledge, that you may be filled with all the fullness of God" (Ephesians 3:19).

The whole of human history is leading up to the day when Jesus Christ will take His people into the immediate presence of God. The apostle John was given a glimpse of what this will be like. He saw a great city and a great crowd of people. Then he heard "a loud voice from the throne saying, 'Behold, the dwelling place of God is with man. He will dwell with them, and they will be his people, and God himself will be with them as their God'" (Revelation 21:3).

TRAIL MARKERS

The cloud of God's presence in the temple pointed forward to what God would do in Christ. God took human flesh and came down among us in Jesus. When we believe in Him, God's presence enters our lives by the Holy Spirit, giving us a foretaste of the joys that lie ahead when we will live with Him forever.

1. Do you think you would like to live in the presence of God? Why or why not?

2. Who are God's stonecutters in your life right now? How do you think God might use this to make you more like Christ?

3. When in human history did God come down among His people? If we want to meet with God today, where do we need to go?

4. What did the apostle Paul mean when he said to believers, "Your body is a temple of the Holy Spirit" (1 Corinthians 6:19)?

5. How can we get a taste right now of what life will be like in heaven?

To memorize:

> As you come to him, a living stone rejected by men but in the sight of God chosen and precious, you yourselves like living stones are being built up as a spiritual house, to be a holy priesthood, to offer spiritual sacrifices acceptable to God through Jesus Christ. (1 Peter 2:4–5)

King Solomon made a great contribution in building the temple, but he ended badly. In the years that followed, most of the kings after him turned away from the Lord. One of the worst was King Ahab who promoted the worship of idols, as did others. But God raised up the prophet Elijah to call His people back to Himself.

16

WORSHIP

1 KINGS 18

Often the distance between triumph and disaster is very short. When Solomon came to the throne, the people of God had everything going for them: wise leadership, strong unity, and peace in their land. God's presence came among them at the dedication of the temple. But as time passed Solomon's success bred complacency, and the seeds of future disaster were sown in the later years of his reign.

A Recipe for Disaster

Solomon made at least three mistakes. First, he lost touch with hurting people. With the king's attention focused on Jerusalem, the people in the south prospered, while their brothers in the north struggled under a program of forced labor that left them feeling increasingly marginalized.

Perhaps Solomon thought that the people in the north were less important, but his shortsighted leadership had long-term repercussions. By the time of his death, when his son Rehoboam succeeded him, the seeds of disunity had already been planted.

Second, Solomon slid into self-indulgence. He had almost unlimited power and great resources, and so he could do virtually anything he wanted. In his early days, he threw his time, energy, and money into accomplishing something for the glory of God. But later in his life he used his position to indulge himself.

Solomon had 700 wives and 300 concubines (1 Kings 11:3), and this indulgence was the root of his downfall: "When Solomon was old his wives turned away his heart after other gods, and his heart was not wholly true to the LORD his God, as was the heart of David his father" (11:4).

Third, Solomon chose to do what was popular instead of what was right. Having married so many foreign wives, he succumbed to pressure to build altars to the gods they worshiped: "Solomon built a high place for Chemosh the abomination of Moab, and for Molech the abomination of the Ammonites, on the mountain east of Jerusalem. And so he did for all his foreign wives, who made offerings and sacrificed to their gods" (11:7–8).

This was the beginning of flagrant idolatry among the people of God. At the start of Solomon's reign, Jerusalem was the place where the living God had put His name. But by the end, Jerusalem was filled with shrines to other gods. Any visitor to Jerusalem would draw the conclusion that the God of Israel was one among many.

Though Solomon had done great things for God in the first half of his life, he reversed much of the good he had done through the indulgence of his later years. He received a kingdom from his father, David, that was united and at peace, but he handed his son a kingdom that would soon be divided and at war.

When Rehoboam took over, he faced rumbling discontent among the people in the north. They found a leader in Jeroboam, rallied around him, and crowned him as their king. So the ten tribes in the north separated from the line of David that God had promised to bless.

The Story in the North

Jeroboam was a shrewd leader of the ten northern tribes. He understood the cohesive power of religion and saw that if faithful people from the north kept going to Jerusalem to worship in the temple, they would be reminded of the unity they shared with their brothers and sisters in the south.

So Jeroboam decided to establish his own centers of worship. He had two golden calves crafted, and he told the people: "You have gone up to Jerusalem long enough. Behold your gods, O Israel, who brought you up out of the land of Egypt" (1 Kings 12:28). These were the same words Aaron had used when he made the golden calf in the desert (Exodus 32:8).

Worse was to follow. Jeroboam handed the kingdom over to his son Nadab, who followed in the ways of his father until he was murdered by Baasha. He was followed by Elah, who was a drunkard and murderer. Then there was Zimri, who was guilty of treason and only lasted seven days, and then Omri, who "did more evil than all who were before him" (1 Kings 16:25). Finally there was Ahab, who then surpassed Omri by doing "evil in the sight of the LORD, more than all who were before him" (16:30). Ahab married the infamous Jezebel who used the power of the palace to initiate a campaign of persecution in which the prophets of God were hunted and killed.

In the years after the death of Solomon, Israel had changed beyond recognition. At the beginning of Solomon's reign, the king said, "There is one God." By the time of Jeroboam, the official position was that "there are many gods." And by the time of Ahab, those who said that there is one God were subject to violent persecution. So God sent the prophet Elijah to restore true worship among His people.

Authentic Worship Is a Response to Revealed Truth

Mount Carmel was the scene of a great confrontation. Ahab sent 450 prophets of Baal and 400 prophets of Asherah, together with people from across the country (1 Kings 18:19). When everyone was gathered, Elijah challenged the people with a question: "How long will you go limping between two different opinions? If the LORD is God, follow him; but if Baal, then follow him" (18:21). Elijah did not appeal to tradition; he appealed to the truth. The single reason for worshiping the Lord is that He is God.

Nobody has the right to say that you should be a Christian because your parents were Christians, or because Christianity is the dominant religion in your culture. Christianity stands or falls on the claim that it is true: "If the LORD is God, follow Him."

Elijah's question assumed categories of truth and error, and the people found it very difficult to think in these terms. They had been brought up with the idea that the God you worship is simply a personal choice, that faith is a private matter, and that every individual must find a way to worship that fits his or her own personality.

But before you can worship, you need to know who God is. Authentic worship is a response to revealed truth. When we worship, we should sing, read, pray, and preach the truth.

Authentic Worship Focuses on the Living God

Elijah wanted the people to know that there is only one living God, so he invited the prophets of Baal to prepare a sacrifice and then call on Baal to answer by sending fire. The prophets of Baal gave themselves to the challenge, and they called on their god: "Oh, Baal, answer us!" (18:26). They danced around the altar and worked themselves into a frenzy.

What started out so bright, colorful, and lively soon turned dark, and a more sinister element began to show. The prophets of Baal began to "cut themselves" (18:28), putting themselves through self-inflicted agonies before they were ready to admit defeat.

But after all this intense activity, "no one answered; no one paid attention" (18:29). The worship of Baal was nothing more than an exercise in self-expression. The prophets were talking to themselves. No one else was listening.

Baal worship evolved because at some point in history people made up mythical stories about a god called Baal and wrote them down. Then other people made images of Baal and carved them out of wood. But there was nothing in the worship of Baal beyond what human minds had dreamed up and what human hands had made. The whole thing was a cultural creation, and for that reason, it had no power.

Many people today have concluded that Christianity evolved in the same way. They assume that the Bible is also a book of ancient myths, and since they assume that it is a creation of human culture, they insist that it has no authority. If they were right in their assumption, they would be right in their conclusion. A religion created by one culture should not be imposed on another and a religion that was merely the choice of one generation should not be foisted on another. If all religions are human creations, then none of them can claim to be true.

Authentic Worship Focuses on an Acceptable Sacrifice

But Elijah knew that the living God was no cultural creation. He longed for the knowledge of the living God to be restored in the land, so he built an altar and poured water over it to drench the sacrifice.

Then Elijah prayed: "O LORD, God of Abraham, Isaac, and Israel, let it be known this day that you are God. . . . Answer me, O LORD, answer me, that this people may know that you, O LORD, are God" (1 Kings 18:36–37).

"Then the fire of the LORD fell and consumed the burnt offering and the wood and the stones and the dust, and licked up the water that was in the trench" (18:38). You can sense the intensity of a fire that not only burned up the wood but even the stones and the dust! When the people saw the fire, they fell prostrate and cried, "The LORD, he is God; the LORD, he is God" (18:39).

Try to imagine yourself in the crowd. You have bought into the prevailing belief of your culture that one religion is essentially the same as another. But as you watch Elijah praying, the sky is filled with fire. Suddenly it is clear to you, Elijah has been speaking the truth. The Lord is God, and now the fire of His judgment is about to fall!

Think about this wonderful truth: The fire of God fell on the sacrifice, not on the people. This points us to the cross where the judgment of God was poured out, not on the soldiers who crucified Jesus or on the crowds who mocked Him, but on Jesus Himself, who became the sacrifice for us. Jesus absorbed the judgment that was due to sinners. It fell on Him so that it would not fall on us. God diverted the judgment away from us and onto Jesus, and in this way, He reconciled us to Himself.

TRAIL MARKERS

True worship will be fostered where God's truth is proclaimed, where Jesus Christ is exalted, and where God's people submit to the work of the Holy Spirit in their lives.

If you want to grow in your worship, open your Bible and soak your mind in what God says about Himself. The Holy Spirit will use the truth to stimulate worship in your heart.

1. Where might you be sowing seeds that will lead to future disaster? Sliding into self-indulgence? Choosing what is popular instead of what is right?

2. What have you learned in this chapter about worship?

3. How did you become convinced that Christianity is true?

4. How would you answer someone who says that all religions are the same?

5. How does the fire of God falling on the sacrifice, and not on the people, help us to understand what was happening on the cross?

To memorize:

"How long will you go limping between two different opinions? If the Lord is God, follow him; but if Baal, then follow him." (1 Kings 18:21)

Despite God's revelation of Himself through the fire on Mount Carmel, God's people continued to worship idols. Every one of the kings in the north did evil in the eyes of the Lord and eventually God allowed enemies to overrun the northern kingdom. The king of Assyria deported the entire population, but later he repopulated the area with people from many nations. God was advancing His purpose to bless all people.

17

SIN

2 KINGS 17

For many people in our culture, *sin* has become a word that describes slightly indulgent things that are entirely legitimate, like eating too much chocolate.

Imagine a thirty-five-year-old husband and father at home on a Sunday morning. Let's call him Bob. After he has finished his morning cup of coffee, he decides that he will tackle that long postponed task of cleaning out his basement. As he sorts through the boxes, Bob comes across a Bible that had belonged to his grandmother. Something inside tells him he should not throw it away; after all, it's old, and there are notes in his grandmother's handwriting on many of the pages. He opens it up and reads that "Christ Jesus came into the world to save sinners" (1 Timothy 1:15).

This strikes Bob as rather quaint. Jesus came to save overindulgent people! Bob enjoys a good bowl of ice cream now and then and knows that he probably shouldn't, but he works out and is generally in good health, so what does he need saving from? He flicks over a few pages and reads that God was angry with people who sinned (Hebrews 3:10). This doesn't make any sense to Bob. Why would sin, as he understands it, make God angry? What kind of God would be angry toward people who indulge in a little bit of pleasure?

So Bob closes the Bible, reassured that he made the right choice to spend his Sunday morning at home. He loves his wife and his kids, and he cannot see why his grandmother thought the Bible was such a wonderful book.

Sin is always being redefined in ways that make it seem like it's no big deal. But sin is not a harmless pleasure. Sin is rebelling against God, and when you see that sin is your greatest problem, you will discover your need of Jesus.

The Priority of Godliness

Sin is a destructive power. It can ruin a life, a family, or a church, and 2 Kings 17 tells us how it destroyed a nation. After the death of Solomon, the ten tribes in the north declared their independence from the two tribes in the south, separating themselves from the blessing God had promised to the royal line of David. There were nineteen northern kings, and every one of them did evil in the eyes of the Lord. After about two hundred years, God allowed enemies to overrun the northern kingdom. The people were deported, and the whole area became a kind of wasteland.

The first king of the ten northern tribes, Rehoboam, was determined that his people would not go to Jerusalem to worship God. So, as we saw, he established his own religion at Dan and Bethel, where he set up two golden calves.

This man-made religion led to a culture where the rich lived in opulence and showed total disregard for the poor. The streets were filled with violence, and God's people indulged in the obscene practice of giving up unwanted children to be burned in a fire.

But the first charge God brought against His people was not the violence, the murder, the greed, or even the cruelty to children. It was that God's people had worshiped other gods (2 Kings 17:7).

The first four of the Ten Commandments are all about God Himself: "You shall have no other gods before me. You shall not make for yourself a carved image. . . . You shall not take the name of the Lord your God in vain. . . . Remember the Sabbath day, to keep it holy" (Exodus 20:3–8).

Our first calling is to a God-centered life. The Bible calls this "godliness" (e.g., 1 Timothy 4:7), and this priority is confirmed by the teaching of Jesus. When asked about the greatest commandment, Jesus replied: "You shall love the Lord your God with all your heart and with all your soul and with all your mind" (Matthew 22:37).

Godliness Leads to Righteousness

After He calls us to godliness in the first four commandments, God calls us to righteousness in our relationship to others: "Honor your father and your mother. . . . You shall not murder. You shall not commit adultery. You shall not steal. You shall not bear false witness. . . . You shall not covet" (Exodus 20:12–17).

God calls us to reflect His love in our relationships with other people. Christ confirmed this when He said that the second commandment is to "love your neighbor as yourself" (Matthew 22:39).

Righteousness is built on the foundation of godliness, so when people reject God, righteousness slips beyond their grasp. When a nation turns away from the living God, the result will be moral confusion and the unleashing of sin and evil.

The collapse of the northern kingdom began with people rejecting God, and it ended, tragically, with them putting their children in the fire. The reason they lost the morality of the Bible is that they rejected the God of the Bible. You cannot have righteousness without godliness.

We want all the benefits of righteousness. We want our marriages to succeed, we would like the people we do business with to be honest and keep their word. We expect public officials not to tell lies. And we want our children to be safe. We want all the benefits of righteousness, but sometimes we do not want God. And that is our greatest sin.

Provoking the Anger of God

God is immensely patient. For two hundred years He restrained judgment and sent the prophets to call His people back to godliness and righteousness, but they would not listen (2 Kings 17:14). Instead, "they did wicked things, provoking the LORD to anger" (17:11).

Notice the word "provoking." Anger is not in God's nature. God is always holy, He is always love, but He is not always angry. The ancient gods were angry by nature, always smoldering and constantly needing to be appeased. Offerings were given to placate them, but their anger never went away. It was never spent; it was only contained. But the God of the Bible is entirely different: "The LORD is . . . slow to anger and abounding in steadfast love" (Psalm 103:8).

Though it is not God's nature to be angry, He can be provoked to anger, and for this we should be thankful. We do not admire those who stand idly by while others are being abused. How could we worship a god who was indifferent when people put their children into the fire?

Notice what God does when He is provoked to anger: "Therefore the LORD was very angry with Israel and removed them out of his sight" (2 Kings 17:18). This happened when the king of Assyria invaded the promised land and "carried the Israelites away" (17:6).

God's Mercy in Action

When God removed His people from His presence, the land He had promised to bless lay desolate and uninhabited. But the king of Assyria repopulated the area by bringing people from all over his empire and settling them there (2 Kings 17:24).

When these immigrants arrived, they faced an unexpected problem. Several of them were attacked by lions. When word of this problem got back to the king of Assyria, he thought the best way to deal with the situation would be to find a priest from among the people who used to live there. He assumed that a local priest would know what to do to placate whatever god was causing this problem. So he gave orders for a Jewish priest to be sent back to Israel, and "one of the priests whom they had carried away from Samaria came and lived in Bethel and taught them how they should fear the LORD" (17:28).

Here was God's mercy in action. He brought people from the north, south, east, and west into the place He had promised to bless, and He sent one of His priests there so that these people could come to know Him.

People from many nations were brought to a knowledge of the truth, but over time they became confused because they continued to worship their own gods as well (17:29). These people came to be known as the Samaritans.

When Jesus went through Samaria (John 4:4), He met a woman there who was ungodly and unrighteous. Jesus did not begin by telling her that God is angry over her sins. He began by guiding her toward a right relationship with God. He told her that God is seeking "worshipers [who] will worship the Father in spirit and truth" (4:23).

Godliness is the root of righteousness, and Jesus began by speaking to the

Samaritan woman about knowing God, because this is where lasting change begins.

Christ died to deal with both our ungodliness and our unrighteousness. On the cross, the Father dealt with the Son as if He had lived a godless life and as if He were guilty of every kind of unrighteousness. The Father turned away from His Son, and He was shut out from the presence of God. That is why He cried out, "My God, my God, why have you forsaken me?" (Matthew 27:46).

Christ "suffered once for sins, the righteous for the unrighteous, that he might bring us to God" (1 Peter 3:18). If you will come to Jesus in faith and repentance, He will lead you into a godly life that will be the beginning of your growth in righteousness.

TRAIL MARKERS

God calls us to godliness and righteousness. We are to love God with our whole heart, and we are to love our neighbor as ourselves. Morality cannot be sustained when we lose the knowledge of God. But when we come to Jesus Christ, He will reconcile us to the Father and lead us in paths of righteousness.

1. What has been your working understanding of sin?

2. What is the difference between godliness and righteousness?

3. Do you think a person can be good without God?

4. What difference does it make to you whether God is *provoked* to anger, or anger is part of God's nature?

5. If you wanted to become a more righteous person, how could Jesus help you?

To memorize:

> Christ . . . suffered once for sins, the righteous for the unrighteous, that he might bring us to God. (1 Peter 3:18)

After the collapse of the northern kingdom, the two tribes in the south struggled on. Many of their kings did great evil, but one of them had a desire to seek after God. Josiah led a great moral reformation in which idols were removed from the land. But the hearts of the people were not changed, and after Josiah's death, God's people returned to their idols.

18

RIGHTEOUSNESS

2 KINGS 22

How would you feel if, in the news one morning, you discovered that forty-two of the fifty American states had left the union? Then, what if several years later, those forty-two independent states collapsed and were overrun by enemies?

As a citizen in one of the eight remaining "United States," you would no longer be part of a world superpower. Instead, you would be a citizen of a rather small country. What once seemed strong and secure would now seem weak and vulnerable.

That's how it was for the people of God in the two tribes that made up the southern kingdom of Judah. In the time of David, Israel had been a dominant power, with the twelve tribes united. But after ten of the twelve tribes declared their independence, things changed radically for the south. The nation was diminished militarily and economically, and within two hundred years, the northern kingdom was overrun by enemies and the ten tribes were scattered.

God's promise to bless the descendants of Abraham and then to bring blessing to the nations of the world through them must have looked very doubtful. But God's promise to bless His people had never been revoked.

A Turn for the Worse

The people of Judah had the benefit of better leadership than their brothers and sisters in the north. But things took a turn for the worse when Manasseh came to the throne. He reigned for fifty-five years (2 Kings 21:1) and brought more trouble to

God's people than anyone else: "Manasseh led them astray to do more evil than the nations had done whom the LORD destroyed before the people of Israel" (21:9).

God had driven the Canaanites out of the land because of their many sins. But now, ironically, God's own people were doing things that were even worse! Manasseh promoted the worship of Molech, which included an evil rite in which children were sacrificed in a fire (21:6). If God judged the Canaanites for their sins, how could He restrain judgment on His own people (21:11)? God's people were called to be a light in a dark place, but the reality was that they were living in the same darkness as the people around them.

At the end of Manasseh's reign, his son Amon came to the throne. But he lasted only two years before he was murdered, leaving his eight-year-old son, Josiah, as king.

The Influence of a Godly Leader

In contrast to his father and grandfather, Josiah "did what was right in the eyes of the LORD and walked in all the way of David his father, and he did not turn aside to the right or to the left" (2 Kings 22:2).

Josiah began to seek the Lord in the eighth year of his reign (2 Chronicles 34:3), which would be at the age of sixteen. As a teenager he developed a heart for God that shaped his entire life. What you pursue now will shape the person you will become. It is never too early to seek the Lord.

Josiah wanted to get God's people back on the right track, but he had no knowledge of the Bible to draw on and no godly example to follow. He had grown up in a spiritually confused and biblically illiterate culture, and yet deep within his heart there was a longing to know God.

Here is the obvious question: If you are seeking God, how are you going to find Him? Maybe you say, "I want to be different. I don't want to continue the things that have been passed down the line in my family. I want to change, and I know I need the help of God, but how do I find Him?"

Rediscovering the Bible

Josiah knew that God was to be worshiped in the temple, so he decided to repair the house of God (2 Kings 22:3–5). While the work was in progress, Hilkiah the high priest found a dusty old book that would change the direction of the nation. He said, "I have found the Book of the Law in the house of the LORD" (22:8). This book was almost certainly a copy of Deuteronomy. How could God's Word have become lost in, of all places, the temple!

The Word of God roundly condemned what Manasseh had done, and it is not difficult to understand why the priests ignored the Scripture. If they had preached from the Bible in the time of Manasseh, they would have found themselves on a collision course with the culture. So they buried the Book of the Law, and fifty years later a new generation arose that did not know God or His law.

The amazing thing is that the priests continued their work in the temple without ever using the Scriptures! Maybe that was your experience. You were seeking God and you went to church, but the Bible was rarely opened. If it was read it was never explained, and you were left with a great hunger in your soul.

Rediscovering Right and Wrong

The book of Deuteronomy was read to Josiah, and "when the king heard the words of the Book of the Law, he tore his clothes" (2 Kings 22:11).

Don't be surprised if the first effect of God's Word in your life is to make you feel like tearing your clothes. When you see the life to which God calls you, you will see how far you are from it, and how far you are from Him. You will begin to say, "Why did I not know this? Nothing in my life conforms to what God requires of me!"

Josiah gathered the elders and the people and read the whole book of Deuteronomy aloud. Standing by the pillar of the temple, he made a public pledge to obey the Lord. Then all the people joined in making the same commitment (23:2–3).

The Word of God lit a fire in Josiah's life, and he determined that he would put what God had said into practice. This vision gripped his mind and soul: By God's grace, he would rescue the nation from idolatry.

Josiah traveled throughout the country, and wherever he found altars or other evidence of idolatry in the land, he completely destroyed them. It was the greatest onslaught against idolatrous practices in the history of Israel. Nothing like this had ever happened before. The idolatrous altars Solomon built for his foreign wives had stood for three hundred years, as did the golden calf set up by Jeroboam (23:13, 15). No other king dared to touch them, but Josiah destroyed them completely.

Josiah was unrelenting in his pursuit of righteousness: "Before him there was no king like him, who turned to the LORD with all his heart and with all his soul and with all his might, according to all the Law of Moses, nor did any like him arise after him" (23:25). You couldn't ask for a better epitaph than that!

God held back judgment on the nation during Josiah's lifetime: "Because your heart was penitent, and you humbled yourself before the LORD, . . . your eyes shall not see all the disaster that I will bring upon this place" (22:19–20).

Righteousness Begins in the Heart

But there were limitations to Josiah's achievement. Most of the change came as the direct result of the king's own activity. It was not a grassroots movement; it was all done by state intervention.

A strong element of coercion was involved in all of this. So it is not surprising to find that as long as Josiah lived, "they did not turn away from following the LORD, the God of their fathers" (2 Chronicles 34:33). But as soon as Josiah died, things went back to the way they had been before.

The prophet Jeremiah gives us a fascinating insight into the limitations of Josiah's reform: "Judah did not return to me with her whole heart, but in pretense, declares the LORD" (Jeremiah 3:10). Is that you? Pretending one thing with parents and family and another with friends? One thing at work, another at home, and another at church? If you keep pretending, you will soon lose sight of who you are.

Good behavior can sometimes be little more than a reflection of your environment. True righteousness comes from a heart that has been changed by God, and for this reason God promised a new covenant: "I will put my law within them, and I will write it on their hearts" (Jeremiah 31:33). God was promising to do what no parent, church, or state can ever do: Get His law into our minds and hearts so that we will want what He has commanded.

When you come to Jesus in faith and repentance, He will put a desire for righteousness in you. That is the promise of the new covenant (Luke 22:20). God gives us more than His law; He gives us Himself! God's Spirit will create new desires and new capacities within you. You will come to love God and long for righteousness. You will want to pray, and when you sin, it will not be long before you feel the need to come to Christ and be forgiven.

This hunger and thirst for righteousness is one of the greatest blessings of the Christian life. Those who hunger for what God forbids will, in the end, experience emptiness and frustration, but those who desire righteousness will be satisfied (Matthew 5:6). Don't settle for an outward conformity to Christian values when Christ can give you a new heart.

TRAIL MARKERS

Left to ourselves, we would not be able to tell right from wrong. But righteousness is revealed in God's Word, and where His Word is put into practice blessing will come to our families, our churches, and even our nation.

Good laws are better than bad ones, and we need them to restrain evil. But the law cannot bring a change of heart, and that is why attempts to impose religion always fail.

God's purpose is not to impose an outward conformity to His law. It is to cultivate an inward desire for righteousness. This is the promise of the new covenant and the work of the Holy Spirit. It involves changing our hearts to give us a new hunger for righteousness and a new ability to pursue a life that is pleasing to God.

1. Talk about a rule you had to follow growing up. What was its effect on your heart?

2. Josiah grew up in a spiritually confused, biblically illiterate culture, but deep down he had a desire to know God. Where do you most relate to his experience?

3. What is the value of moral laws? What are their limitations?

4. Where does true righteousness come from?

5. What is God able to do that no parent, church, or government can ever do?

To memorize:

> For this is the covenant that I will make with the house of Israel after those days, declares the Lord: I will put my law within them, and I will write it on their hearts. And I will be their God, and they shall be my people. (Jeremiah 31:33)

Some years after Josiah's failed attempt to call people back to Scripture, God allowed enemies to reduce His own city to a pile of rubble. The Babylonian army laid siege to Jerusalem. There was a terrible loss of life, and those who survived either fled for their lives or were taken prisoner and marched off to resettlement camps in Babylon. But God had not abandoned His people, and after seventy years, a small community returned to rebuild the city.

19

JOY

NEHEMIAH 8

The city where God put His name became a smoldering ruin, and silence reigned where a community of believers once lifted their voices in worship. The temple that once was filled with the cloud of God's presence was now completely destroyed.

But the Babylonian empire gave way to the rising empire of the Medes and Persians, and a new king, Cyrus, gave the decree that any Jewish exiles who wished to return to Jerusalem and rebuild the temple were free to do so. About fifty thousand people responded to the challenge (Ezra 2:64–67).

Rebuilding the City of God

It was a small group for such a large task, but they were fired up by a vision of rebuilding the temple and forming a new community in the city of God.

Their leader was Zerubbabel, a builder, and his first challenge was to oversee the building of homes. When their ancestors came into the promised land, God gave them homes they had not built and vineyards they had not planted. But when the exiles returned, they had to cut every timber and hammer every nail. After building their homes, God's people began the task of rebuilding the temple (Ezra 3).

Then God raised up a Bible teacher named Ezra. He was skilled in the Law of Moses and "the hand of the Lord his God was on him" (Ezra 7:6). When Ezra arrived in Jerusalem, he could hardly believe that the people of God in the city of God knew so little about the Word of God. He sat down appalled and remained in a stunned silence until the end of the day (Ezra 9:2–4).

Sometime later God raised up a gifted planner and organizer named Nehemiah. When he came to Jerusalem, he saw that the city had no defenses, and God put it into his heart to rebuild the walls.

The story of the rebuilding of Jerusalem is a wonderful example of how God brings people with different gifts together to get His work done. God used a builder, a Bible teacher, and a strategic planner and together, God's people achieved great things.

Bring Out the Bible!

Ezra was faced with the challenge of teaching the Bible to a community of people who thought they knew the Lord, but who knew very little of His Word. How could these people who had spent their lives in a secular culture be molded into a worshiping community who loved and obeyed the Lord?

Ezra's strategy was to gather the entire community, around fifty thousand people, in the public square. As they gathered, "they told Ezra the scribe to bring the Book of the Law of Moses that the Lord had commanded Israel" (Nehemiah 8:1).

How do fifty thousand people make a request? They chant. This crowd gathered with a great hunger for the Word of God, and growing impatient for events to get underway, they began to shout: "We want the Bible; bring out the Bible!" It must have been a great joy for Ezra to bring out the Scriptures and to teach this vast crowd the Word of God.

Ezra the priest brought the Law before the assembly, which was made up of men and women and "all who could understand what they heard" (8:2). That means children were there too. It is a powerful thing to bring children into an environment where they see adults worshiping and taking the Word of God seriously.

Great Expectations

The crowd watched expectantly, and when Ezra opened the Scriptures, the people stood (8:5). Then "Ezra blessed the Lord, the great God, and all the people answered, 'Amen, Amen,' lifting up their hands. And they bowed their heads and worshiped the LORD with their faces to the ground" (8:6).

A thousand years had passed since God had given His Word to Moses, but when the Scripture was opened and explained, the people knew that God was speaking to them. When they heard this book, they knew that they were not listening to the words of a man; they were hearing the very words of God.

Notice, Ezra did not take a trip to Mount Sinai to hear a new word from God. He opened the Book of the Law, which was a thousand years old, believing that when God's Word is opened, God's voice is heard.

Making the Meaning Clear

Ezra's preaching started from the text of the Bible. He explained the message that had already been given. God has promised to bless His own Word (Isaiah 55:11). So the task of the preacher is to fill his words with God's words so that God's people will be blessed.

Ezra was supported by the Levites in his task: "They read from the book, from the Law of God, clearly, and they gave the sense, so that the people understood the reading" (Nehemiah 8:8). It seems that the Levites were interspersed in the crowd. Ezra would read a part of the law and explain the meaning. Then the Levites would gather people around them in smaller family groups and ask if they had understood what was read. When everyone was ready, Ezra would continue reading (8:7–8).

There was a direct connection between Ezra's preaching and a small group setting in which people had the opportunity to ask questions and apply God's Word. Reading, explaining, and applying the Bible was Ezra's central strategy for building up the people of God.

The Happiness of God

As Ezra read the law of God, the people mourned and wept because they realized how far they were from what God was calling them to be. So Ezra, Nehemiah, and the Levites said to the people, "'This day is holy to the LORD your God; do not mourn or weep.' For all the people wept as they heard the words of the Law" (8:9).

When you open God's Word, you will discover sins in your life that you didn't see before. And what grieves the heart of God will grieve your heart as well. The Word of God is sharper than a two-edged sword. It pierces and cuts and wounds (Hebrews 4:12).

God's Word will convict you of sin, but it is never God's purpose to leave you there. Conviction of sin is always a means to an end, and the end is that we come to a deeper appreciation of God's grace. That's why Nehemiah said, "This day is holy to our Lord. And do not be grieved, for the joy of the LORD is your strength" (Nehemiah 8:10).

Notice that our strength lies in God's joy, not ours. God is supremely happy in Himself. He is "the blessed and only Sovereign, the King of kings and Lord of lords" (1 Timothy 6:15).

There could be no joy in communion with an unhappy god. But when you know that God is blessed, that He is supremely happy in Himself, you will be drawn to walk with Him, and as you do, the joy that is in God will increasingly be in you.

The Joy of Obedience

On the second day, the heads of each family gathered. The Bible was read again, and "they found it written in the Law that the LORD had commanded by Moses that the people of Israel should dwell in booths during the feast of the seventh month" (Nehemiah 8:14).

This festival involved each family making a temporary dwelling from branches and living in it for seven days. The festival reminded the people of how God had kept their forefathers in the desert. It was also a reminder that everything in this world is temporary and that, like Abraham, they were looking for a heavenly city.

I love the spontaneity of their response. They heard the Word of God and they obeyed it: "So the people . . . made booths for themselves, each on his roof, and in their courts and in the courts of the house of God" (8:16).

The obedience of these men to the Word of God was contagious. The whole community built booths and lived in them, "and there was very great rejoicing" (8:17). Great joy will be yours when you are obedient to God.

About five hundred years after the time of Nehemiah, Jesus came to Jerusalem to celebrate the feast of booths (John 7:2). And "on the last day of the feast, the great day, Jesus stood up and cried out, 'If anyone thirsts, let him come to me and drink'" (John 7:37).

This invitation is for you. Jesus speaks of Himself as a fountain, and says, "Come to me and drink." Faith is like drinking from an inexhaustible fountain. It is the means by which you receive Christ and all that He offers.

TRAIL MARKERS

Scripture has the power to change a human life and reshape an entire community. When God's Word is taught, God's voice is heard. The Bible read and applied will expose our sins and reveal God's grace. When this leads to repentance and obedience, you will experience great joy.

1. When and where have you seen God bring a group of people with different gifts together to get His work done?

2. As you were growing up, what was your experience of your parents or other adults worshiping and interacting with God's Word?

3. Respond to this statement: "When God's Word is opened, God's voice is heard."

4. When have you experienced God's Word convicting you of your sin? Did it lead you to joy? Why or why not?

5. How does Jesus' offer "Come to me and drink" sound to you today?

To memorize:

All Scripture is breathed out by God and profitable for teaching, for reproof, for correction, and for training in righteousness, that the man of God may be complete, equipped for every good work. (2 Timothy 3:16–17)

We have been following the story of how God's people rebelled against Him, were taken into exile, and then brought back to the promised land. During these years, God spoke to His people through the prophets. The last seventeen books of the Old Testament contain the writings of these prophets, the first of whom was Isaiah.

20

HOLINESS

ISAIAH 6

When crises happen, it's natural to ask, "Where is God in this?" A child dies, a home is destroyed by a flood or by fire, a country is ravaged by war or by famine. Pastors try to discern how best to apply the Word of God to these tragic events, but we cannot answer the question "why?" It was different for the prophets . . .

Growing Casual Toward God

Isaiah, one of the best-known prophets, spoke the Word of God over a period of more than sixty years. His ministry spanned the reigns of four kings: Uzziah, Jotham, Ahaz, and Hezekiah (Isaiah 1:1).

In the year that King Uzziah died, Isaiah was given a vision of God that shaped his life and ministry. Uzziah ruled in Jerusalem for fifty-two years, and during that time, the nation enjoyed a remarkable period of prosperity. This generated a feeling of confidence among God's people, and as their confidence grew, they became increasingly casual toward God.

Vast crowds pressed into the temple, offering their sacrifices and observing the feasts and festivals. But their religion made little difference to their lives. The temple that was once filled with God's glory had become a mere symbol of traditional values. Far from being pleased by this religious activity, God saw it as an obnoxious "trampling of my courts" (1:12). The great issue in Isaiah's time was that people had lost sight of the holiness of God.

A Vision of the Lord

Isaiah had already been preaching for some years when God spoke to him in a vision: "In the year that King Uzziah died I saw the Lord sitting upon a throne, high and lifted up; and the train of his robe filled the temple" (Isaiah 6:1).

"God revealed Himself to me," Isaiah was saying, "but I could not look at His face. All I can tell you is that He was high and lifted up. I could only see the end of His robe."

God's brilliance is overwhelming. When God revealed Himself to Moses, he could only describe what lay beneath God's feet: "Under his feet as it were a pavement of sapphire stone, like the very heaven for clearness" (Exodus 24:10).

Then Isaiah heard angelic creatures calling out to one another: "Holy, holy, holy is the LORD of hosts" (Isaiah 6:3). If you want to give emphasis to a statement, you can underline it, put it in italics, or use a bold typeface. You could also give something emphasis by saying it twice, as Jesus did when He said, "Truly, truly, I say to you . . ." (John 3:3).

The only truth that is repeated three times in the Bible is the truth that God is holy. The holiness of God is so foundational to who God is, that if we do not grasp His holiness, we do not know Him.

The Angels Who Couldn't Bear to Look

If we ask "What is holiness?" it is rather like asking "What is fire?" The best way to understand fire is by observing its effect, and the best way to understand the holiness of God is by observing what happens when God comes near.

You would think that angels who inhabit heaven would be comfortable in the immediate presence of God, but Isaiah saw that even the angels covered their faces when God came near.

Why would they do that? These angels hadn't sinned as we have. They had nothing to be ashamed of. Their whole lives were spent in serving God. The angels covered their faces because they were creatures, overawed in the presence of their Creator. Even if you lived a perfect life and then entered the presence of God, you would still shrink back in awe and wonder as a creature before the glory of your Creator.

Coming Apart at the Seams

When God came near, the temple shook and was filled with smoke (Isaiah 6:4). Isaiah said, "Woe to me! . . . I am ruined!" (6:5 NIV). The word *ruined* literally means coming apart at the seams. If someone is competent or successful, we sometimes say, "He or she has got it all together." Isaiah experienced the opposite. When he saw God, he fell apart.

Isaiah was one of the most respected people of his time. He was known, and no doubt celebrated, for his marvelous ministry. If he were around today, thousands would be crowding into conferences to hear him speak, and millions would be following him on social media. But in the presence of God he could only say, "Woe is me." The holiness of God makes even the best people feel ruined.

As a prophet, Isaiah's lips were the tools of his ministry. Speech was his spiritual gift, but in the presence of God, he found that even his greatest gift had to be cleansed: "I am a man of unclean lips," he said (6:5). when we begin to grasp the holiness of God, we see that what needs to be cleansed is not just our sins, but our gifts, and our strengths as well.

Touched by the Mercy of God

After a momentary glimpse of the glory of God, Isaiah was plunged into darkness as smoke filled the temple. He was conscious of the presence of God, but God was hidden from his view. Then the foundations of the temple began to shake. It must have been absolutely terrifying!

Then, as Isaiah peered into the smoke, he saw one of the angels flying toward him with a live coal in his hand taken from the altar. The angel pressed the hot coal onto Isaiah's mouth: "Behold, this has touched your lips," he said. "Your guilt is taken away, and your sin atoned for" (Isaiah 6:7).

The altar was the place where sacrifices were offered. So when the coal was brought from the altar to Isaiah, God's provision for sin was applied personally to him. And notice that it was applied to the place where Isaiah was most deeply aware of his own need. Isaiah had confessed, "I am a man of unclean lips," and now the angel of God said, "Behold, this has touched your lips; your guilt is taken away."

Having discovered the grace of God in this deep and personal way, Isaiah had a new readiness to serve the Lord. When God said, "Whom shall I send, and who will go for us?" (6:8) Isaiah responded, "Here I am! Send me" (6:8). So God sent Isaiah.

It was as if God said, "You go, Isaiah, because you've understood who I am, and you know what sin is, and you have experienced My grace." Filled with a new sense of the privilege of serving God, Isaiah went out to make Him known.

Isaiah's encounter with God points us to the coming of Jesus Christ. John tells us that "Isaiah . . . saw his [Jesus'] glory and spoke of him" (John 12:41). The Father and the Son share the same glory (John 17:5). The Holy One, whose glory Isaiah had seen, was placed on the altar of the cross and He became the sacrifice for our sins.

As Isaiah was surrounded by darkness in the temple, so Jesus was plunged into darkness on the cross (Matthew 27:45). As the foundations of the temple shook when the presence of God came down, so the earth shook and the rocks split when Jesus laid down His life (Matthew 27:51). The earth trembled when Christ bore the sins of the world and the Father poured out His judgment on the Son.

Jesus died so that people like us who are unraveled by the holiness of God may be touched and healed by His grace. In Jesus Christ, God draws near and says, "Your guilt is taken away, and your sin atoned for."

TRAIL MARKERS

God is holy, holy, holy. His holiness is foundational to His character. In Isaiah's day thousands of people crowded into the temple, but they had no experience of the God they claimed to worship. Eventually this kind of worship becomes boring. But if you think God is boring, you have never encountered the God of the Bible.

Sin is an offense against a holy God, and an atonement is needed. Without it, sinners would be ruined in His presence. The good news of the gospel is that Jesus, God's Son, satisfied the judgment of a holy God by becoming the sacrifice that atoned for all our sins.

When you discover the awesome holiness of God, then, like Isaiah, you will begin to appreciate the wonder of what God has done for you in Jesus Christ. And you will feel that your greatest privilege in life is to serve this awesome, glorious, holy God.

1. What does it mean to "grow casual" toward God? Have you seen any of this in your own life?

2. What is holiness? How would you explain the holiness of God to someone else?

3. How would you know whether or not you have grasped the holiness of God?

4. What is the most striking thing to you about Isaiah's encounter with God?

5. What area of your life would you identify as a strength? How might this need to be cleansed?

To memorize:

> As obedient children, do not be conformed to the passions of your former ignorance, but as he who called you is holy, you also be holy in all your conduct, since it is written, "You shall be holy, for I am holy." (1 Peter 1:14–16)

Thirteen hundred years before the time of Isaiah, God promised that His blessing would come to the nations. But in all that time, little progress was made. God kept blessing His people, but they kept turning to other gods. And now they were coming under the judgment of God themselves. So what hope was there of God's blessing reaching the ends of the earth?

21

SERVANT

ISAIAH 53

Picture the worst place you have ever been. A place that seemed dark, despairing, hopeless. *What would it take for the will of God to be done there?* The same question may come to mind in more ordinary places—your workplace, your neighborhood, or your extended family. Isaiah faced the same question. *What would it take to get God's will done?*

The One Who Gets God's Will Done

God's answer was: "Behold, my servant . . ." (Isaiah 42:1). A servant is a person who gets his master's will done. If you are a servant, your job description is very simple: whatever your master tells you to do, you do it!

So when God introduces His servant, He is saying, "Let Me tell you about the person who will get My will done in the world." God's words about the servant give us a pattern for the kind of ministry that gets His will done and the kind of person He uses to bring His blessing to the world.

God's servant has remarkable privileges: "Behold my servant, whom I uphold, my chosen, in whom my soul delights; I have put my Spirit upon him; he will bring forth justice to the nations" (42:1).

The servant is chosen, loved, anointed, and sustained, and his calling is to bring justice to the world. Justice is more than getting right decisions in a court of law. The servant's task is to put things in order and make them as they ought to be—no more corruption, deception, or exploitation.

By any standards, bringing justice to the nations would be an extraordinary achievement. Who could bring this about? And how could this be done?

If you were given the job of bringing justice to the world, where would you begin? Would you call a press conference, initiate an education program, or declare martial law and put the army on the streets? God's servant would do none of these things. Instead, we are told, "He will not cry aloud or lift up his voice, or make it heard in the street" (42:2).

God's servant will not promote himself. He will not be the kind of person who tries to dominate everybody else. He will not shout. In fact, the outstanding thing about him will be the quietness of his ministry. God's will is accomplished not by angry people who promote their own agendas but by grace-filled people who seek the good of others.

The Power of Compassion

The will of God does not get done in this world through the genius of spectacular programs or by the glamour of celebrities. The servant's style is altogether different: "A bruised reed he will not break, and a faintly burning wick he will not quench" (42:3).

When a reed bends, it usually gets trampled on. And if a candle is burning low, you snuff it out and light another one. But God says that His servant will not do that. He will not break a bruised reed, and he will not quench a faintly burning wick.

Perhaps you can identify with the bruised reed. You have been trampled on and you struggle to stand up under a crushing weight that seems too great to bear. Or perhaps you can relate to the picture of a smoldering candle. There was a time when your faith burned brightly, but now you are running out of fuel. Your inner resources of patience, hope, and love seem to be burning low, and the light within you is flickering.

Broken, bruised, and burned-out people will never be drawn to the loud-mouthed showman. The servant who gets God's will done has a quiet ministry that touches the lives of wounded and weary people with compassion.

The Scale of the Challenge

The people to whom God sends His servant are not only bruised and broken, but also blind and bound. So the servant faces an overwhelming challenge. He has to "open eyes that are blind" and "bring out the prisoners from the dungeon" (42:7).

If people had the capacity of spiritual sight, it would be relatively easy to flood the world with the good news of the gospel. People would immediately see their need and come to Christ. But the problem God's servant faces is that even when he describes the glory of God, his hearers are blind to the truth and lack the capacity to respond to it.

If sin were simply a choice, it would be relatively easy to educate people toward better choices. But sin is a power that binds us. Apart from the work of the Holy Spirit, we are all like blind people in an art gallery.

Who Fits the Profile?

When God first spoke about the servant, it must have seemed to Isaiah that He was talking about Israel: "But you, Israel, my servant, Jacob, whom I have chosen, the offspring of Abraham, my friend; you whom I took from the ends of the earth, and called from its farthest corners, saying to you, 'You are my servant'" (Isaiah 41:8–9).

God's people, Israel, were called to fulfill the role of His servant among the nations. They had been given the light of God's truth, the law, and the sacrifices. God's people were to be the means by which His blessing would come to the world.

But God's people could not live up to their calling. The servant was called to bring sight to the blind and release to the prisoners, but God said, "Who is blind but my servant? . . . This is a people . . . trapped in holes and hidden in prisons" (42:19, 22). The people who were supposed to bring sight and freedom to others turned out to be blind and bound themselves.

Could Isaiah Be the Servant?

Since Israel was clearly not in a position to fulfill the role of God's servant, could Isaiah be the means of getting God's will done? Speaking directly to Isaiah, God said, "You are my servant, Israel, in whom I will be glorified" (49:3).

Isaiah knew that the job of restoring Israel was beyond him. When he said, "I have labored in vain" (49:4), he was saying, "There is no way that my little ministry can fulfill the role of the servant!"

But God went even further: "It is too light a thing that you should be my servant to raise up the tribes of Jacob. . . . I will make you as a light for the nations, that my salvation may reach to the end of the earth" (49:6). This was mission impossible! No prophet ever achieved this or even came close. So who could fulfill the calling of the servant and get God's will done?

Who Would Believe It?

When God revealed the person who would bring love, justice, light, and salvation to the world, Isaiah was so staggered, he feared that no one would believe what he had seen. "Who has believed what he has heard from us? And to whom has the arm of the LORD been revealed?" (53:1). "If I told you what I saw," Isaiah was saying, "you would never believe it."

What Isaiah couldn't get over was that the servant who would get the will of God done was despised and rejected. Violence was poured out on him, and the servant was so disfigured that people hid their heads in their hands. They could hardly bear to look at him.

Isaiah must have winced as he saw what would happen to the servant on whom the hope of God's blessing depends: "He was pierced for our transgressions; he was crushed for our iniquities; upon him was the chastisement that brought us peace, and with his wounds we are healed" (53:5).

Then God told Isaiah something that must have made him gasp. "It was the will of the LORD to crush him" (53:10). How could the suffering inflicted on the humble, compassionate servant of the Lord be the will of God? Did this mean that God's servant would fail? Isaiah must have wondered. But God said: "The will of the LORD shall prosper in his hand" (53:10). God's servant would bring blessing to the nations. And it would come through His suffering and death.

Quoting Isaiah, Matthew clearly identifies Jesus as the gentle, compassionate Servant of God. His ministry fulfilled what was spoken by the prophet Isaiah: "Behold, my servant whom I have chosen, my beloved with whom my soul is well pleased. I will put my Spirit upon him, and he will proclaim justice to the Gentiles. He will not quarrel or cry aloud, nor will anyone hear his voice in the streets; a bruised reed he will not break, and a smoldering wick he will not quench, until he brings justice to victory; and in his name the Gentiles will hope" (Matthew 12:18–2).

Jesus opens our blind eyes to know God, and He sets us free from the power of sin that binds us. He has compassion on the bruised, the burned out, and the broken and, knowing this, you can come to Him.

TRAIL MARKERS

Jesus Christ is the Servant who gets the will of God done. He said to His disciples, "As the Father has sent me, even so I am sending you" (John 20:21). Those who know Jesus are to go out into a broken world and show the compassion of Christ. We are to proclaim the truth of what God has done in Jesus, so that people who do not know Him may come to enjoy the freedom that He gives.

Christ sends His servants to all the nations of the earth. As we minister in His name, the blessing of God will come to many people, and Christ will see the fruit of the travail of His soul and be satisfied.

1. What is a servant? Would you consider yourself a servant of God?

2. Why do you think God chooses to get His work done through compassion?

3. What makes God's work in the world particularly challenging?

4. Contrast the way God gets His will done with the way the world gets its will done.

5. What is the means by which God's servant brings blessing to the world?

To memorize:

Behold my servant, whom I uphold, my chosen, in whom my soul delights; I have put my Spirit upon him; he will bring forth justice to the nations. He

> will not cry aloud or lift up his voice, or make it heard in the street; a bruised reed he will not break, and a faintly burning wick he will not quench; he will faithfully bring forth justice. (Isaiah 42:1–3)

Salvation is a free gift, but Isaiah invites us to "Come, buy" (Isaiah 55:1). He uses the word buy because there is a definite transaction in which we must receive what God offers. Even though we do not pay for it, we must receive it. And unless this transaction takes place, what God offers remains, as it were, on the shelf.

22

CALLING

ISAIAH 55

In the town where my wife, Karen, and I used to live in north London, market days were every Thursday and Saturday. Crews would arrive at around six in the morning and set up the scaffolding and the canopies for the stalls.

There were stalls with fruit and vegetables, a luggage rack, clothing stalls, and a man who strangely seemed to do nothing but sell parts for vacuum cleaners. The market was always milling with people looking for a bargain.

God uses the picture of a marketplace to explain His incredible offer to us: "Come, everyone who thirsts, come to the waters; and he who has no money, come, buy and eat! Come, buy wine and milk without money and without price" (Isaiah 55:1).

Centuries later, Jesus took up these words and applied them to Himself. "If anyone thirsts," He said, "let him come to me and drink" (John 7:37). The street trader is the Son of God, and He offers to satisfy the deep thirsts within your soul.

Jesus' invitation goes out, but not everyone who hears it responds. One reason for this is that some people in the marketplace are preoccupied at other stalls. They are within earshot of the invitation, but it is not heard because it is drowned out by other voices and other interests.

In today's market, many are preoccupied at the sports stall. Others are looking for what will satisfy them on the marriage stall. Others are rummaging around in the career, travel, or entertainment stalls.

These stalls offer good things, but Christ says to us, "Come over here; I have something to offer that you will not find anywhere else." He asks, "Why do you spend your money for that which is not bread, and your labor for that which does not satisfy?" (Isaiah 55:2).

The Son of God offers something of great value. He calls out, "Incline your ear, and come to me; hear, that your soul may live" (55:3). That sounds like a great offer. Let's go over and find out what it costs.

The Price Is Right!

Bargaining on market day is usually about the trader arguing the customer up to his price, but here we have Jesus arguing the price down: "Come, buy . . . without money and without price" (55:1). It's like an auction in reverse where everything is turned on its head, because Christ has chosen to sell to the *lowest* bidder.

So let's take a trip to this auction. Jesus is standing in the stall, and He says, "I am pleased to offer total forgiveness and reconciliation with God. The offer includes the ultimate value of everlasting life, and it is available today to the lowest bidder."

A man in a pinstripe suit steps forward with the first bid. "I've led a good life and run an honest business," he says. "I have been faithful to my wife and have been a good father to my children. I have served on the boards of three charitable organizations. I would like to offer these good works."

A murmur rises from the rest of the bidders. That's a pretty impressive offer. "It's with the man in the pinstripe suit," says the auctioneer. "Can anyone make me a lower offer?"

Then a woman in a blue coat lifts her hand. "I haven't done as much as the man in the pinstripe suit," she says, "but I have attended church faithfully, and I think that I have become a spiritual person."

"It's with the woman in the blue coat," says the seller. "Does anyone have a lower offer?"

A casually dressed teen raises her hand. "I haven't attended church like the woman in the blue coat, but I have tried to live a good life."

"Well," says the auctioneer, "that's not very much, but it's going to the lowest bidder, so you have it. Am I hearing any other bids?"

A man in a red sweater and a red face to go with it, gets up slowly. "I've not lived up to my own expectations," he says. "I have let people down, and I've done some terrible things, but at least I am sorry. I didn't mean to do what I did, so let me offer the fact that I am truly repentant."

"Well," says the seller, "that *really* isn't much. But it's going to the lowest bidder, so your meager bid has it right now. Is anyone going to make me a lower offer?"

This is not a battle of pride; it is a battle of blushes. Many people have opted out of the bidding, not because the cost is too high, but because the offers are embarrassingly low. Most people are just watching to see if anyone would dare to offer less than the man in the red sweater. How could anyone offer so little to God?

Finally someone steps forward, and says, "I don't have anything to offer. My repentance isn't what it should be; my faith isn't what it should be; my works aren't what they should be. Nothing is as it should be! I have nothing to offer."

The auctioneer brings down His hammer. "It's yours," he says. "It's yours."

What Do We Bring?

Maybe you're saying, "Okay, but don't we have to bring something to God? Don't we have to be sorry? Don't we have to believe?"

Yes. But we do not receive salvation because we offer these things. Salvation is a gift. Some people become confused at this point. They think of salvation as a deal in which God offers forgiveness and life in exchange for our repentance and faith. But that's not the gospel.

If God were to ask you why you should be admitted to heaven, what would you say? If you are trusting in your repentance or in your faith you will never have assurance, because your faith could always be stronger and your repentance is never complete. Your salvation depends entirely on Jesus Christ and what He has done for you. Faith is simply the open hand that receives what He offers, and repentance is the response of a heart that receives.

Offering the Lowest Bid

If you find it difficult to love God, could it be that you have not yet received what Christ offers? Perhaps you are following a moral code and offering that to God. Your hands are full, and you have never come to Christ to receive.

God has made it so that every one of us can make the lowest offer. Only pride stands in your way. The man in the pinstripe suit and the woman in the blue coat may have this blessing also, but they must stop trying to buy it. They must lay aside their works and come to Christ empty-handed.

One reason we find this so difficult is that we don't like debt. This came home to me when a friend offered to fix a problem in our home. He spent a couple of hours working on it, and I was grateful. I tried to slip some money in his pocket, but he wouldn't take it.

Why did I want to pay him? Because I didn't want to be in his debt. If I got some help and he got some money, we were level on the deal. And somewhere deep in our hearts that's how we think when it comes to God: "He offers me something that I need. Let me offer Him something that He wants in return." That gives me some credibility, some self-respect. And Christ says, "On that basis, no deal."

The only basis on which we can receive what Christ offers is with the empty hand that receives from Him and that leaves us incalculably in His debt for the rest of our lives and for all eternity.

Making the Purchase

If what Christ offers is to become yours, you must close the deal. Some people enjoy just looking in shops or browsing online, and there is nothing wrong with that. It's where some people are spiritually. They have come over to Christ's stall and started asking questions about the Bible and salvation. Looking is great, but looking isn't buying. The greatest commitment of your life is worthy of the deepest investigation, so look into the claims of Christ carefully. But don't confuse looking with buying.

And trying isn't buying. You could be in a store trying on clothes from nine until five, Monday to Friday, and never buy. And you can come to church, read the Bible, say your prayers, and still never close the deal with Christ. You can feel that you come close to buying but still never do.

And knowing isn't buying. The last time we were looking at washing machines, we found a helpful sales assistant. "This one," he said, "rotates with twenty-three minutes of agitation; and this one has the cork-screw spindle, but it does not have the automatic temperature gauge."

We began talking with him, and eventually he told us that he didn't own a washing machine himself because he lived on his own and went to the laundromat every couple of weeks. He knew all about the products but had never bought one himself. To make matters worse, we didn't buy the washing machine either!

Maybe that is where you are spiritually. You have learned many things about Jesus, but what He offers has not yet become yours. Knowing isn't buying.

There's a time for doing your research, but if you are going to buy, there must come a point where you make a decision and close the deal. And when you buy, what Christ offers becomes yours.

TRAIL MARKERS

Jesus Christ offers to meet the deepest thirsts of your soul. He offers to bring you into a relationship with God in which your sins are forgiven, and you begin a new life that will continue beyond death for eternity.

You cannot buy this gift, but you can receive it. In order to receive it, you must lay aside the idea that there is something that you can offer to God. You must ask Him to give you what you do not have. Faith is like a hand being opened to receive what Christ offers, and He stands ready to give to all who are willing to receive.

1. Why doesn't everyone respond to Jesus' invitation?

2. Would you be better off if Jesus offered forgiveness, reconciliation, and eternal life to the highest bidder or to the lowest bidder? Why?

3. What would you say if God were to ask you on the last day, "Why should I let you into heaven?"

4. What, if anything, is standing in the way of you receiving what Jesus offers?

5. Where are you in the buying process with Jesus? Are you just looking? Are you trying it on? Are you learning more? Have you closed the deal?

To memorize:

> Seek the Lord while he may be found; call upon him while he is near; let the wicked forsake his way, and the unrighteous man his thoughts; let him return to the Lord, that he may have compassion on him, and to our God, for he will abundantly pardon. (Isaiah 55:6–7)

Some people have the idea that in the Old Testament God was only interested in rules, regulations, and duties, but in the New Testament He saw that wasn't working and so introduced a new religion of the heart. But from the beginning, God said, "Love the LORD your God with all your heart" (Deuteronomy 6:5).

23

HEART

JEREMIAH 31

John's credit card debt had spiraled out of control. His wife had insisted on him seeing a counselor, and so, reluctantly, he agreed to go. The counselor made an assessment of his income and his expenses. It wasn't going to be easy, but eventually the counselor came up with a plan. It would involve a radical change in John's lifestyle, and it would take five years to solve the problem.

John winced as he looked at the figures. "I know what I need to do," he said. "The problem is that I don't want to do it." John's predicament illustrates why change is so difficult. Knowing what to do is easy; finding the heart to do it is hard.

God has given us His commandments, showing us how we are to live. The commands are not difficult to understand. The problem is finding the heart to obey them. But God has given us a promise that makes real, deep, lasting change possible in our lives.

God told the prophet Jeremiah that He would make a new covenant. And the heart of the new covenant is a change in the heart: "This is the covenant that I will make with the house of Israel. . . . I will put my law within them, and I will write it on their hearts" (Jeremiah 31:33).

Someone said to me recently: "Pastor, I was taken to church as a child and I got nothing out of it. I didn't understand what was being said, and when I did, it made me feel bad. It was boring, and I could not see how it was relevant to my life. The whole thing was a matter of duty imposed on me, and as soon as I had the opportunity, I left it behind."

If that was your experience, you may find yourself wondering, "Is it really possible to love God from the heart?"

The Problem with the Heart

The heart is devious and sometimes quite baffling. You cannot predict the direction your heart will go: "The heart is deceitful above all things, and desperately sick; who can understand it?" (Jeremiah 17:9).

The reason the heart is perplexing is that sin has defaced it: "sin . . . is written with a pen of iron; with a point of diamond it is engraved on the tablet of their heart" (17:1). Like thieves breaking in and spraying obscenities on the walls of your living room, sin is an enemy that has vandalized your heart!

When sin gets written on your heart, it becomes engraved in your character. It creates the power of habit, and it is the source of the struggles within you. The intensity of the struggle will vary. For some, the heart has become a place where foul and ugly things are deeply engraved. For others, the defacing effects of sin are less severe, but the Bible is clear in telling us that, in some degree, sin is scrawled over every human heart.

No one ever spoke more powerfully about the problem of the human heart than Jesus. He said, "For from within, out of the heart of man, come evil thoughts, sexual immorality, theft, murder, adultery, coveting, wickedness, deceit, sensuality, envy, slander, pride, foolishness. All these evil things come from within, and they defile a person" (Mark 7:21–23).

When King David repented of his sin of adultery, he asked God for two things. First, he said, "Purge me with hyssop, and I shall be clean; wash me, and I shall be whiter than snow" (Psalm 51:7). David knew that he needed to be forgiven, washed, and cleansed.

But he did not stop there. He knew that he needed more than forgiveness, and so he prayed, "Create in me a clean heart, O God" (Psalm 51:10). David asked God to deal with his heart, because he knew that unless his heart was changed, it would lead him down the same sinful path again. So he prayed, "Lord, deal with the heart that led me to do this!"

Cleaning Up the Graffiti

Your heart is the control center of your life. We sometimes talk about "the way we are wired." That gets at it. There is an inclination within us that drives our choices. So when we talk about the heart, we are talking about the core of a person's being.

When God said that He would write His law on our hearts, He was describing a fundamental change that every one of us needs. If you are going to live the life God calls you to lead, what He commands must become what you desire.

No one can live a righteous life simply because God says, "You shall." If you are to become what God wants you to be, there must be an inner transformation that brings you to the point of saying freely, "I will." The question is this: How can that happen?

Neither Fear or Prosperity Can Change Your Heart

Some people think strict discipline and fear of consequences will deliver good character. And yes, fear does have its place. It can modify behavior, but it cannot change the heart. When God gave the law at Mount Sinai, the people were absolutely terrified. But within a few weeks, they were dancing around the golden calf (Exodus 32). Fear did nothing to change their hearts.

There are others who think that the answer to the human condition is primarily social and economic. The argument is that if people do not have enough money or suffer from low self-esteem, they will have no hope, and the way to change this is through programs of economic aid and social reform.

Again, there is some truth in this. But when God brought His people into a land flowing with milk and honey and blessed them with freedom, prosperity, and opportunity, their hearts were no different than when they were in the desert. You cannot erase the graffiti of sin on the human heart by changing a person's circumstances.

Religion Cannot Change Your Heart

Could coming to church, saying prayers, or reading the Bible bring about a change of heart? Again, these are good and right things, but they do not have the power to change the heart.

Before his conversion, the apostle Paul was devoted to a religious life. He wanted to pursue God's law, but found that his heart was pulling him in a different direction: "I do not understand my own actions," he said. "For I do not do what I want, but I do the very thing I hate" (Romans 7:15). The law was powerless to change him. It was overwhelmed by the prevailing disposition of his heart.

Parents often assume that if they exercise appropriate discipline, encourage self-esteem, and bring their children to church, they will have good hearts. But often they are alarmed to find that there is an inclination in their children's hearts that takes them in the wrong direction.

Perhaps you see that same struggle in yourself. You feel that you need to change and live a better life. But when you try, you find to your astonishment that the impulse of your heart toward selfishness, pride, lust, and greed are every bit as strong as they were before. So how can your heart be changed?

How New Life Begins

God says, "I will put my law within them, and I will write it on their hearts. And I will be their God, and they shall be my people" (Jeremiah 31:33). God alone can change your heart. No matter how hard you try, you cannot align your heart with the law of God. It's impossible. So God says, "I will do what you are incapable of doing. I will write My law on your heart."

The Bible calls this change of heart "regeneration" (Titus 3:5). This work of God gives you a new love for Him, a new hunger for His Word, and a new desire to walk in His ways.

The best illustration I know of regeneration is the way a human life begins. The living seed comes, and in a secret, mysterious, and wonderful way, a new life is conceived. It is instantaneous. It happens in a moment. A new life has begun within the woman's body even though, at that moment, she may not even be aware of it!

The next day she goes to work, and it seems that everything is the same, but some weeks later, she begins to feel that something is changing inside her. Something feels different, and she wonders, *Could I be pregnant?*

Perhaps you can look back and see how God has changed your heart. There was a time when you were unresponsive to God. But then things began to change. You had a new hunger for God, a new sense of your own need, and a new desire to be clean.

Here is the explanation: You have been regenerated. New life has been implanted within you by the power of the Holy Spirit. You may not know precisely when this happened, but like every pregnancy, it will eventually show. Repentance and faith in the Lord Jesus Christ are the first visible evidence of the new life that comes from God.

A New Heart

On one occasion, Nicodemus, a highly respected Pharisee, came to talk with Jesus. In the course of the conversation, Jesus explained that to see the kingdom of God, a person "must be born again" (John 3:7). Nicodemus was confused. How could a middle-aged man return to his mother's womb and be born again?

Jesus explained that He was not talking about a physical birth but a spiritual one: "That which is born of the flesh is flesh, and that which is born of the Spirit is spirit" (3:6). Nicodemus was a moral and religious man, but he needed a work of the Holy Spirit within him that would give him a new heart.

When you are in heaven, what is at the heart of you will become the whole of you. If God has implanted new life in your heart, your deepest desire will be satisfied. In God's presence, you will become the person you long to be.

TRAIL MARKERS

The problem of the human heart is that it is defaced with the graffiti of sin. Our great need is that the law of God should be written on our hearts so that what He commands becomes what we desire. Only God can write His law on our hearts, and He came to us in Jesus Christ to make this possible. "If anyone thirsts," Jesus said, "let him come to me and drink. Whoever believes in me, as the Scripture has said, 'Out of his heart will flow rivers of living water'" (John 7:37–38).

1. Can you think of a time when you knew what to do, but you didn't want to do it?

2. How does the Bible explain the unpredictable nature of the human heart?

3. Why do we need more than forgiveness (according to Psalm 51) when we sin?

4. Where have you seen an attempt to change the human heart through fear, prosperity, or religion?

5. How would you know if you had the new life that comes from God? What are some of the signs?

To memorize:

> Purge me with hyssop, and I shall be clean; wash me, and I shall be whiter than snow. Let me hear joy and gladness; let the bones that you have broken rejoice. Hide your face from my sins, and blot out all my iniquities. Create in me a clean heart, O God, and renew a right spirit within me. (Psalm 51:7–10)

A lament is a long and loud cry that ascends to God from a person who endures unspeakable pain or loss. You find laments in the book of Job and in the Psalms, and God has given us an entire book of the Bible called Lamentations, which describes in excruciating detail the grief and sorrow that resulted from the destruction of Jerusalem. Lamentations is the cry of a broken heart. It is God's gift to all who grieve.

24

TEARS

LAMENTATIONS 3

The smoke was still rising from the ashes, as Jeremiah picked his way through the rubble of the once great city, and what he saw broke his heart. The city that had once thrived under the blessing of God now seemed like a ghost town: "How lonely sits the city that was full of people!" (Lamentations 1:1).

Jeremiah had the unenviable task of being God's mouthpiece at this desperate time. His ministry began during the reign of Josiah, the young king who led a campaign of religious and moral reform. But Josiah's son Jehoiakim chose a very different path. He asked for the Word of God to be read to him, then slashed the scroll with a knife, and threw the Scriptures into the fire. It was during the reign of this king who burned the Scriptures that God's judgment on His people began.

Nebuchadnezzar, the king of Babylon, laid siege to Jerusalem. And when the people were too weak to defend their city, his army rounded up the most talented people, including a young man called Daniel (whose story we will come to later), and deported them to Babylon.

God's people endured five disasters—one on top of the other: Enemies laid siege to the city (Jeremiah 52:5), the people starved (Lamentations 1:11), the city fell (1:7), then it was occupied (1:5), and the temple was destroyed (4:1).

Those who survived lost their homes, and many of them lost children as well. The youngest would have been the first to die of hunger in the siege. And when the city fell, those who had older children endured the pain of seeing their sons and daughters marched off into exile, knowing that they would never see them again: "Her children have gone away, captives before the foe" (1:5). Their grief must have been overwhelming.

Grief is the painful process of adjusting to the loss of something or someone you love. It may be the loss of a role or a position that brought you great fulfillment. It could be the loss of the physical ability or mental agility to pursue something you greatly enjoyed. Or it could be the loss of a dearly loved person without whom your life will never be the same.

Soaked in Tears

Lamentations is a book soaked in tears: "She weeps bitterly in the night, with tears on her cheeks" (1:2); "My eyes flow with tears; for a comforter is far from me" (1:16); "My eyes are spent with weeping . . . because infants and babies faint in the streets of the city" (2:11). The references to tears continue throughout the book.

Tears are the shuddering of the body at the pain of the soul. They are a gift from God because they act as a release valve for your pain. God has given you a Savior who knows what it is to weep, so let your tears flow and don't hold them back.

> Lamentations puts grief into words, and it models how grieving people pore over every detail of their loss. Help comes from facing the dark corners of your grief, and bringing it out into the light of God's healing presence in the company of others who love you.

The Hand of God

The people who suffered in Lamentations believed that God is sovereign. When they suffered, they did not say, "This has nothing to do with God." They said, "Though he cause grief, he will have compassion according to the abundance of his steadfast love" (Lamentations 3:32).

Believing that God controls all things raises hard questions that we cannot answer. When our Lord Jesus suffered on the cross, He cried out, "Why . . . ?" (Matthew 27:46). And heaven was silent. So when the agonized "Why?" rises from your soul, remember that Jesus has been there and that He too had to trust the Father without being given an answer.

So what are you to do with the grievance you may feel toward God?

In Lamentations 3, there are nineteen grievances or complaints against the Lord. Notice the repeated use of the word *He,* referring to the Lord: "*He* has walled me about so that I cannot escape" (3:7); "*He* shuts out my prayer" (3:8); "*He* has filled me with bitterness" (3:15). It's not just that God has allowed these things; it's that God has done them! He has brought them about!

Grievance toward God is not an expression of unbelief. In a profound way, it can be an expression of faith. The people who raised so many complaints against God in Lamentations did not believe that what they suffered happened by random chance. They knew that God is sovereign in all things, including the disaster that had befallen them, and it was precisely because they believed this that they struggled with grievance toward God.

Somewhere in your life you may face the same struggle. You may find yourself in great darkness. You may feel trapped, weighed down, afraid, and exhausted. And you may feel as if God has turned against you.

Lamentations models what you should do. God wants you to bring your grievance to Him. A friend or a pastor may be able to help you with this, but what matters most is that you tell God the truth about what you are feeling. Don't complain about God behind His back! Tell Him your grievance face to face. There is no better place to pour out your complaint than in the presence of God.

Hope for Today

In a book about grief, you might expect to find a great deal about the hope of heaven. But there is very little about heaven in Lamentations. Why? The fulfillment of God's ultimate purpose is very wonderful, but heaven may seem a long way from the painful reality faced by a grieving person. When you grieve, your first question is "How am I going to get through today?" Heaven is not the answer to that question; God's love and mercy is.

"This I call to mind, and therefore I have hope: The steadfast love of the LORD never ceases; his mercies never come to an end; they are new every morning; great is your faithfulness. 'The LORD is my portion,' says my soul, 'therefore I will hope in him'" (Lamentations 3:21–24).

God's mercy will be sufficient to get you through today. And when you wake up tomorrow, His love and mercy will be waiting for you. Christ will give you the strength you need to match the load you carry at any given time.

Is God Really for Me?

A question that often rises in the mind of a grieving person is "How can I believe that God is for me when He has brought such pain into my life?"

The answer to this question lies in "the man," who is introduced to us in Lamentations 3:1: "I am the man who has seen affliction under the rod of his wrath." Who is this man?

The man in Lamentations clearly anticipates our Lord Jesus Christ.

The man said, "My soul is bereft of peace" (3:17). And in the garden of Gethsemane, Jesus said, "My soul is very sorrowful, even to death" (Mark 14:34).

The man said, "I have become the laughingstock of all peoples, the object of their taunts all day long" (Lamentations 3:14). And of Jesus, we read: "Kneeling before him, they mocked him, saying, 'Hail, King of the Jews!'" (Matthew 27:29).

The man said, "He has driven and brought me into darkness without any light" (Lamentations 3:2). And when Jesus hung on the cross, darkness covered the whole land (Matthew 27:45).

The man said, "Though I call and cry for help, he shuts out my prayer" (Lamentations 3:8). And on the cross Jesus cried out, "My God, my God, why have you forsaken me?" (Matthew 27:46).

How extraordinary that when Pontius Pilate put Jesus on display before the crowds, with that crown of thorns on Jesus' head, he said, "Behold the man!" (John 19:5). He would have had no idea that, in saying this, he was fulfilling Lamentations 3:1.

Jesus is the man anticipated in Lamentations. The Son of God became the Man of Sorrows, and He is "acquainted with grief" (Isaiah 53:3). Because Jesus has suffered, He is able to help us when we suffer.

A suffering world needs a suffering Savior, but we also need a Savior who has triumphed over suffering. The good news is that suffering was not the end for Jesus. He came through it and triumphed over it in His resurrection. And this Savior offers Himself to you: "Weeping may tarry for the night, but joy comes with the morning" (Psalm 30:5), and one day God will wipe away all tears from your eyes.

TRAIL MARKERS

When you pass through the valley of sorrow and loss, you are in a place where Christ can be found. The Savior knows what it is to walk sorrow's path, and He is well acquainted with grief. Any path on which you come closer to Jesus will be blessed, even if it is a path you would never have chosen to walk.

1. Describe something or someone you lost and what that has been like for you.

2. What do you think it looks like to grieve properly?

3. What did you find most helpful in the way Lamentations models the processing of grief?

4. Have you felt a grievance toward God? And if so, how did you handle it?

5. How can you know if God is for you or against you?

To memorize:

> But this I call to mind, and therefore I have hope: The steadfast love of the Lord never ceases; his mercies never come to an end; they are new every morning; great is your faithfulness. (Lamentations 3:21–23)

Ezekiel's thirtieth birthday may have been the hardest day of his life. He had been preparing for ministry in the temple of God, but at the age of twenty-five, in the middle of his training, war broke out and he was carted off to the Chebar canal. A priest's thirtieth birthday was the day on which his ministry in the temple would begin. But what can a new priest do if he is seven hundred miles away from the temple?

25

GLORY

EZEKIEL 1

Ezekiel was a man with crushed hopes and shattered dreams. If only he had lived at another time. If only he could be in another place. If only! Circumstances seemed to have blocked his path to ministry, and he found himself among a group of confused and discouraged people in a backwater near Babylon.

Perhaps you can relate to Ezekiel. Maybe you had high hopes and big dreams, and you never imagined you would be where you are today.

God's People in Two Places

God's people were in two places in Ezekiel's day. Ten thousand of them were at the Chebar canal in Babylon, and the rest were back in Jerusalem where King Zedekiah was holding on to power by the skin of his teeth.

Ezekiel was called to speak the Word of God to the exiles. And at the same time, Jeremiah was speaking the Word of God to the remaining community in Jerusalem.

Families were divided, and everyone was wondering what would happen next. Would the beleaguered community in Jerusalem survive? When would the exiles be able to return? Next month? Next year? Ever?

There was no shortage of answers from people claiming to speak the Word of

God. False prophets were eager to assure God's people that what had happened was only a temporary setback: "God would never leave His temple. The exiles would soon be home. How could Jerusalem ever fall?"

The prophet Jeremiah had a different message, and it was not good news. In a letter to the exiles, he told the ten thousand deportees that seventy years would pass before God would allow them to return. Their entire lives would be spent in a strange and foreign land (Jeremiah 29). They needed encouragement and God gave it to them through a fresh vision of His glory.

The Glory Appears

There are seven elements in Ezekiel's vision of the glory of God.

First, there was a massive platform made of glass that sparkled in the sunlight (Ezekiel 1:22). Second, the platform was being held up by living creatures, one at each corner. They held up the platform on their wings, but they had more than one pair of wings, so they could also fly. The platform could take off vertically, rather like a helicopter (1:19).

Third, Ezekiel saw wheels: "I saw a wheel on the earth beside the living creatures . . . as it were a wheel within a wheel" (1:15–16). Picture a wheel facing north to south, being intersected by another wheel going east to west. These wheels could move in any of four directions, which would be useful if you needed to parallel park your car in a tight space. You could just switch to lateral mode and slide in!

These wheels gave mobility to the platform. What we are being told here is that God's presence is not fixed or limited to any one location. God is free to move wherever He chooses and in any direction. There is no place on earth where one of God's people is ever beyond His reach.

Fourth, above the platform, the living creatures, and the wheels "there was the likeness of a throne, in appearance like sapphire" (1:26). Notice the word "likeness." Ezekiel is struggling for language to describe what he sees, and the higher he looks, the more difficult it is to express.

Fifth, above the throne Ezekiel saw "gleaming metal, like the appearance of fire enclosed all around" (1:27). The fire and lightning that speak of the judgment of God came from the throne of God. And sixth, something else that you would not expect to see at the same time: "The appearance of the bow that is in the cloud on the day of rain" (1:28). Ezekiel saw a rainbow that speaks of the grace of God, also coming from the throne.

As Ezekiel gazed into this vision, he kept looking higher. Above the creatures was the platform. Above the platform he saw "the likeness of a throne" (1:26). And seventh, above the throne he saw a glorious person, "a likeness with a human appearance" surrounded by brilliant light (1:26–27).

What Ezekiel most needed to see when he was far from where he wanted to be was that God was on the throne and that God's presence was with him. What you most need when you are far from where you want to be is a fresh vision of the glory of God.

The Glory Departs

Sometime later Ezekiel was given a very different vision in which he saw a massive idol in the temple of God. He saw grotesque images of idols scrawled on the temple walls (Ezekiel 8:7–10). Obscene things were going on in secret, even in the temple, and people were saying, "The Lord does not see us" (8:12).

Then Ezekiel saw the same glory of the Lord that he had seen in his earlier vision (8:2–4). It was as if God was squaring off with the idol. The Lord was getting ready to destroy the false worship that had desecrated His temple.

When Ezekiel saw the vision of God's glory again, he saw the platform, the wheels, and the throne of God moving toward the door. God was about to leave His temple and His city (Ezekiel 10:4, 18; 11:22–23).

God's presence, symbolized by the flying platform, was leaving Jerusalem, but He had not abandoned His people or His promises. The focus of His redeeming work was moving away from Jerusalem. God was leaving the temple, but His presence would now be made known among the exiles beside the Chebar canal.

Ezekiel was far from his home and far from the temple, but he was right in the center of the will of God.

You may not be where you want to be, but God has you where you are for a reason. And His great eternal purpose of conforming you to the likeness of Jesus Christ will be wonderfully advanced wherever you are.

The Glory Returns

Twenty years after Ezekiel's first vision, God spoke to him again. And what Ezekiel saw must have brought joy to his heart: "The glory of the LORD entered the temple by the gate facing east . . . and behold, the glory of the LORD filled the temple" (43:4–5). God's glory would one day fill a temple that would serve as a center of worship for people of every tribe and nation.

This Is Jesus' Story

Ezekiel saw "the likeness of the glory of the LORD" (Ezekiel 1:28). The book of Hebrews tells us that Jesus "is the radiance of the glory of God" (Hebrews 1:3). The glory of God came down among us: "We have seen his glory, glory as of the only Son from the Father, full of grace and truth" (John 1:14).

Think of it this way: God came off His platform! The eternal Creator, the Lord of glory, came down from His throne. This indescribably glorious person, surrounded by the rainbow and the fire and the lightning, took on human flesh and was born in Bethlehem. The one who sat on the throne upheld by angels lay in a manger, and angels looked down on Him.

Not only did the Lord of glory come down from the platform, He came to His temple and spoke the Word of God. And the Lord of glory, who had come down, left the temple, not on a platform, but carrying a cross.

But the glory that appeared and departed will one day return. This is where all history is headed. We wait with eager expectation for the day when the Lord of Glory will descend from heaven. We will see Him, we will be like Him, and we will be with Him forever!

This Could Be Your Story

Ezekiel was a gifted man in the prime of life, yet he found himself relegated to an obscure backwater in Babylon. His prospects seemed bleak, and his personal hopes for the future seemed shattered. Maybe you have felt like that. Something happened in your life and you find yourself saying, "This isn't how it was supposed to be!" Or perhaps God has taken you from a place where you were happy and moved you somewhere else.

Ezekiel's flying platform reminds us that God's presence is not limited to one place. If God moves you on, His presence will go with you. He says, "I will never leave you nor forsake you" (Hebrews 13:5). There is no place on earth where His presence cannot go. Ezekiel discovered that it was better to be in Babylon with the presence of God than to be in Jerusalem without it.

TRAIL MARKERS

The glorious presence of God came down among us in Jesus Christ. The Lord of glory came to His temple, but the people rejected Him and Jesus left Jerusalem carrying a cross. The Glory appeared and the Glory departed, but thank God, the Glory will return. Jesus Christ rose from the dead, and one day He will return in power and glory. The Bible story points forward to the time when the great exile of human history will be over and when God's people will be brought into His presence to enjoy Him forever.

1. Have you ever said (or thought), "I'm not where I'm supposed to be"?

2. What is your reaction to Ezekiel being far from home, and far from the temple, but still being right in the middle of God's will?

3. How do Ezekiel's visions anticipate the story of Jesus?

4. Explain in your own words why it is "better to be in Babylon with the presence of God than to be in Jerusalem without it."

5. How does Ezekiel's vision of the glory of God compare with the way you normally think about God?

To memorize:

In the beginning was the Word, and the Word was with God, and the Word was God. . . . The Word became flesh and dwelt among us, and we have seen his glory, glory as of the only Son from the Father, full of grace and truth. (John 1:1, 14)

The experience of every family, school, business, church, and nation will largely depend on the quality of its leadership. If you have suffered the effects of poor leadership, this chapter is for you. It describes how God's people languished under abusive leadership and how God Himself intervened. If you have been trusted with the privilege of leadership in any sphere of life, Ezekiel will show you what God requires of you and how you can fulfill your calling.

26

SHEPHERD

EZEKIEL 34

The three distinct leadership roles in the Old Testament are prophet, priest, and king. The prophets stood in the presence of God and heard the word of God so that they could speak that word to the people. The prophets gave leadership in the realm of truth.

The ministry of the priests related to worship. They offered prayers and sacrifices in the temple, and they brought people into the presence of God through a ministry of pastoral care and counsel.

The kings led the people into battle and protected them from their enemies. They were also responsible for leading the people in right paths so that they would continue to enjoy the blessing of God.

These three ministries, taken together, show us God's plan for leadership. The prophet was to lead people into truth, the priest was to bring people to God, and the king was to lead and protect the people. The ministry of the prophet was about revealing, the ministry of the priest was about reconciling, and the ministry of the king was about ruling.

The Shepherd Leader

The image of a shepherd brings the roles of prophet, priest, and king together into one beautiful picture that encompasses all three dimensions of biblical leadership.

The shepherd *feeds* the sheep—sustaining the people of God on a healthy diet of the Word of God. The shepherd *seeks* the sheep—finding the sheep that is lost and bringing it back. The shepherd *leads* the sheep—giving direction and protection to the flock. So when God speaks about shepherds, He is speaking about everything that is involved in leading His people.

Most professions have a system of making an annual review or appraisal of how employees have performed in their duties. God had entrusted the shepherds of Israel with great responsibility, and in Ezekiel 34 He gives an evaluation of their performance. It was not a good review: "Son of man, prophesy against the shepherds of Israel; prophesy, and say to them, even to the shepherds, Thus says the Lord GOD: Ah, shepherds of Israel who have been feeding yourselves! Should not shepherds feed the sheep?" (Ezekiel 34:2).

God brought three charges against the leaders of His people: they abused their power, they subverted the truth, and they neglected the Lord.

Leaders Who Abuse Their Power

God's people suffered under a consistent pattern of abuse. Many kings were wicked, and even the best kings ended up placing great burdens upon the people. God indicted them for their complete failure to care for His flock: "The weak you have not strengthened, the sick you have not healed, the injured you have not bound up, the strayed you have not brought back, the lost you have not sought, and with force and harshness you have ruled them" (34:4).

Leaders Who Subvert God's Truth

God also indicted those who claimed to be prophets but replaced the Word of God with their own opinions: "Son of man, prophesy against the prophets of Israel, who are prophesying, and say to those who prophesy from their own hearts: 'Hear the word of the LORD!' Thus says the Lord GOD, Woe to the foolish prophets who follow their own spirit, and have seen nothing!" (Ezekiel 13:2–3).

These leaders studied the culture to discover what people wanted to hear. Then they shaped their message to fit the felt needs of the hour. In Ezekiel's time, these prophets led God's people astray by saying "peace" when God had said that there would be no peace (13:10). What God said did not concern them. Their ministry was not driven by truth but by demand.

Leaders Who Neglect the Lord

The priests were given a ministry of bringing people to God, but they focused on helping people be at peace with themselves instead of helping them find peace with God. They were not exercising a ministry of prayer or showing people how to be reconciled with God: "Her priests have done violence to my law and have profaned my holy things. They have made no distinction between the holy and the common, neither have they taught the difference between the unclean and the clean . . . so that I am profaned among them" (22:26).

When God looked at the shepherds of Israel, He saw terrible abuses of power, a deliberate subversion of the truth, and a neglect of God Himself. The effect of all this was that God's flock was malnourished, the sheep were not cared for, and they were not protected.

Time for a New Shepherd

God found the situation among His people intolerable, so He determined to intervene: "I myself will be the shepherd of my sheep . . . declares the Lord God" (34:15). God was saying, "I will be the prophet, priest, and king to My people. I will personally bring the truth to them. I will come to My people and care for them Myself. I will personally protect them and lead them in right paths."

How would God do that? Roll the story forward another six hundred years, and Jesus Christ is born into the world. He saw that God's people were "like sheep without a shepherd" (Matthew 9:36) and He had compassion on them. He said, "I am the good shepherd" (John 10:11). "All who came before me are thieves and robbers" (10:8). They exploited the sheep, but Jesus laid down His life for the sheep (10:11). They slaughtered the sheep, but Jesus came that the sheep may have life (10:10).

Jesus is the Good Shepherd who feeds the sheep, seeks the sheep, and leads the sheep. He will nourish you in the truth. He will bring you back and restore you when you go astray (Luke 15:5–6). He will protect you from your enemies, and when death comes, He will bring you into everlasting life: "My sheep . . . will never perish, and no one will snatch them out of my hand" (John 10:27–28).

The Tenderness of Jesus

Jesus has a special tenderness toward people who have suffered under abusive leaders because He has suffered this way Himself. When large crowds were drawn to Jesus, the religious leaders of the day saw the danger of losing their flock. So they had Jesus arrested, and the Good Shepherd was brought to trial by the shepherds of Israel.

When Jesus was tried before Caiaphas, He was spat on, slapped, and struck (Matthew 26:67). When Jesus was sent to Herod, the king did nothing to defend Him. When Jesus was brought before Pilate, the governor showed no interest in the truth (John 18:38). His decision about Jesus was not based on justice but on the prevailing mood of the people. Pilate washed his hands and gave Jesus over to be crucified.

Jesus knows what is it like to suffer under shepherds who abuse power, subvert truth, and care more for themselves than for God. If you have suffered in this way, you have a Savior to whom you can come.

The Good Shepherd

Jesus, the Good Shepherd, says, "I will seek the lost, and I will bring back the strayed, and I will bind up the injured, and I will strengthen the weak, and the fat and the strong I will destroy. I will feed them in justice" (Ezekiel 34:16).

"Lost" means you don't know where you are, and you can't find your way back to where you need to be. If you feel lost today, Jesus came to seek you and save you. And if you will give yourself to Him, He will bring you home.

"Strayed" means that you have drifted away from the other sheep. You're isolated, and because you are alone, you are vulnerable. But Jesus can bring you back.

"Injured" means that something happened in your life that really hurt you. If you have been injured, Jesus says to you today, "I will bind up your wounds." Now you may say, "My wounds are too deep!" But there is no wound that Christ cannot heal.

"Weak" means you do not have the strength to do what you need to do. If you don't know how you're going to face this week, Jesus offers to give you strength.

It is a marvelous thing to be wholly owned and led by the Son of God. When you can say, "The LORD is my shepherd" you will also be able to say, "I shall not want" (Psalm 23:1).

But then God says, "The fat and the strong I will destroy" (Ezekiel 34:16). The fat and the strong are those who feel they have no need of the shepherd. God will bring justice to all who abuse power and to all who resist His rule.

TRAIL MARKERS

Shepherding God's flock involves the ministries of the prophet, priest, and king. Those who are trusted by God with the responsibility of leadership in the church must not abuse their positions by teaching their own opinions, neglecting the spiritual needs of God's people, or imposing unnecessary burdens on them.

Effective leaders will teach God's truth, pastor God's people, and lead God's flock in paths that are pleasing to Him. They will focus on these duties because they are accountable to the Great Shepherd, Jesus Christ, who gave His life for the sheep (Acts 20:28).

1. Where has God entrusted you with the privilege of leadership? (e.g., family, work, church, community)

2. What are the roles of the prophet, priest, and king? In which area do you think you are strongest?

3. Have you personally suffered under abusive leadership? How did it affect you?

4. What do you see in Jesus that would encourage you to ask for His help?

5. "Lost," "strayed," "injured," or "weak"—which of these do you most relate to?

To memorize:

> "I am the good shepherd. The good shepherd lays down his life for the sheep. . . . My sheep hear my voice, and I know them, and they follow me. I give them eternal life, and they will never perish, and no one will snatch them out of my hand." (John 10:11, 27–28)

The story of Daniel is about one of God's people in an alien land, and it shows us how to live in a secular and materialistic culture. Daniel was one of a small group of talented students who were taken to Babylon after the first siege of Jerusalem. He would have been a teenager when he arrived, and he remained in Babylon for the rest of his life.

27

EXILES

DANIEL 1

The Bible uses the word *exiles* or *sojourners* to describe God's people (1 Peter 2:11). You do not belong to this world in a permanent way. You belong to another city "whose designer and builder is God" (Hebrews 11:10), and you cannot understand your life in this world until you have grasped that this is not what God created you for.

If you are a Christian, you are like a person who carries two passports. One of them will expire, because when Christ returns, the nations to which we belong will be relegated to history. But your passport as a citizen of heaven will never pass away. It will remain forever.

The art of the Christian life is to live in this world without being consumed by it. We are to use our short lives here to prepare for the eternal life that is to come.

Teenager Abducted!

Imagine Daniel sitting at his school desk in Jerusalem. There is a knock on the door. A moment later, three soldiers from Nebuchadnezzar's army burst in, and Daniel is taken seven hundred miles to Babylon. His parents are distraught, and there's nothing they can do to stop it.

But when Daniel arrives in Babylon, he finds that far from being tortured and imprisoned, he is treated like royalty and enrolled in a top flight school. He has been selected to participate in a premier education program that will fast-track him into the king's service. If he plays his cards right, he will land a top job in Babylon.

The Pressure to Conform

Daniel was placed in a new environment where he was completely anonymous. Those who travel know all about this pressure. When you check into a hotel, nobody knows who you are. You can be whoever you want to be, and that brings its own pressure.

Daniel was placed under the care of a tutor called Ashpenaz, who was assigned to teach him the literature and language of the Babylonians (Daniel 1:4). Back in Jerusalem, Daniel would have studied Hebrew and learned the Hebrew Scriptures. But that was not on the curriculum in Babylon.

Instead, Daniel was exposed to a whole spectrum of learning, most of which would have been in direct conflict with what he had been taught from Scripture as a child. By filling Daniel's mind with Babylonian learning, Ashpenaz was attempting to erode Daniel's distinctive faith in God, so that at the end of three years in college, he would emerge with a thoroughly Babylonian worldview. He would still be Jewish, of course, but he would think and act like a Babylonian.

In addition to the challenges of the curriculum, Daniel would face pressure from his tutor and from other students: "How can you seriously believe that your God is the only God? How can you possibly think that you are the only one who has the truth?" Christian young people face the same pressure in universities today.

Parents are sometimes distressed over what their children are taught in school. Students are often studying literature that directly contradicts the truth. But this is nothing new. It is exactly the situation that Daniel faced, and God has given us a model of how to stand against that pressure. Far from overwhelming him, Daniel's secular education was actually the making of him. In the goodness of God, it became the anvil on which his faith was hammered into maturity.

A Taste of the High Life

Throughout their history, God's people lived under two very different kinds of oppression. Pharaoh's plan was to persecute God's people. He was ruthless and subjected them to hard labor. Satan uses the same tactic today in many places where Christians are persecuted for their faith.

But Nebuchadnezzar's plan was more subtle. His strategy was to absorb God's people into the culture of Babylon, opening doors of opportunity for them and putting them on the fast track to success.

The enemy of our souls is still using the tactics of Nebuchadnezzar, and they are proving very effective. The strategy is simple: First, intoxicate the people of God with the sheer fascination and splendor of this world. Second, erode their distinctive practices and values until they are so assimilated into the culture that their distinctive calling to live for the glory of God is overwhelmed.

Daniel was offered "a daily portion of the food that the king ate" but he "resolved that he would not defile himself with the king's food" (1:5, 8). Some suggest that this had to do with Jewish dietary laws, but I think Daniel discerned that Nebuchadnezzar wanted to lure him with the opportunities of life in Babylon, and he was determined that this would never happen. He would live, serve, and prosper in Babylon, but he would never allow Babylon to capture his heart.

Daniel needed a way of keeping this fixed in his mind. So he chose to establish a discipline for himself. He turned down the offer of a daily visit to the top restaurant in town and ate a brown bag lunch of vegetables instead. He did not do this because of some external law, but because of an internal desire. It was a voluntary discipline, designed to remind him of his own distinctive calling.

Like Daniel, we are constantly bombarded by a view of life that has no room for God. We need to be realistic about the pressures the world places on us, and we need a strategy for resistance.

Cultivating the Ability to Say No

Like Daniel, we need to cultivate the ability to say no to ungodliness (Titus 2:11–12), and that begins with the small stuff.

Christians sometimes make decisions based on one question: "Is this right or wrong?" If something isn't immoral, we conclude it is ours to enjoy. But there's another question we should ask: "Is this wise?"

What entertainment should you choose? What company should you keep? On what should you spend your money? Daniel's example reminds us that as we make these decisions, we need to consider the long-term potential of being sucked into the values and lifestyles of the world.

Daniel could not change what they taught him at school, but he could create a space in his life that was a daily reminder to him that he was a servant of God.

Faithful and Successful

God gave Daniel and his friends great success in their studies. He "gave them learning and skill in all literature and wisdom" (Daniel 1:17).

Faithfulness and success need not be alternatives; they are natural partners. Daniel had proved faithful in small things, and God trusted him with greater things. He was appointed to a premier position within the most powerful government of his day.

Never assume that faithfulness to Christ means settling for small things. Daniel proved that he could be trusted. He was faithful to God, and the Lord opened the door of opportunity for him. He became second-in-command to the king of Babylon, and he was given influence beyond what he had ever dreamed.

Like Daniel, Jesus faced the seductive enticements of the world when He was tempted, and He faced the open hostility of the world on the cross. He triumphed over both and He was able to say to His disciples, "Take heart; I have overcome the world" (John 16:33).

TRAIL MARKERS

Daniel lived a godly and successful life in an affluent and ungodly culture by exercising voluntary restraint. God does not call us to lives of austerity, but undisciplined indulgence erodes godliness.

The attractions of wealth, power, and pleasure are strong and can easily capture our hearts. We need a love for God that is stronger than the attractions of the world. As love for Christ fills your heart, it will increasingly expel the lesser loves that would otherwise take you captive.

 1. Where is the pressure of the culture the greatest on you, personally? What effect is it having on you? Think about specifics.

 2. Think about a decision you have made in the past month. Did you simply ask, "Is this right or wrong?" Would it have helped to ask, "Is it wise?"

 3. How are you intentionally resisting the pressures of the world around you? Where could you start?

 4. Do *faithfulness* and *success* seem like alternatives? Or have you thought of them as natural partners? Why or why not?

 5. How can you best use the time you have on earth to prepare for the life to come?

To memorize:

> For the grace of God has appeared, bringing salvation for all people, training us to renounce ungodliness and worldly passions, and to live self-controlled, upright, and godly lives in the present age. (Titus 2:11–12)

Malachi was the last of the Old Testament prophets. He spoke the Word of God at the time of Nehemiah when a small community rebuilt Jerusalem. Sixteen hundred years after the time of Abraham, our human problem was unchanged, and God's people were still waiting for His promise to be fulfilled. After Malachi, nothing significant happened in the Bible story for four hundred years.

28

HOPE

MALACHI 4

As we come to the end of the Old Testament, it's worth asking: Where do things stand in the relationship between God and His people after all these years? Malachi does not give us an encouraging answer.

Alienated from God

A pattern of resistance to God runs through the book of Malachi.

God begins by affirming His love: "'I have loved you,' says the LORD" (Malachi 1:2). But God's people fold their arms in defiance: "How have you loved us?" (1:2).

Then God rebukes the priests who despise His name. They say, "How have we despised your name?" (1:6).

Then God raises the issue of tithes. "Will man rob God? Yet you are robbing me" (3:8). But God's people push back: "How have we robbed you?" (3:8).

Then God accuses His people of speaking about Him harshly. "Your words have been hard against me" (3:13). But with feigned innocence they ask, "How have we spoken against you?" (3:13).

This discussion is getting nowhere, and the pattern runs right through the book—denial, denial, denial. When God raises the issue of repentance—"'Return to me, and I will return to you,' says the LORD of hosts" (3:7)—the response has a note of defiance about it: "How shall we return?" (3:7).

Relationships are restored when issues that have caused offense are brought to light and dealt with honestly. But when God reached out to reconcile with His people, they were in denial about the problem.

Human Conflict

Besides being alienated from God, the Old Testament ends with people in conflict. In the garden, Adam and Eve enjoyed a beautiful relationship in which their love for each other was a mirror of the love of God for them.

They were at ease together, and their trust in each other was complete. But the knowledge of evil changed all that. Adam blamed his wife for what had gone wrong, and for the first time, suspicion developed between the man and the woman. The knowledge of evil put strain on the first marriage.

No one imagines on their wedding day that they will end up divorced. But in Malachi's time, as in ours, marriages were breaking apart: "The Lord was witness between you and the wife of your youth, to whom you have been faithless, though she is your companion and your wife by covenant" (2:14).

The story of the Old Testament began with a man and a woman sharing the joy of a perfect life in the garden, and it ends with men and women unable to sustain relationships of faithfulness and love.

Sin broke trust in the first marriage and led to a world of conflict in which families, communities, and nations continue to be torn apart.

A Promise and a Curse

As if alienation from God and estrangement from one another weren't enough, a dreadful curse hangs over every person born into the world.

God's curse on evil permeates the book of Malachi: "I will send the curse upon you and I will curse your blessings" (2:2). "You are cursed with a curse, for you are robbing me, the whole nation of you" (3:9).

The last verse in the Old Testament ends with the threat of a curse: "Lest I come and strike the land with a decree of utter destruction [a curse]" (4:6). So at the end of the Old Testament, no progress has been made in dealing with the human problem of alienation from God, our conflict with each other, or the dreadful curse that hangs over us all.

The Unfulfilled Promise

The problem of sin pervades the Old Testament, but the heart of the Bible story beats with a promise. When sin entered the world, God promised that someone, born of a woman, would destroy the evil one and all his works (Genesis 3:15).

God sent Malachi to remind His people not only of the problem but also of the promise: "The sun of righteousness shall rise with healing in its wings. You shall go out leaping like calves from the stall" (Malachi 4:2).

The day will come when all the wounds of God's people will be healed, and they will experience the freedom that calves enjoy when they are released. But at the end of the Old Testament, we are still looking for this promise to be fulfilled.

Time for the Intermission

If the Bible were presented as a drama, it would unfold in two parts, like a two-act play. The Old Testament is Act 1, and as it comes to a close, we are ready for an intermission before coming back to see what happens in act two.

As we spill out into the foyer to reflect on the first act, people are talking about what they have seen.

"Some of that was a bit heavy," says a large man as he pulls out his phone.

"Some of it made me want to cry," says a woman with a wine glass in her hand.

"I hope that act two has a happier ending than this," adds a third.

"Well, it must," says someone else. "All the way through there have been promises and pointers; something good is going to happen."

"Well, whatever it is, it hasn't happened yet," says a man who is clearly irritated. "Nothing has happened in the whole of act one that has dealt with the basic problem."

"What do you mean nothing has happened?" his wife interjects. "We've had the Law, and the sacrifices. We've had kings and priests. We've seen the cloud of God's presence in the temple—"

"So what?" snaps the frustrated man. "The main problem isn't solved. They are still alienated. They are still in conflict. And they are still under the curse."

The bell rings for the end of the intermission, and they all file back to their seats in the theater for act two.

Don't Miss Act 2!

When you come to the end of the Old Testament, with its laws, priests, and sacrifices, you are left asking, "Who can end our alienation from God, change our hearts, and remove the dreadful curse?"

The New Testament answers this question.

Jesus Christ came into the world to reconcile us to God: "Christ also suffered once for sins, the righteous for the unrighteous, that he might bring us to God" (1 Peter 3:18).

Jesus came to reconcile us to each other: "He himself is our peace, who has made us both one and has broken down in his flesh the dividing wall of hostility" (Ephesians 2:14).

And Jesus came to set us free from the curse by "becoming a curse for us" (Galatians 3:13).

But if our hope is only found in Jesus, what is the point of the Old Testament?

Properly understood, the Old Testament prepares us to recognize Jesus as the Savior we need and to welcome Him with faith. So let's review what we have gained from our hike through the Old Testament.

God is the Creator and owner of everything. Your *life* is a gift from His hands (chapter 1), and you were made to enjoy and *worship* Him forever (chapter 16). The God who made you is *holy* (chapter 20), and your deepest problem is that you were born into a world that is under a *curse* (chapter 2), plagued with the knowledge of evil and excluded from the presence of God.

The inclination to love yourself more than God and care for yourself more than others lies deep within you and causes you to break God's *law* and *sin* against Him (chapters 7 and 17). You need a Savior, and Jesus is the Savior you need.

Jesus is the *glory* of God who came to this *alien* world (chapters 25 and 27). He is the true *temple* in whom God's presence has come down (chapter 15). He is the *servant* who gets the will of God done (chapter 21). He is the man who suffered in this world of *tears* (chapter 24). He is the Good *Shepherd* who laid down His life for His sheep (chapter 26). He is our *prophet*, our *priest*, and our *king* (chapters 14, 9, 12).

In His life, He fulfilled the *righteousness* that God requires of us (chapter 18). In laying down that perfect life, He bore the *judgment* that was due to us (chapter

4), making *atonement* through the shedding of His *blood* (chapters 8 and 6). He fulfills the *promise* given to Abraham (chapter 5), and He will reign on the *throne* of David forever (chapter 13).

Jesus stands ready to forgive your sins and to reconcile you to God. He is the *Deliverer* who can set you free (chapter 11). He is able to change your *heart* (chapter 23), and He can give you new *courage, hope,* and *joy* (chapters 10, 28, 19). In love He is *calling* out (chapter 22), offering His *salvation* freely to you (chapter 3).

The Old Testament, properly understood, will lead you to faith in Jesus.

TRAIL MARKERS

It would be easy to get the idea that all religions lead to God, but the Old Testament teaches the opposite. No religion can bring us to God, not even the religion of the Old Testament itself. The Old Testament tells us why we need a Savior and prepares us for His coming. God destroys all false hopes so that we may find our true hope in His Son, who came to deal with the problem of sin and to fulfill the promise of God.

1. If you were in the foyer at the end of act one, what would you be saying?

2. The Old Testament ends with people far from God. Has there been a time when you felt far from God?

3. When have you experienced conflict with others? Why do you think human conflicts are so prevalent?

4. What were some of the limitations of religion in the Old Testament?

5. Do you believe that Jesus is able to reconcile you to God and bring you peace? Why or why not?

To memorize:

Christ redeemed us from the curse of the law by becoming a curse for us—for it is written, "Cursed is everyone who is hanged on a tree." (Galatians 3:13)

The Old Testament story set the stage for God's greatest intervention in human history. God had given many clues about the identity of a promised person, often referred to as the Messiah or Christ. Whoever this person turned out to be, His entrance into the world would be the greatest event in the entire history of the human race. Everything God had promised to do would be fulfilled by Him.

29

BORN

LUKE 1

Envision yourself living on a beautiful island with breathtaking views.[5] The beaches extend for hundreds of miles, and the island is home to a vast population.

Over the years, the islanders have often wondered what may lie beyond the horizon. But nobody has ever left the island, so no one really knows.

The islanders have spent many hours studying wildlife, plants, weather, and rock formations. They have also paid a great deal of attention to cultivating family life. The islanders are all descended from castaways who were washed up after a great disaster that happened many years ago—so long ago that most residents know little or nothing about it.

At the center of the island is a volcano. Some islanders fear that one day it may erupt, but most have come to the conclusion that it never will.

Message in a Bottle

One morning, as you are out strolling on the beach, you see a reflection in the sand. As you look more closely, you notice that a green bottle has been washed up

5. Original idea adapted from a piece in Eugene Petersen, *Working the Angles* (Eerdmans, 1987), 139ff. Petersen adapted it from an essay/parable by Walker Percy, *The Message in a Bottle* (Farrar, Straus & Giroux, 1975).

on the shore. Inside you find a message: "Help is coming."

Strange. You have never seen anything like this before. "Help"? What kind of help could possibly be needed on such a beautiful island?

A few weeks later, you see another bottle, with another message: "Help will arrive soon!" Two bottles with the same message. Where could they have come from?

The discoveries are strangely unnerving. After all, you are living on an idyllic island and are enjoying a very full and satisfying life. But the notes in the bottles suggest that there is some kind of problem.

Perhaps there is someone out there beyond the horizon. And perhaps he, she, or it is telling you that you are in danger and that there is a plan to do something about it.

But then again, the messages might have been written by children on the other side of the island. If they threw the bottles out to sea, the tide could easily have washed them back in.

Whatever happened, you can't get the bottles and their message out of your mind: "Help is coming."

The Islanders' Problem

The story of the islanders can help us grasp the big picture of the Bible. God created you to know Him, enjoy Him, and live in His presence. But there was a great disaster. Sin ruptured our relationship with God, and now we live in a fallen world, which for all its beauty, has a curse hanging over it. We all face many problems living on the island, but our greatest problem is that the island itself will one day be destroyed.

From the beginning, God promised that help would come. Over hundreds of years He repeated the same message through the Old Testament prophets: "Don't despair. I am sending help. Someone will come to rescue you from a danger that you do not yet fully understand."

You were born for a land that you have never seen, but you can only get there if someone comes to rescue you. This is why Jesus Christ came into the world. He is the help that God promised from the beginning of the Bible story.

God Takes the Initiative

The birth of Jesus was entirely at the initiative of God. Mary was a young woman, preparing for marriage to a man named Joseph. She was a virgin, and God had chosen her as the one who would bring Jesus Christ into the world. So He sent the angel Gabriel to tell her: "Do not be afraid, Mary, for you have found favor with God. And behold, you will conceive in your womb and bear a son, and you shall call his name Jesus" (Luke 1:30–31).

"How will this be . . . ?" Mary asked (1:34).

The angel's answer takes us to the heart of the greatest mystery in the Bible: "The Holy Spirit will come upon you, and the power of the Most High will overshadow you; therefore the child to be born will be called holy—the Son of God" (1:35).

Mary's child was born as the result of the direct initiative of God. Joseph made no contribution to his conception whatsoever. The Bible contains other stories of miraculous births. Abraham and Sarah had longed for a child, and Isaac's birth was a miracle because they were both well past the age of conceiving children. The same was true for Zechariah and Elizabeth when John the Baptist was born.

These children were born as a result of a special intervention of God, working through the union of a father and a mother. But Mary was a virgin. Joseph had no union with her before the child was conceived, and he had no union with her until after the child was born (Matthew 1:25).

The life in Mary's womb came to be there through a creative miracle of God that is beautifully described in the words of the angel: "The Holy Spirit will come upon you, and the power of the Most High will overshadow you" (Luke 1:35).

The New Testament teaches us three foundational truths about the identity of Jesus: He is God. He is man. And He is holy.

Jesus Is God

The angel announced to Mary that her child would be "the Son of the Most High" (Luke 1:32). He would be "the Son of God" (1:35). He would be "God with us" (Matthew 1:23).

Before He was born, God the Son already enjoyed the most marvelous life. Your life began when you were conceived in your mother's womb. Before that moment, you did not exist. God used the union of your father and your mother to bring you into being.

But with Jesus, it is different. His life did not begin in the virgin's womb. Before He was born in the stable, He shared the eternal life of God: "In the beginning was the Word, and the Word was with God, and the Word was God." This Word "became flesh and dwelt among us" (John 1:1, 14). The one who shared the life of the Father came to us. He did not arise from the human race, but He came to the human race.

The wonderful truth that Jesus is God is good news, because only God can reconcile us to Himself.

Jesus Is Man

Once we have grasped that Jesus is God, it is every bit as important for us to grasp that God became a man. This had never happened before, and it has never happened since.

In the Old Testament, there were many occasions when God appeared in visible form. These appearances are called theophanies, and they could be compared to an actor dressing up. When the show is over, the actor takes off his costume and leaves the theater. But the birth of Jesus was entirely different. The Son of God took human flesh to Himself. He did not cease to be God. But He became a man, and He remains a man forever.

We'll never be able to fathom the mystery of how God could become a man, but knowing that He did makes sense of everything else. When we see that God became a man in Jesus, His claims, His miracles, and His resurrection all begin to make sense.

Since Jesus is "God with us," no one should be surprised when He tells us that He is the way to God and that there is no other way. And when you know that God has come to us in Jesus, you may be astonished that He would allow His enemies to nail Him to a cross, but you will not be surprised when He rises from the dead. What other outcome would you expect?

Jesus Is Holy

Jesus Christ is like us in every respect except one—He is holy (Luke 1:35). This means that Jesus did not at any time commit a single sin. But it means more than that. He was holy in His thoughts, in His intentions, and in His character. His nature was holy. He was not drawn to sin, and He had no inner propensity to sin. There has never been anyone else in all of human history about whom this could be said.

The apostle Paul was a good man who desperately wanted to live a holy life. He was born into a privileged family and educated in the finest schools. His parents gave him everything he could want, except for one thing: They could not give him holiness. The nature he inherited from his parents was far from holy.

Parents pass on many good things to their children, but holiness is not one of them. We do not have it in us. What is born is not holy, and what is holy was not born until Jesus Christ came into the world.

Jesus blazes the trail of a new humanity that will be holy, free from sin, and no longer subject to death. The purpose of God has always been that Jesus will be the first of many who, through Him, will triumph over death and live forever in the joy of God's holy presence.

TRAIL MARKERS

Throughout the Old Testament, God had promised that help was coming. In Jesus Christ, that help has come. God the Son came on an amazing journey. He took human flesh to Himself and was born of a virgin. He came down, lived among us, and went to the cross to bear our sins. As God, He reconciled us to Himself. As man, He delivered us from the wrath of God. As the holy one, He empowers us for a holy life, and one day He will welcome us into the joy of His holy presence.

1. What is your response to the Bible's message that help is coming? Are you unnerved by it? Curious? Relieved? Skeptical? Other? Why?

2. What makes the birth of Jesus unique in the history of the world?

3. Jesus is God. He is man. He is holy. Which of these do you find easiest to believe? Which is most difficult? Why?

4. How well do you think Jesus understands your experience of life?

5. Think about the journey of the Son of God. What is most amazing to you? Why?

To memorize:

> Have this mind among yourselves, which is yours in Christ Jesus, who, though he was in the form of God, did not count equality with God a thing to be grasped, but emptied himself, by taking the form of a servant, being born in the likeness of men. (Philippians 2:5–7)

Jesus was thirty years of age when He began His public ministry. When He was baptized in the River Jordan, the Holy Spirit descended on Him and an audible voice from heaven said, "This is my beloved Son, with whom I am well pleased" (Matthew 3:17). Filled with the Holy Spirit, Jesus went into the desert, where He endured a period of intense temptation that lasted for forty days.

30

TEMPTED

MATTHEW 4

Visualize an office building with hundreds of computers all linked on a network. An enemy could sabotage the entire network by devising a computer virus which, once loaded into the server, would transfer itself to every machine in the building. The virus would gradually corrupt the programs on each computer in such a way that, although some parts might work reasonably well, nothing would work as it used to.

The computer geeks would be called in. But if nobody could find an antidote for the virus, the whole system would be destroyed from within. The enemy would not need to personally sabotage every terminal in the building, because the network would spread the virus for him. One virus would corrupt every terminal, because all the machines are networked together.

Now imagine one computer that is not linked to the network. While all the other machines in the office are corrupted, this one machine remains free from the destructive power of the virus. If the enemy wants to destroy it, he will have to attack from the outside what he could not corrupt from the inside.

The standalone computer can help us to understand how Jesus is fully human and yet free from the corrupting power of sin. Every other member of the human race has been affected by the virus of sin, but sin had no access to Jesus. He was free from its corrupting power.

The Spread of the Virus

Human beings are not like pebbles on a beach; we are like leaves on a tree. The disease of sin flows from the root, and its blight appears on every leaf. We are not disconnected units; we are one family, and we are descended from one stock.

When foot-and-mouth disease is found in one cow, the whole herd has to be slaughtered. And this is the tragedy of the human race: "In Adam all die" (1 Corinthians 15:22). Adam sinned as the head of the human race, and his sin brought death to the whole herd. To change the analogy, through Adam's sin a virus has entered into the human network and communicated itself to every terminal. "By the one man's disobedience the many were made sinners" (Romans 5:19).

Stalking the Enemy

Adam and Eve sinned in the garden, but the Spirit of God led Jesus into the desert to be tempted and to triumph where Adam had failed (Matthew 4:1). Satan used the same strategies that had proven successful with Adam and Eve: confusion, presumption, and ambition.

First, Satan attempted to create confusion in the mind of Jesus about His own identity: "If you are the Son of God . . ." Satan was raising a question. Was Jesus really the Son of God? If so, His Father didn't seem to be taking very good care of Him. Perhaps He should take matters into His own hands and "command these stones to become loaves of bread" (4:3).

Then the enemy switched tactics and used an alternative argument. Instead of questioning Christ's identity, he now affirmed it and attempted to use Jesus' position as the divine Son as the basis for a second temptation. "Given that God is Your Father, You can be confident that He will take care of You in every circumstance. You can attempt things that other people wouldn't dream of. You could even throw yourself off this temple, and God's angels would float You to the ground. So go ahead—do it!"

The third temptation revolved around how costly it would be for Jesus to obey the will of His Father. "Think of what this will cost You! There must be an easier way. I can give You the kingdoms of this world, if only You will worship me."

Satan knew that Jesus had come to crush him, so he did what any general would do when faced with overwhelming opposition: He offered a truce. He would gladly have settled for a world filled with the teaching of Jesus, so long as Christ did not proceed with the Father's plan and go to the cross. But Jesus was not negotiating.

Facing Temptation's Full Force

We are enticed by our own evil desire (James 1:14). But since Jesus did not have a sinful nature, how could He know our struggle? This raises the question of whether the temptations of Jesus were real.

Three airmen fly jets over enemy territory during a war. They are shot down, captured, and then taken by the enemy for interrogation. One by one they are brought into a darkened room.

The first airman gives his name, rank, and serial number. They press him for information that he knows he must not give, but he also knows that the enemy is cruel and eventually they will break him. So why go through all that? He tells them what he knows.

A second airman is brought in. He also gives his name, rank, and serial number, and they begin to pump him for information. He is determined not to give in. So the cruelty begins. Eventually it overwhelms him. He breaks and tells them what he knows.

Then the third airman comes in and gives his name, rank, and serial number. "You will not break me," he says.

"Oh, yes we will. We have broken every man who has ever come into this room. It is only a matter of time; you'll see."

The cruelty begins, but he does not break. It is intensified, and still he does not break. So it is intensified again, until it becomes unbearable, but still he does not break.

Finally, there comes a point when they have tried everything they know. "It's no use," they say. "He is not like any other person we've had in this room. We can't break him."

Now, which of these three airmen faced the full force of the enemy?

The only one to know the full force of the enemy's assault is the one who did not break.

So let's not think that the temptations Jesus faced are less than ours. Only He knows the full power of the enemy, because He alone withstood the assault.

Jesus was tempted in every respect as we are, but He was without sin (Hebrews 4:15).

Plugging into the Network

We are all descended from Adam by nature, and so we are networked to him. And when we believe in Christ, we are networked to Him, or as the Bible puts it, "united with him" (Romans 6:5).

Just as the consequences of Adam's failure flow to us through our union with him, so through our union with Christ the consequences of His triumph will flow to us. "For as by the one man's disobedience the many were made sinners, so by the one man's obedience the many will be made righteous" (Romans 5:19).

The first man sinned in the garden, and the result was the condemnation of the whole human race. But God did not leave us there. The Son of God took our human flesh and became "the second man" (1 Corinthians 15:47). This second man confronted our enemy. And just as the first Adam's failure spelled death for all his family, so the last Adam's triumph spells life for all who are His (1 Corinthians 15:45).

The Power of the Network Principle

Human history revolves around two men: Adam and Jesus. The whole human race is networked to Adam, and so we all suffer from the disease called sin, which leads to death. If God had left us there, we would be without hope: "In Adam all die" (1 Corinthians 15:22).

But God decided to build another network—a network of those who are united with Jesus Christ. They are joined to Him not by physical birth, but by a new birth through the Holy Spirit.

Just as the consequences of Adam's sin run through his network, bringing corruption and death to all his descendants, the consequences of Jesus' righteousness run through His network, changing the eternal destiny of all who are joined to Him. "For as in Adam all die, so also in Christ shall all be made alive" (15:22).

God's network principle is devastating when we consider Adam's sin, but it is wonderful when we consider Jesus' righteousness. God's network principle means that one man's triumph can open the door to everlasting life for many, on the single condition that they are joined to Him.

When we come to Jesus in repentance and faith, the Holy Spirit joins us to Him. We are still in Adam—we fail in many ways, and one day we will die. But when you come to Jesus, the most important thing about you is that you are in Christ. And that means you will share in His triumph.

TRAIL MARKERS

The Bible makes it clear that Jesus was tempted in every way as we are, yet He was without sin (Hebrews 4:15). The difference between Jesus' temptations and ours is that sin resides in us, and we are tempted by our own evil desire (James 1:14). Jesus' temptations were not less than ours; they were greater. Christ stood against everything the enemy threw at Him—and triumphed. When you are united to Jesus by faith, you will be able to overcome the power of the temptations you face.

1. What evidence do you see that the human race has been infected by the virus of sin?

2. Can you identify a time when you were tempted? How did you deal with it?

3. Which of the airmen do you most relate to? Why?

4. What are some of the effects of being networked to Adam? How about Jesus?

5. How do you think a person gets united to Jesus? Why?

To memorize:

For we do not have a high priest who is unable to sympathize with our weaknesses, but one who in every respect has been tempted as we are, yet without sin. Let us then with confidence draw near to the throne of grace, that we may receive mercy and find grace to help in time of need. (Hebrews 4:15–16)

After Jesus was tempted Mark tells us that He came into Galilee, proclaiming the gospel of God, and saying, "The time is fulfilled, and the kingdom of God is at hand; repent and believe the gospel" (Mark 1:15). A kingdom means that there is a king, and the good news is that this king has come. In this chapter we look at four stories that unveil Jesus as the sovereign king and show why this is good news for us today.

31

SOVEREIGN

MARK 4–5

When I was five years old, my father took me to a junkyard outside Edinburgh. The place was filled with scrap cars and trucks, and it was a marvelous place for a child with a vivid imagination to play.

Dad used to go there to get spare parts that he needed for our car. The system was simple: You could strip pieces that you needed off the cars, and then pay for them at the gate as you left. The problem was that some people were in the habit of throwing parts over the perimeter fence, walking past the gate without paying, and then picking up the stuff in the wasteland outside.

So the owners cleared a "no go" area inside the perimeter and brought in guard dogs leashed to a railing. As long as you did not go close to the fence, you were perfectly safe.

One day when my father was working on a wrecked car, I found a truck and climbed up into the cab. I was lost in an imaginary world of truck driving, when suddenly one of the dogs broke free from its chain and came bounding toward me.

I don't think that I have ever been more terrified in my life. I screamed as any small child would. My father rushed over, grabbed a stick and, after a struggle, overpowered the dog. My father saved me by subduing the animal. If he had not been able to subdue the dog, he would not have been able to save his boy.

Christ is able to save us from our enemies because He is sovereign over them and is able to subdue them. It is the fact that He is Lord that qualifies Him to act as our Savior. That is why Scripture says, "Everyone who calls on the name of the

Lord will be saved" (Romans 10:13).

So what are the enemies that we need saving from?

Dimensions of Darkness

Our world is filled with what we sometimes call natural disasters: earthquakes, mudslides, volcanoes, storms, fires, and floods.

We are also plagued by human evil—school shootings, gang murders, acts of terror, human trafficking—the list goes on and on. Every time another atrocity happens, we ask, "How could we have stopped it, and how can we make sure it never happens again?"

Then for all the wonders of medical science, for which we are profoundly grateful, sickness remains rampant: Cancer, stroke, heart disease, dementia, and many forms of mental illness are all around us.

Which brings us to what the Bible describes as our last enemy—death. Everyone who has faced it with a loved one knows what a terrible enemy death is.

Our news is dominated by these four dimensions of darkness: disasters, evil, sickness, and death. For all the joys of this life, we find ourselves asking, "Who shall deliver us? Who has the authority to subdue the destructive powers that bring such darkness?"

Mark records four stories that illustrate the sovereign power of Jesus over all the dimensions of darkness. Each story shows us that Jesus is Lord, and for this reason we can trust Him as Savior.

Lord over Natural Disasters

One evening the disciples found themselves caught in a storm as they were crossing the Sea of Galilee in a boat. They were terrified and cried out: "Teacher, do you not care that we are perishing?" (Mark 4:38).

Jesus "rebuked the wind and said to the sea, 'Peace! Be still!' And the wind ceased, and there was a great calm" (4:39). The disciples were astonished and said, "Who then is this, that even the wind and the sea obey him?" (4:41).

The human spirit does not have power over the elements. We do not have power over the rain, the tornado, the volcano, or the tsunami. But when Jesus spoke, He stilled the storm.

Lord over the Demons

When Jesus and His disciples reached the other side of the lake, they were immediately confronted by a man who was out of his mind. He lived among the tombs, and night and day he would cry out and cut himself with stones (5:5).

This man was public enemy number one, and though he had been bound many times, he "wrenched the chains apart, and he broke the shackles in pieces. No one had the strength to subdue him" (5:4). So the whole community lived in fear. Every night they would hear this man crying out, and there was nothing they could do to stop him.

It is clear from Scripture that evil spirits (or demons) were behind these great outbreaks of violence (5:8, 13). This is not the case with every violent act or self-destructive person, but it was the case with this man. Jesus described the devil as a thief who comes "to steal and kill and destroy" (John 10:10), and where stealing, killing, and destroying are most rampant, there his activity can be most clearly seen.

When Jesus came to this community, He commanded the evil spirits to leave the man and enter a herd of pigs. The evil spirits had to obey Him, and when they left the man, he was completely changed. When the people in the town heard, they came out to see what had happened, and they found the man who had been possessed by the demons "sitting there, clothed and in his right mind" (Mark 5:15).

Lord over Disease

When Jesus returned to the other side of the lake, a large crowd was waiting. Among them was a woman who had been subject to "a discharge of blood for twelve years" (5:25). She had spent all that she had in consulting various doctors, but in spite of their efforts, her condition was no better.

This woman felt that if she could just reach Jesus, she would be healed. When she managed to touch Him, she was immediately aware of a change in her body: "The flow of blood dried up, and she felt in her body that she was healed of her disease" (5:29).

This woman had come to the place where there was nothing more the doctors could do. But Jesus was able to heal her because He is Lord over disease.

Lord over Death

A ruler of the synagogue named Jairus came to Jesus and pleaded earnestly with Him: "My little daughter is at the point of death. Come and lay your hands on her so that she may be made well and live" (5:23). Jesus went with him, but there was a delay as He ministered to the woman with the incurable disease.

While He was speaking with her, some men from Jairus' house came with the tragic news that his daughter had died. "Why trouble the Teacher any further?" they said (5:35). You see their point: As long as the girl was alive there was some prospect of Jesus healing her, but when she died all hope was gone.

But Jesus said to Jairus, "Do not fear, only believe" (5:36).

When Jesus came to Jairus' home, the wake was already in process. He sent the mourners out of the house, and only the girl's father and mother, along with Peter, James, and John, remained. Jesus took the girl's hand and said, "'Talitha cumi,' which means, 'Little girl, I say to you, arise'" (5:41). To the absolute amazement of everyone in the room, "the girl got up and began walking" (5:42).

For anyone who has lost a loved one, the pattern of this story is beautiful and profound. Jairus' daughter was ill. There was a delay in Jesus' coming. The girl died during the delay. But when Jesus came, she rose from the dead.

Jesus is giving us a glimpse of the full blessing we will know when His kingdom comes. In this world there will be death and there will be delay. The resurrection will come when Jesus Christ returns in power and glory.

Why Doesn't He Do It?

Jesus is sovereign over all the dimensions of human darkness. He is able to subdue disaster, demons, disease, and even death. As Lord over these enemies, He is able to save us from their destructive power.

So why doesn't He do it?

Mark gives us the answer. When Jesus delivered the demon-possessed man, "they began to beg Jesus to depart from their region" (5:17). You would think they might have said, "You have solved our biggest social problem in this community. Would you please stay, because we have other problems? And if you can solve this, you can solve these too." But that was not their reaction. They asked Jesus to leave.

And if the one who is able to subdue the dog leaves the junkyard, what will happen to the boy?

We live in a Christ-rejecting world: "He came to his own, and his own people did not receive him" (John 1:11).

The rejection of Jesus led to the cross, which was the ultimate expression of our world's contempt for God. We rejected the Lord of glory. We mocked Him, spat on Him, and nailed Him to a cross. A world that rejects Jesus is a world that continues to ache under the curse of disasters, demons, disease, and death.

But this is not the end of the Bible story. On the third day, Jesus rose from the dead. When He ascended into heaven, the Father said to Him, "Sit at my right hand until I make your enemies a footstool for your feet" (Hebrews 1:13).

Jesus is reigning, but He is also waiting. The reigning and waiting are not in conflict. "He must reign until he has put all his enemies under his feet. The last enemy to be destroyed is death" (1 Corinthians 15:25–26).

So we continue to live in a suffering world. But those who belong to the kingdom of Jesus Christ wait for the day when He will subdue our enemies. Under the blessed rule of our sovereign Lord, there will be no more disasters, no more demons, no more diseases, and no more death.

TRAIL MARKERS

I sometimes hear people say that they received Jesus as Savior but did not make Him Lord. The assumption is that we can somehow separate the Savior from the Lord—that we can have faith without repentance, blessings without commands, and the forgiveness of sins without the pursuit of holiness.

This is a fundamental misunderstanding of the gospel. We cannot receive what Jesus offers and at the same time resist what He commands. God calls us to give up our resistance to the lordship of Christ and receive His salvation: "Everyone who calls on the name of the *Lord* will be saved" (Romans 10:13). Submit yourself to Christ as Lord and you will find that He is a mighty Savior.

 1. Which of the four enemies (disaster, demons, disease, death) are you most concerned about right now? Why?

 2. How does it help you to know that Jesus is Lord over this enemy?

 3. What qualifies Jesus to be your Savior?

 4. In your own words, why doesn't Jesus defeat all our enemies now?

 5. How do you react to the promise that "Everyone who calls on the name of the Lord will be saved" (Romans 10:13)?

To memorize:

> God has highly exalted him and bestowed on him the name that is above every name, so that at the name of Jesus every knee should bow, in heaven and on earth and under the earth, and every tongue confess that Jesus Christ is Lord, to the glory of God the Father. (Philippians 2:9–11)

If you had been at the cross, you would have heard nails being driven through the hands and feet of Jesus. You would have seen two criminals crucified on either side of Him. And you would have seen the inscription over His head that read: "This is the King of the Jews" (Luke 23:38). Jesus hung on the cross for six hours, and what happened during that time takes us to the heart of the Bible story.

32

CRUCIFIED

LUKE 23

The day that Jesus died was the darkest day in human history, and yet this was the day when God's plan of salvation was accomplished. Our sin reached its full horror and its most awful expression at the cross. Having disobeyed God's commands, we were now crucifying God's Son.

If ever there was a moment in human history when God's judgment had to fall, this was it. But Jesus cried out, "Father, forgive them, for they know not what they do" (23:34).

Jesus knew that God's judgment would come that day, but He was saying, "Don't let it fall on them. Let it fall on Me, and on Me alone. Let Me be the lightning rod for Your judgment on their sin."

This is the heart of the gospel. Jesus stood under the judgment of God for our sins. He called on the Father to divert the punishment away from us, and He absorbed it in Himself. That is how forgiveness is released.

When Jesus prayed, "Father, forgive *them*," His prayer included the priests who condemned Him, the crowds who mocked Him, and the soldiers who crucified Him. It also included the disciples who deserted Him and the Old Testament believers who had waited for Him.

The prayer of Jesus covered the sin of every person who would come to Him. And if His prayer could cover the sins of those who nailed Him to the cross, it is big enough to cover our sin as well.

Paradise Is Opened

A few feet away from Jesus was a man who had made a tragic waste of his life. Having pursued a life of crime, he had faced human justice and was now paying the price. Soon death would relieve his suffering, but then he would enter the presence of God where he would face divine justice. His position seemed hopeless.

A short while earlier, he had joined with another criminal in ridiculing Jesus' claims. But as death drew near, he seemed to have a new awareness of what it would mean for a sinner to enter the presence of God, and ridiculing Jesus no longer seemed appropriate.

When Jesus was crucified, He prayed for those who nailed Him to the cross. *Perhaps*, the man thought, *if Jesus could forgive these soldiers, He could forgive me too*. So he turned to Jesus and said, "Jesus, remember me when you come into your kingdom" (23:42). And Jesus answered, "Truly, I say to you, today you will be with me in paradise" (23:43).

Paradise! This man's life had been a series of disastrous choices, but Jesus promised him an immediate translation, through death, into a life of unending joy. Before the day was over, Jesus would usher him into the presence of God. Suddenly this man, for whom the world held nothing, found that because of Jesus he was about to enter the greatest joy a human being can ever know.

This man's story is a stunning example of what Jesus Christ is able to do for any person who turns to Him in faith and repentance, no matter how late in life. Heaven is Christ's home. He holds the keys, and He opens it to all who turn to Him in repentance and faith, whatever they may have done.

What Jesus Suffered

Jesus was crucified at nine o'clock in the morning, and during the first three hours of His suffering, He prayed for His enemies and answered the prayer of a criminal who reached out to Him in faith. Then, at midday, "there was darkness over the whole land" (23:44), and for the next three hours Jesus entered into the heart of His sufferings.

What took place in the darkness is beyond our understanding, but there are some things that we know because God has told us.

Jesus carried our sins when He died on the cross.

He . . . bore our sins in his body on the tree. (1 Peter 2:24)

For our sake he made him to be sin who knew no sin. (2 Corinthians 5:21)

The L*ORD has laid on him the iniquity of us all.* (Isaiah 53:6)

Jesus carried your sins into His death, so that you would not carry them into yours. Bearing our sins meant that Jesus endured the punishment that was due to us:

Upon him was the chastisement that brought us peace (Isaiah 53:5).

Jesus endured all that hell is on the cross. He was in conscious suffering, in blackest darkness, surrounded by demonic powers. He bore the guilt of sin, He absorbed divine wrath, and He endured all this alone, separated from the comfort of the Father's love.

People often talk about whether hell is real or not. Hell is as real as the cross. Christ entered into all the dimensions of hell in the darkness, and He did this so that you would never know what hell is like.

In the depth of His suffering, Jesus cried out, "My God, my God, why have you forsaken me?" (Matthew 27:46). No words can express the depth of this suffering. God the Father and God the Son have always shared one life, one love, one purpose, and one will. But when the Son of God became our sin bearer, the comforts of the Father's love were beyond His reach. He was completely alone, suspended between heaven and earth—and rejected by both.

How Jesus Died

After three hours, while darkness was over the land, the judgment poured out on Jesus was spent. Justice was satisfied, and Jesus shouted in triumph, "It is finished" (John 19:30). God's righteous judgment for our sin fell on Jesus. He absorbed it. He drained it. He exhausted it. Hell burned itself out on Jesus for all who trust in Him.

Having released forgiveness and opened paradise by offering Himself as the sacrifice for our sins, Jesus had completed all that the Father had given Him to do. The battle was over, and the victory was won. All that remained was for Jesus to lay down His life. He called out in a loud voice: "Father, into your hands I commit my spirit!" (Luke 23:46). When someone dies, their strength diminishes and their voice weakens. No one speaks in a loud voice at the moment of death. But Jesus did.

Jesus was not overwhelmed by death. He said, "No one takes it [my life] from me. . . . I have authority to lay it down, and I have authority to take it up again" (John 10:18). Christ's life was not taken, it was given. He *gave Himself* for us (Galatians 2:20).

The Bible speaks of death as a dark valley that we all have to walk through. Dark valleys are scary places, especially if enemies are hiding there. But Christ has gone through the valley of death and cleared out the enemies. Death is still a dark place, but it is a safe place for all who belong to Jesus.

If you are in Christ, when the moment of death comes for you, you will be able to say with Jesus: "Father, into Your hands I commit my spirit." And you will be safe in the Father's hands. Death will not lead to a long period of unconsciousness or of preparation. If you are in Christ, to be away from the body is to be at home with the Lord (2 Corinthians 5:8).

Why Jesus Died on the Cross

Many people go through life with the feeling that God is against them. But here is what you need to know: Jesus did not come into the world and die on the cross *in order* to make the Father love you. He came into the world and died on the cross *because* the Father loves you.

One way to measure God's love for you would be to list the joys and blessings of your life. So if you have good health, are surrounded by people who love you, and have work that you enjoy, you can rejoice in these gifts as signs of His love.

But what if you lose that great job? Or what if someone in your family becomes sick? Or what if a person you love loses interest in you? How will you know that God loves you then?

If you gauge God's love for you by your changing experiences in life, you will find yourself confused. When blessings come, you will feel that God loves you. When hardship comes, you will feel that He must be against you, and you will lose the sense of His love when you need it the most!

This is why we must walk by faith, not by sight. Faith looks beyond our changing circumstances and knows that God's love was demonstrated decisively at the cross.

God shows his love for us in that while we were still sinners, Christ died for us. (Romans 5:8)

In this the love of God was made manifest among us, that God sent his only Son into the world, so that we might live through him. (1 John 4:9)

TRAIL MARKERS

Everything God had planned to do since the beginning of time was accomplished at the cross. Jesus bore our sin, endured our hell, and was forsaken by the Father. Through His suffering, He purchased our forgiveness, reconciled us to God, and secured our entrance into heaven.

If you ever find yourself doubting God's love for you, look to the cross: "God so loved the world, that he gave his only Son, that whoever believes in him should not perish but have eternal life" (John 3:16).

1. What are some of the things you would have seen and heard if you had been there on the day that Jesus was crucified?

2. When Jesus prayed "Father, forgive them," who did that prayer include?

3. Do you think Jesus could do for anyone what He did for the thief on the cross? Why or why not?

4. What was happening during the three hours of darkness while Jesus was on the cross?

5. Do you believe that God loves you? Why or why not?

To memorize:

He was pierced for our transgressions; he was crushed for our iniquities; upon him was the chastisement that brought us peace, and with his wounds we are healed. All we like sheep have gone astray; we have turned—every one—to his own way; and the Lord has laid on him the iniquity of us all. (Isaiah 53:5–6)

Mary Magdalene, Joanna, and some other women traveled with Jesus and the twelve disciples (Luke 8:1–3; 24:10). They had heard Christ speaking about what would happen on the third day (24:6–7), but as they made their way to the tomb, they did not expect anything unusual. Their journey was motivated by love, but it was devoid of faith. Their confidence in Jesus had been overwhelmed by the agony of the cross. Faith was gone; all that was left was love.

33

RISEN

LUKE 24

When the women arrived, they found that the stone in front of the tomb had been moved and, going inside, they found to their great astonishment that the tomb was empty. Notice that the women did not conclude Jesus had risen from the dead. They were "perplexed" and completely lost for an explanation (Luke 24:4).

It was not that Mary found the body missing, and said, "I have a feeling that Jesus must have risen from the dead," and Joanna replied, "I think you're right. I have that feeling too." The thought did not even occur to them.

So how did they know that Jesus had risen? God told them.

God Gives the Explanation

"While they were perplexed about this, behold, two men[6] stood by them in dazzling apparel. And as they were frightened and bowed their faces to the ground, the men said to them, 'Why do you seek the living among the dead? He is not here, but has risen'" (24:4–6).

God called two angels, and said, "Go and tell them what I have done. These women love My Son, but there is no way in the world that they are ever going to work out what happened. Go and tell them."

---

6. Matthew tells us that they were angels (Matthew 28:5). Luke tells us what they looked like.

Christian faith rests on believing God's explanation of what He has done.

How could Mary, the mother of our Lord, have known what was happening when she conceived? God gave the explanation. It was the same with the shepherds. How could they possibly have known that the child in the manger was God in human flesh? God sent the angels to tell them.

And it was the same when Jesus was crucified. Many people saw Him die, but how could they understand what God was doing? God tells us that, on the cross, Jesus bore our sin and laid down His life as a sacrifice.

The women would never have figured out why the tomb was empty. God told them what happened. Christian faith does not rest on feelings, impulses, or personal insights. It is believing God's explanation of events, given to us in the Scriptures. He is risen!

"Risen" Means That Death Is Defeated

Throughout history, death has been like a tyrant exercising a reign of terror over the human race. No one can escape it. Abraham, Isaac, Jacob, Moses, and David all believed God's promise, but death got every one of them. Sooner or later, death sucks all of us in. The question is, how do we get out?

When I was in grade school, our class had a pet mouse, and on weekends we got to take the mouse home. On one occasion, the mouse became intrigued by my red plastic double-decker London bus. And after sniffing around, it decided to climb inside.

This was tremendous entertainment—until the mouse reached the front of the bus. Then we had a problem. The mouse couldn't move forward, and it didn't have room to turn back. It was completely stuck.

I remember my father saying, "There's only one thing to do, son. We'll have to destroy the bus!" He took a knife and cut the roof open. The mouse was free. I can't tell you what a relief that was. But my bus was never the same. It really was rather curious; a bright red London bus with the roof cut open! Of course, this made things even more interesting for the mouse. Before the mouse had a way in, but no way out. Now it could go in through the door and come out through the roof!

When Jesus died, He cut a hole in death. For Christ's people, death is not a prison, but a passage that leads right into the presence of God.

"Risen" Means the Whole Person Will Be Redeemed

All religions have some idea of survival after death, but the resurrection of the body is unique to Christianity. The good news is not simply that Jesus is *alive,* but that Jesus has *risen* (Luke 24:6). It is worth thinking about the difference.

The Son of God was alive in heaven before He took human flesh. So why did He not simply leave His crucified body in the tomb and return to the Father? After all, it was only flesh and bone. Why bother with it?

The angels could still have appeared on Easter morning and said, "His body is here in the tomb, but don't worry, His Spirit is with the Father in heaven." After all, is this not precisely what we say at a funeral service when a Christian dies?

The resurrection tells us that the body matters. You are a marvelous union of soul and body, and Jesus came into the world not to save part of you but to redeem the whole of you. He came to bring you, body and soul, into the joy of a new creation.

Death separates your soul from your body, and that is why is it such a terrible enemy. It is the tearing apart of what God has joined together, and it will only be defeated when your body and soul are reunited in the power of a new life.

When Jesus appeared to the disciples, their first thought was that they were seeing a ghost (Luke 24:37). But He drew their attention to His body: "See my hands and my feet, that it is I myself. Touch me, and see. For a spirit does not have flesh and bones as you see that I have" (24: 39).

Taking a Virtual Vacation

Suppose you have planned the vacation of a lifetime in Hawaii, but just before you are due to take the trip, you fall down the stairs and break just about every bone in your body. In good cartoon style, you wind up in the hospital bandaged from head to toe, with a thermometer sticking out of your mouth.

A friend, who is a computer geek, offers to take you on a virtual tour instead. He sets up his laptop, and sure enough, you see wonderful views of Honolulu. "It's so beautiful," you say. "I just wish that I had been able to go."

"But you have," says your friend. "You have been there on a virtual tour."

Whatever he says, you know that as long as your body is stuck in the hospital, you haven't been to Hawaii. Going there in your mind, or via the internet, simply isn't the same.

The life God promises to His people in heaven is not like a virtual tour. It is not a spiritual experience or a mind game. God sent His Son to redeem the whole of you, and bring you, body and soul, into His presence. The good news is that Christ is risen, and the resurrection of the body is the glorious future that lies ahead of every Christian believer.

What Will the Resurrection Body Be Like?

When the body of Jesus was raised, it was also changed. His body was no longer subject to aging or death. His flesh was transformed and adapted for eternity. That's why Christians can look forward to heaven.

Scripture gives us four descriptions of the resurrection body.

1. *Imperishable*

> *What is sown is perishable; what is raised is imperishable.*
> (1 Corinthians 15:42)

Lazarus was raised from the dead, but he came out of the tomb as he had gone into it. He continued aging, and at some point, the poor fellow had to go through the whole miserable business of dying again! But Jesus rose in the power of an endless life (Hebrews 7:16), and your resurrection body, like His, will be a body that will never die. Your resurrection body will never age, it will never be sick, and it will never decline.

2. *Glorious*

> *It is sown in dishonor; it is raised in glory.* (1 Corinthians 15:43)

When Peter, James, and John went up the mountain with Jesus, they saw the brightness and radiance of His glory (Mark 9:2–8). When you are clothed with your resurrection body, you will reflect Jesus' glory: "The righteous will shine like the sun in the kingdom of their Father" (Matthew 13:43).

3. Powerful

> *It is sown in weakness; it is raised in power.*
> (1 Corinthians 15:43)

You will have more energy, more stamina, more speed, better coordination, and greater capacity in your resurrection body than you ever did before.

4. Spiritual

> *It is sown a natural body; it is raised a spiritual body.*
> (1 Corinthians 15:44)

A spiritual body is one that is fully responsive to the Holy Spirit. We will no longer say, "The spirit indeed is willing, but the flesh is weak" (Matthew 26:41). Our resurrection bodies will be as eager to do the will of God as our redeemed spirits.

Here's what you have to look forward to in the new heaven and the new earth: A body that is adapted to life forever and will never decline. A body that is glorious and powerful. A body that is fully responsive to the Holy Spirit.

Wait Until Everyone Is Ready

The gift of the resurrection body is so wonderful that God holds it in reserve until the day when He will gather all His children together.

Christian loved ones who have died are with Jesus, consciously enjoying the glory of His presence. That is better by far than anything they could know here. But God has another gift for them and for us that He is keeping for the day when He gathers His whole family together.

When Christ returns, our Christian loved ones will come with Him (1 Thessalonians 4:14). Then "the dead in Christ will rise" (4:16) and their souls will be clothed with resurrected bodies adapted for everlasting life.

At the same time, believers who are still alive will be "caught up together with them in the clouds to meet the Lord in the air" (4:17). We will experience the same transformation in which our bodies are adapted for everlasting life.

TRAIL MARKERS

On the third day, the tomb was empty. Jesus rose from the dead. We know this because God said so. When Christ comes again in glory and gathers all His people, we too will be given resurrection bodies. God will redeem not just a part of you, but the whole of you. Get this settled in your mind and you will have far greater anticipation of the joys that lie ahead.

1. Have you experienced a personal tragedy that made it hard for you to trust Jesus?

2. Respond to this statement: "Christian faith rests on believing God's explanation of what He has done."

3. In your own words, how does the story of the London double-decker bus illustrate what Jesus accomplished in His death and resurrection?

4. What difference do you think it makes whether or not Jesus' body was raised from the dead?

5. What stands out to you when you think about the resurrection body?

To memorize:

"Thus it is written, that the Christ should suffer and on the third day rise from the dead, and that repentance for the forgiveness of sins should be proclaimed in his name to all nations, beginning from Jerusalem." (Luke 24:46–47)

Forty days after the resurrection, Jesus ascended into heaven. Luke records the scene when Jesus said goodbye to His disciples: "He led them out as far as Bethany, and lifting up his hands he blessed them. While he blessed them, he parted from them and was carried up into heaven. And they worshiped him and returned to Jerusalem with great joy*" (Luke 24:50–52). Why "great joy"?*

34

ASCENDED

ACTS 1

It's never easy to say goodbye. I remember struggling when we said goodbye to my parents at Glasgow Airport. We were well prepared, and everyone agreed that our move from Britain to the United States was the right thing. But we were leaving our home country, and however well prepared you are to say goodbye, it is never easy when the moment comes.

If our family and friends had thrown a party when our plane left, we would have found that rather strange. So what are we to make of the disciples' joy when Jesus left them?

The disciples' joy is all the more strange when we remember how horrified they were when Jesus had spoken about leaving during the Last Supper. Something must have happened so that what they once dreaded now became a cause for celebration. In this chapter we will discover what that was.

Lifted into the Cloud

When Jesus ascended, "a *cloud* took him out of their sight" (Acts 1:9). This reference to "a cloud" is not a report on the weather conditions in Jerusalem. Why does Luke tell us about the cloud?

When God's people were in the desert, He revealed Himself in a pillar of cloud. Similarly, in the time of Solomon, the cloud of God's presence came down and filled the temple (1 Kings 8:10–13). When the disciples saw the glory of Jesus in the transfiguration, they heard the voice of God speaking from a cloud: "This is my beloved Son; listen to him" (Mark 9:7).

The cloud speaks of God's presence, and when the cloud took Jesus away from the disciples, they knew that Jesus was returning to His Father in heaven.

Adam was expelled from the garden of Eden, and all of his children were alienated from God. But Christ was welcomed into heaven, and all His children will be reconciled to God. The first Adam led us all out. The last Adam leads us all in. That's why the disciples went back to Jerusalem with joy.

An Advocate in Heaven

When Jesus ascended into heaven, the disciples knew that He was exactly where they needed Him to be.

Suppose you are in prison on a charge that carries the death penalty if convicted. You need a good attorney, the best you can get.

You find a good attorney, and as you get to know him, you discover that he is not only a skilled lawyer, but also a man of great compassion. His visits to your cell bring you great comfort, and as you build a relationship, you find that you can talk to him about the difficulties of your life.

This is of great value, but what you need most from your attorney is not his comfort in the cell. You need him to defend you in the courtroom.

Our greatest need, as sinners, is not comfort on earth, but defense in heaven. We need an advocate who will plead our case, and "we have an advocate with the Father, Jesus Christ the righteous" (1 John 2:1).

The Accuser

Picture yourself standing in the courtroom of heaven. Satan, your accuser, has a case to present against you. The courtroom is filled with angels, who rise as God takes His place as the Judge. Your accuser takes his papers and begins to stride around the court as he makes his case. The sum of it is that you are guilty of sin and that you should be condemned.

He begins by stating that you were born in sin and that your nature is corrupt. He then proceeds to accuse you of particular sins that you committed when you were young. He follows your life story, identifying moments of cowardice, complacency, pride, pettiness, and greed. You cringe as you listen, overwhelmed by a sense of your own shame.

Finally, the accuser clinches his argument by pointing out that even though you professed to be a believer in Christ, your faith was often weak, and you had many doubts. His case is compelling, and you fear that you will be condemned.

Then Jesus steps forward. He takes His brief in hand and begins to argue in your defense. "My client admits that every word spoken by the prosecution is true. We do not contest any of the charges, nor do we claim any mitigating circumstances. My client is guilty as charged."

But then, lifting His nail-scarred hands, He says, "I have here a full pardon purchased with My own blood."[7]

The accuser has no answer to this. His whole case against you crumbles and is thrown out of court. Our defense is that Jesus Christ has died for our sins. They have already been judged at the cross, and once a charge has been dealt with, it cannot be brought again. "Who is to condemn? Christ Jesus is the one who died—more than that, who was raised—who is at the right hand of God, who indeed is interceding for us" (Romans 8:34).

The Continuing Work of Jesus

Anyone who has lost a loved one knows that last impressions make a powerful impact. We remember people as we last saw them. The last glimpse the disciples had of Jesus was with His hands raised to bless them: "While he blessed them, he parted from them and was carried up into heaven" (Luke 24:51).

The ascension speaks to us both of the completed work and the continuing work of Jesus. He has completed the work of offering Himself as the sacrifice for sin. There is no more sacrifice to be offered, no more atonement to be made, nothing more that needs to be done to placate the wrath of God and release forgiveness to His people. That work is complete. It is finished!

But Jesus also has a continuing work. As He sits at the right hand of the Father, He continues what He was doing when He ascended, pouring out His blessing on

7. Adapted from C. H. Spurgeon, *The Gracious Lips of Jesus* (sermon #3081), 1908.

His people. "He always lives to make intercession" for us (Hebrews 7:25), and this work will go on until He returns.

The Promise of His Presence

Jesus ascended into heaven, but He was still with His disciples through the Holy Spirit. This is what Christ was referring to when He said, "It is to your advantage that I go away, for if I do not go away, the Helper will not come to you. But if I go, I will send him to you" (John 16:7; see also Acts 1:4–5).

Our Lord Jesus Christ is at the right hand of the Father, and at the same time, He is present in the hearts of believers by the Holy Spirit. The Son of God represents us to the Father, and the Spirit of God represents the Father and the Son to us.

Though we have never seen Jesus, His presence with us is as real as it was when He walked with the disciples. Christ calls us to "go . . . and make disciples" (Matthew 28:19). We are to be his "witnesses . . . to the end of the earth" (Acts 1:8). And as we go in His name, Jesus says, "I am with you always, to the end of the age" (Matthew 28:20).

The Promise of His Return

When Jesus ascended, two angelic figures appeared and said to the disciples, "Men of Galilee, why do you stand looking into heaven? This Jesus, who was taken up from you into heaven, will come in the same way as you saw him go into heaven" (Acts 1:11).

God has promised that just as Jesus was snatched up into the cloud, when He returns, we will be caught up to meet Him in the air (1 Thessalonians 4:17). What happened to Jesus in His ascension will happen to us when He comes in glory.

Christians are waiting for the great day when Christ will come again. Every believer will be part of that day, including those who have already died. Those who are already with the Lord and those who are alive when He comes will be with the Lord forever.

TRAIL MARKERS

As a believer, you can have great joy today, knowing that your ascended Lord is at the right hand of the Father and that His hands are raised in blessing over you. Through the Holy Spirit, His presence is always with you, empowering you to do all that He calls you to do. And when He comes again, He will take you up into His presence forever.

1. When have you had a difficult goodbye? What made it so hard?

2. Why did the disciples have joy when Jesus left them?

3. Respond to the statement: "Our greatest need, as sinners, is not comfort on earth, but defense in heaven."

4. As you think about standing in the courtroom of heaven, what would your defense be?

5. What does the ascension of Jesus point forward to?

To memorize:

"As they were looking on, he was lifted up, and a cloud took him out of their sight." (Acts 1:9)

When Jesus ascended, two angels said to the disciples: "Men of Galilee, why do you stand looking into heaven? This Jesus, who was taken up from you into heaven, will come in the same way as you saw him go into heaven" (Acts 1:11). Christians await the great day when Christ will come again. Every believer will participate in that day. Those who have already died will come with Him, and we who are still alive will meet the Lord in the air (1 Thessalonians 4:14, 17).

35

RETURNING

JOHN 14

Jesus spoke about His return often, but never more clearly than on the night before He died. The Last Supper was a dinner in which everything seemed to go wrong. Early in the evening, Jesus shocked His friends by telling them that someone at the table would betray Him. One after another they began to say, "Is it I, Lord?" (Matthew 26:22). Nobody said, "Lord, is it Judas?" Clearly, Judas was trusted and respected. He had been put in charge of the money, and you don't give a man your money unless you trust him.

John, who was sitting next to Jesus, asked Him who He was speaking about, and Jesus said, "It is he to whom I will give this morsel of bread" (John 13:26). Then He offered the bread to Judas.

Judas already had plans to betray Jesus, but now the final decision was made in his mind. John tells us that "after he had taken the morsel, Satan entered into him" (13:27). Notice the order of events. Satan entered into a mind that had been fully opened to his activity. Then, Judas went out, and John says, "It was night" (13:30).

There was more bad news to come. Jesus said, "Little children, yet a little while I am with you" (13:33). The disciples had left everything to follow Jesus. They had staked everything on Him, and now after just three years, He was telling them that He would be with them only a little longer.

To be told that the person who means most to you in the world will only be with you for a little while longer is one of the hardest experiences a human being can endure, and this was what the disciples faced at the Last Supper.

Peter could not bear to think of being separated from Jesus, and he announced that he was ready to lay down his life for Him. But Jesus answered, "Will you lay down your life for me? Truly, truly, I say to you, the rooster will not crow till you have denied me three times" (13:38).

There had never been a day when the disciples had to deal with so much bad news. In one evening, they discovered that a trusted leader would betray the Savior, Jesus Himself would be taken from them, and His leading disciple would deny his faith.

When You Hear Disastrous News

What Jesus said next must have seemed absolutely staggering: "Let not your hearts be troubled" (John 14:1). How could Jesus possibly say this in the light of all that had just happened?

Imagine a church meeting where the congregation gathers for a few items of business. The chairman opens the meeting in prayer and says that he has three important announcements.

"First, I have to announce, with regret, that our senior pastor is leaving in a few days' time. Second, you need to know that the church treasurer has resigned, and at this point we are not sure what he has done with the money. Third, our senior elder has denied the faith and no longer wishes to be associated with the church."

The congregation is reeling at this triple announcement of disastrous news, but the chairman continues. "I know that some of you may have questions," he says, "but the first thing I want to say is, do not let your hearts be troubled!"

What do you do if someone betrays your trust as Judas did? What do you do when a leader whose example you have looked up to shows himself to have feet of clay like Peter? And how do you cope when the person you have built your life around is no longer with you? The answer lies in the words of Jesus.

Jesus looked around the room, His piercing eyes gazing into the souls of His disciples. "Let not your hearts be troubled," He said. "Believe in God; believe also in me" (14:1).

Jesus was not asking them to take a blind leap of faith. He was saying, "Here's what you need to do right now. Trust God! Trust in Me!" The disciples had seen

His miracles, heard His words, and walked with Him for three years. Now they had to lean into all that they knew of Jesus. In this moment of great darkness, Christ called them to trust what He had taught them in the light.

One House with Many Rooms

Having called His disciples to exercise faith in Him, Jesus spoke to them about the future: "In my Father's house are many rooms" (14:2). The picture is of one great extended family living together in the Father's home.

There is a special irony in Jesus speaking about the many rooms in His Father's house. When Jesus was born, there was no room for Him in Bethlehem. The innkeeper had a small house and every room was taken. I cannot help but think that there must have been a smile on the face of Jesus as He was telling His friends, in effect, "Now don't worry; when you come to My home, it won't be as it was when I came to yours. You won't find it overcrowded like Bethlehem. In My Father's house are many rooms."

Jesus spoke about home again later that evening, when He said, "If anyone loves me, he will keep my word, and my Father will love him, and we will come to him and make our home with him" (14:23). Literally Jesus said, "We will room with him." Jesus is telling us that God will "room" with us by the Holy Spirit until He returns again, and then we will "room" with Him. God will move in with you until the day you move in with Him.

The future home of Jesus' disciples is certain. Listen to the candor of Jesus: "In my Father's house are many rooms. If it were not so, would I have told you that I go to prepare a place for you?" (John 14:2). If the disciples' future were in doubt, Jesus would have told them. But their future in heaven was assured, and for this reason they were not to be troubled.

The Way to the Father's House

Having described the Father's house, Jesus went on to explain how His disciples would get there: "I go to prepare a place for you" (14:2).

We are not to think of Jesus working round the clock to get heaven ready for our arrival. Christ created the cosmos out of nothing with a word; He can get heaven ready for believers with a single command.

When Jesus said that He was going "to prepare a place," He meant that through His going the place would be prepared. Through His death, resurrection, and ascension, Christ opened the way for all who believe to enter the glory of the Father's house. His death and resurrection guarantees a place in heaven for all who will believe. And for this reason, Jesus said, "Let not your hearts be troubled."

"I Will Come Again"

"If I go and prepare a place for you, I will come again and will take you to myself, that where I am you may be also" (14:3). Jesus was saying, "If I go through the agony of death and then rise on the third day and ascend into heaven to prepare a place for you, I will surely bring you there."

If you were to spend your entire life savings on a priceless ring, it is inconceivable that, having made the purchase, you would then leave the ring on the counter of the jewelry store. Having paid the price, the ring would become your treasured possession, and you would bring it home.

This is why Jesus told the disciples that they were not to be troubled but rather to trust in Him. They had seen Judas leave, they had heard that Peter would fail, and they had been told that Jesus would be taken from them. It seemed that their world was falling apart, but it was not. Jesus was going to prepare a place for them, and they could be certain that He would bring them home.

An Unfinished Project

The glorious prospect of heaven may seem a long way off, but the promise is given to sustain us when our lives are far from what God calls us to be.

When you remodel a room, studs, pipes, and wires are exposed. The room might be functional, but nothing is as it will be. When you look at the state of the place, you need to remind yourself that you are looking at an unfinished project and that it will not always be like this.

And when you look in the mirror, you are looking at an unfinished project. The new life has already begun in you, but you still battle with the pull of the flesh and you are not yet what you will be. Like Peter, you will have your failures as well as your successes, but it will not always be so. Christ is coming, and when He appears, you will be everything God has made you to be. So do not let your heart be troubled.

TRAIL MARKERS

The return of Jesus is a vital and practical truth that we need to grasp for living the Christian life today. There may be times when you are faced with devastating news. You may wonder what God is doing and what the future holds. But Jesus tells you not to let your heart be troubled. He invites you to trust Him and lean on what He has revealed about Himself. God's work in you and in the world is an unfinished project, but it will be brought to completion when Jesus Christ returns in glory.

1. Try to put yourself in the shoes of the disciples at the Last Supper. Which piece of bad news would have been most troubling to you? Why?

2. Can you think of a time when you were in a dark place and had to lean into all that you knew about Jesus?

3. What is your reaction to Jesus' words, "In my Father's house are many rooms. If it were not so, would I have told you that I go to prepare a place for you"?

4. On a scale of 1 (no confidence) to 10 (completely confident), how confident are you that Jesus has reserved a place for you in heaven? Why?

5. Where in your life do you most need to apply Jesus' words, "Let not let your hearts be troubled"?

To memorize:

"Let not your hearts be troubled. Believe in God; believe also in me. In my Father's house are many rooms. If it were not so, would I have told you that I go to prepare a place for you? And if I go and prepare a place for you, I will come again and will take you to myself, that where I am you may be also." (John 14:1–3)

In the Bible, God reveals that He is one. But the Old Testament raises some questions that are not resolved until later. For example, at creation God said, "Let us *make man in our image" (Genesis 1:26). Why "us" when God tells us so clearly that He is one? In the New Testament, God reveals that He is Father, Son, and Holy Spirit. God is love (1 John 4:8), and when nothing else existed, love flowed between the Father, the Son, and the Holy Spirit (John 17:24).*

36

FATHER

MATTHEW 11

The old pastor's brow was furrowed as he peered over his half-moon spectacles at the scattered congregation and began the message he had been pondering all week. "First," he said slowly, "I am going to search the unsearchable." Then, he said with increasing confidence, "I am going to explain the unexplainable." And finally, he paused as he searched for the words. "I'm going to unscrew the inscrutable!"

I'm not so ambitious, and it is with a sense of awe that I write about the most distinctive but also the most difficult doctrine in the whole of the Christian faith: There is one God, and He is Father, Son, and Holy Spirit.

Don't expect to understand the nature of God. Fish can only have a very limited understanding of human nature, and in the same way, it is beyond our capacity to figure out the nature of God.

Saturated in the Life of God

If we are to know God, we must experience Him as Father, Son, and Spirit. At the end of Matthew's gospel, Jesus tells His disciples that they are to "go . . . and make disciples of all nations, baptizing them in the name of the Father and of the Son and of the Holy Spirit" (Matthew 28:19).

The word *baptize* literally means *to dip* or *to drench*. The Christian life is all about being drenched in the Father, plunged into the Son, and soaked in the Spirit. The Father, the Son, and the Holy Spirit permeate every part of a believer's life. You cannot know the Father apart from the Son or the Son apart from the Spirit.

So while we may not be able to fully comprehend the nature of God, we must grasp what is revealed about the Father, Son, and Holy Spirit if we are to know God as He is.

Fixing the Anchor Points

We may summarize what God has revealed to us about His nature in three statements.

First, there is one God. This is clear in both the Old and New Testaments. God says, "Hear, O Israel: The Lord our God, the Lord is one" (Deuteronomy 6:4). There is "one Lord . . . one God and Father of all" (Ephesians 4:5–6). Christians do not believe in three gods. There is one God.

Second, God exists in three persons. The distinct identities of the Father, Son, and Spirit are written all through the New Testament. The Father sends the Son (Galatians 4:4). The Son prays to the Father (John 17:1). The Spirit glorifies the Son (John 16:14), and the Son sends the Spirit (Acts 2:33). The three persons of the Godhead are not to be confused. The Father did not die on the cross. The Son did not send Himself into the world. The Spirit did not rise from the dead. There is one God, and He exists in three persons.

Third, each person is fully God. The Father is God, the Son is God, and the Spirit is God. Christ said, "I and the Father are one" (John 10:30). He shared the glory of the Father before the world began (17:5). Through the Holy Spirit, the presence of Jesus was with His disciples, even though He was returning to the Father (14:16–18). If the Spirit was with them, Christ was with them, and if Christ was with them, the Father was with them (14:23).

The Father is God, the Son is God, and the Spirit is God, but there are not three gods. There is one eternal God, and He is Father, Son, and Holy Spirit.

The Problem with Analogies

Through the centuries, people have used analogies to try and explain the Trinity. But if there were an analogy in the natural world that would help us grasp the nature of God, surely God would have put it in the Bible.

While analogies of the Trinity may help us to see one part of the truth, they invariably distort or obscure something else. Some people use the analogy of one person playing three different roles. For example, I am a husband and a father and a pastor. But the analogy falls short because there is only one person fulfilling these three roles. God exists in three persons; the Father is not the Son, and the Son is not the Spirit.

Once, when I was climbing a mountain in Scotland, a mist came down and settled over the town in the valley below. I couldn't see the town, but I could see everything around it. The truth of the Trinity is shrouded in mist. We cannot explain how one God can exist in three persons. But we can clearly identify what lies beyond the bounds of truth. For example, if someone says that Christ is less than God, or that there are many gods, we can immediately see from the Scriptures that this lies outside of the truth. The mist covers the truth itself, but that which is outside the truth can be clearly seen.

How to Respond to a Mystery

The nature of God is a mystery, but it is not a contradiction. If Christians believed both that there is one God and there are three gods, that would be a contradiction. Or if we believed that there are three persons and there is one person, that would be a contradiction. But to say that there is one God who exists in three persons is not a contradiction. It is a mystery.

How should you respond to this mystery?

First, don't turn away from it. If you turn away from what you do not understand about God, you will miss the unfathomable splendor of His glory.

Second, don't try to explain it. You will never get to a place where you say, "It all makes perfect sense to me now; I don't know why I didn't see it before." God will never let you get there.

Third, let it lead you to worship. You will spend all eternity marveling at the glory of God, so let your worship begin in response to the wonder of what He has already revealed.

Coming to God the Father

So how can we come to a God who is so great that we cannot fathom His nature? Jesus said, "I am the way, and the truth, and the life. No one comes to the Father except through me" (John 14:6).

If you want to visit the president of the United States there are several approaches you might try. If you knew a family member, that person could make the introduction. Or if you knew the secretary of state or the chief of staff, he or she might grant you access. There are many people next to the president of the United States, but who is next to God the Father?

Since "no one knows the Father except the Son" (Matthew 11:27) and "no one has ever seen God; the only God, who is at the Father's side, he has made him known" (John 1:18), it follows that Jesus is the only one who can bring us to the Father (John 14:6).

Knowing God the Father

If we want to know what a relationship with God the Father looks like, we must begin by looking at what it meant for Jesus.

Christ invites us into a relationship in which we are subject to the Father's authority. You can't miss this in the life of Jesus. His whole life was aligned with the Father's purpose, and that was never seen more clearly than in the garden of Gethsemane, where Jesus said, "My Father, if it be possible, let this cup pass from me; nevertheless, not as I will, but as you will" (Matthew 26:39).

Knowing God as Father involves being subject to His authority, even when that is costly. There will be times when, like Jesus, we say, "Not my will, but Yours be done." If you want to know the Father's love, you must submit to His authority.

Jesus invites us into a relationship in which we enjoy the same love that the Father has for His own Son: "As the Father has loved me, so have I loved you" (John 15:9; see also 17:26). How great is the love of God the Father for His own Son?

God is eternal in His being, unlimited in His power and infinite in His knowledge. His love is beyond anything we can imagine on earth and more than the angels can fathom in heaven.

We will be lost in worship, wonder, love, and praise when the full extent of God's love is unfolded to us in heaven, and it is the special work of the Holy Spirit to let us know that we are loved like this now (Romans 5:5).

Those who share in the Father's love will also share in His glory: "The glory that you have given to me I have given to them" (John 17:22). There will be times when it is costly to submit to the authority of the Father, but Paul reminds us that this is "not worth comparing with the glory that is to be revealed to us" (Romans 8:18).

For Jesus to know God as His Father meant submitting to His authority, enjoying His love, and sharing His glory. When Jesus invites us to come to the Father through Him, He is inviting us into the same kind of relationship.

TRAIL MARKER

There is one God, and He is Father, Son, and Holy Spirit. This is a mystery, but we should not be surprised that the nature of God is beyond our understanding. While we cannot know God fully, we can come to know Him truly. This is why Jesus Christ has come into the world. He came from the Father's side to make Him known and to bring us to the Father.

1. What are the three anchor points about the nature of God that we find in the Bible? Which one of these are you most familiar with? Least familiar?

2. What analogies of the Trinity have you heard? What truth do they distort or obscure?

3. Which of the three suggested responses to a mystery (don't turn away, don't try to explain, let it lead you to worship) is most challenging for you? Why?

4. How can a person come to know God?

5. What do you find most attractive about Jesus' relationship with God the Father?

To memorize:

> "I am the way, and the truth, and the life. No one comes to the Father except through me. If you had known me, you would have known my Father also. From now on you do know him and have seen him." (John 14:6–7)

When did God become Father? The answer is that He has always been Father. He is the everlasting Father, and His nature never changes. When did Christ become the Son? The answer is that He has always been the Son. He is the eternal Son, and His nature never changes. The Father was never without the Son, and the Son was never without the Father.

37

SON

JOHN 5

I became a father in 1986 when my son Andrew was born. Before I had a son, I could not have been described as a father. The birth of a son or daughter makes a man a father or a woman a mother. But God did not gain a son when Jesus was born into the world. God sent His Son, who was already "at the Father's side" (John 1:18).

The Bible makes it clear that the Son is equal with the Father (5:18). Before He took our flesh, God the Son shared the Father's glory (17:5), the Father's life (5:26), the Father's activity (1:3), and the Father's love (17:24). He is in very nature God, but He did not count this equality something to be grasped (Philippians 2:6). He placed Himself at the disposal of the Father and took on the form of a servant.

On one occasion, Jesus said, "The Father is greater than I" (John 14:28). This would be like saying, "The president of the United States is greater than I am." The point of the statement is simply that his position is greater than mine.

Jesus shares the same nature as the Father, so when He said, "The Father is greater than I," He did not mean that the Father is more divine, but that the Father had a more exalted position. The Father was in heaven and Jesus was on His way to the cross. This is why Jesus said to His disciples, "If you loved me, you would have rejoiced, because I am going to the Father . . ." (14:28). Going to the Father meant returning to share His exalted position.

Like Father, Like Son

The Bible uses the word *son* in two ways. It can mean a dependent relative or a reflected nature.[8]

In the ancient world, a son followed in his father's footsteps. If your father was a carpenter, you would be a carpenter as well. And if your father was a good carpenter, the quality of his work would be reflected in yours. As the old saying goes, "Like father, like son."

In the New Testament, we read about a man the apostles nicknamed "Barnabas." Barnabas means "son of encouragement" (Acts 4:36). It's not difficult to see why the apostles gave him this name. They saw that Barnabas was a great encourager. He was encouragement personified, encouragement in human flesh. He was the son of encouragement.

Jesus used the word "son" in the same way in the Sermon on the Mount. "Blessed are the peacemakers," He said, "for they shall be called sons of God" (Matthew 5:9). God is the great peacemaker, and when we make peace, we reflect His character.

So when the Bible described Jesus as "the Son of God" (John 5:25), the word *Son* does not mean that He is a dependent relative of the Father, but that He exactly reflects the Father's nature (Hebrews 1:3). The Son of God is all that God is, in human form.

Doing the Father's Work

Jesus said, "Truly, truly, I say to you, the Son can do nothing of his own accord, but only what he sees the Father doing" (John 5:19). We could never say that we only do what God does. Yet that is exactly what Jesus is saying: "You will not find a single thing in My life that is outside of the range of the activity of God."

Then Jesus makes a second statement that is even more astonishing: "Whatever the Father does, that the Son does likewise" (5:19). We may do some of the things that God does. When we love, show mercy, or keep our promises we reflect the nature of the Father. But there are some things that belong to God alone. Only

---

8. I gladly acknowledge my debt to Professor Don Carson for his insight on the use of the word "son" in the New Testament. See especially D. A. Carson, *The Difficult Doctrine of the Love of God* (Crossway, 2000), 31ff.

God gives life. Only God raises the dead. God alone is the judge. These are God's things, and Jesus tells us that He does them: "As the Father raises the dead and gives them life, so also the Son gives life to whom he will. For the Father judges no one, but has given all judgment to the Son" (5:21–22).

The Son Has Life in Himself

Your life is a gift from God through the union of your father and your mother. Without them you would not exist. Only God has life in Himself. He is the only being whose existence does not depend on anyone else.

But Jesus says, "As the Father has life in himself, so he has granted the Son also to have life in himself" (5:26). These words help us gaze with wonder on the mystery of the Trinity. Notice that Jesus did not say, "The Father has life in Himself and the Son has life in Himself." That would mean that there are two gods, both with life in themselves. Nor did Jesus say, "The Father has life in Himself and He has granted the Son to have life." That would mean that the Son was a created and dependent being just like you and me.

Jesus said, "As the Father has life in himself, so he has granted the Son also to have life in himself." The Father and the Son share in the one eternal life of God.[9]

Put all this together and you will begin to see the glory of our Lord Jesus Christ. One day He will raise the dead and pronounce final judgment on all people, and He is able to give life to all who come to Him.

Knowing God: Speculation or Revelation?

The New Testament places great stress on the identity of Jesus. He is God with us. And this truth is of central importance because if the Son were not God, we could not know the Father.

On one occasion, Philip said to Jesus, "Show us the Father, and it is enough for us." Jesus replied, "Have I been with you so long, and you still do not know me, Philip? Whoever has seen me has seen the Father" (John 14:8–9).

I have a brother in England. He is like me in some ways but very different in

9. See D. A. Carson, *The Difficult Doctrine of the Love of God*, 37–39.

others. I could not say, "If you have seen me, you have seen my brother," because even though we come from the same parents, we are quite different. To know me is not to know my brother.

If the Son were not God, we could not know the Father. The best we could say would be that someone who was with the Father came to tell us about Him. That would make Jesus like an angel or a prophet, but Jesus says, "Whoever has seen me has seen the Father" (14:9).

The Cross: An Act of Cruelty or a Gift of Love?

The Bible tells us that the Father laid the guilt and punishment for our sins on His Son (Isaiah 53:5–6), and that this was a demonstration of God's love: "God shows his love for us in that while we were still sinners, Christ died for us" (Romans 5:8).

But if the Son were not God, the cross would be an act of cruelty, not a gift of love. God would then have picked on some person in His creation and poured out on him what everyone else deserved. What kind of love would that be?

If the Son were not God, we would have to rewrite Romans 5:8: "God shows his injustice in that while we were still sinners, Christ died for us." But the Son *is* God, and at the cross, it was God who bore our sins and gave Himself for us.

Before God created the world, He planned to redeem men and women so that they would share His glory forever. The plan involved great cost. It would mean God giving Himself, and that self-giving would be the ultimate display of His own nature and glory.

God's self-giving would involve each person of the Trinity. The Father would send the Son. The Son would lay down His life. The Spirit would give Himself to every believer.

Consider the roles of the Father and the Son. Which of them had the easier part to play: the one who would give His Son, or the one who would lay down His life? The question is unanswerable. The Father and the Son were one in the infinite cost of self-giving and sacrifice for you and for me.

Salvation: Being Sure or Hoping for the Best?

If the Son were not God, you could never be sure of your salvation.

I phoned my credit card company recently because I wanted to upgrade my card. "Can I do this over the phone?" I asked. The representative was very helpful and assured me that I could.

A few days later I received a letter.

Dear Colin Smith,

Thank you for your recent inquiry regarding your credit card account. Unfortunately, we are unable to change your account as you requested. If you would like to change your account, please contact our customer service at the telephone number listed above.

Clearly, the representative had been overruled. She sincerely believed that my account could be changed over the phone, but she lacked the authority to make it happen.

What if it was like that with Christ? If Jesus were not God, there would always be the possibility of Him being overruled by a higher authority. And we would face the possibility of arriving at heaven's gate only to find that we are not qualified to enter.

But the Father has entrusted all judgment to the Son (John 5:22). Christ presides over the supreme court of the universe. There is no higher authority. So when the Son says you are forgiven, you are forgiven indeed!

TRAIL MARKERS

Jesus is God with us, and for this reason we can truly know the Father through Him. His death on the cross is the ultimate demonstration of God's love for us. God was reconciling the world to Himself in Christ (2 Corinthians 5:19). The deity of the Lord Jesus Christ is our assurance of salvation. Jesus said, "Truly, truly, I say to you, whoever hears my word and believes him who sent me has eternal life. He does not come into judgment, but has passed from death to life" (John 5:24).

1. Which of your family members is most (or least) like you?

2. In your own words, what does it mean when the Bible says that Jesus is "the Son of God"?

3. Respond to the statement: "If the Son were not God, we could not know the Father."

4. How would you respond to someone who says the cross was an act of cruelty?

5. What truth(s) in this chapter could increase your confidence that you will enter heaven? Why?

To memorize:

I have been crucified with Christ. It is no longer I who live, but Christ who lives in me. And the life I now live in the flesh I live by faith in the Son of God, who loved me and gave himself for me. (Galatians 2:20)

Some people who are reasonably clear about God the Father and God the Son are quite confused when it comes to God the Holy Spirit. We understand that without the Father, the Son would never have been sent into the world. We can see that without the Son there would be no sacrifice on the cross, no empty tomb, and we could not be saved. But what if there was no Holy Spirit? What difference would that make? How important is the third person of the Trinity?

38

SPIRIT

JOHN 16

A man named Stavros has amassed a fortune over the years, and now he is fabulously wealthy.

When Stavros dies, his lawyer opens the will. It's a lengthy document, running to hundreds of pages, and the beneficiaries are all over the world. Each of them has to be found and told about the legacy, and according to the terms of the will, every one of them has to be brought to Stavros' home in order to receive what has been promised. The lawyer has his work cut out for years to come.

The Bible tells us that Jesus purchased a marvelous inheritance for us. Through His death and resurrection, He has opened the way for us to be reconciled to God and to enter everlasting life. The will of God has been signed by the Father and sealed by the Son. But what has been signed and sealed still needs to be delivered.

It is one thing for a gift to be offered; it is another for that gift to be received. And all that Jesus has done is of no value to us until we receive what He offers.

So how can the will of God be delivered to us? The answer is by the Holy Spirit. The Holy Spirit brings what Jesus has accomplished on the cross and applies it personally to us.

Without the Spirit of God, salvation would remain a theoretical possibility, but it would never become a reality for anyone. If there were no Holy Spirit, no one would arrive in heaven. Without the Spirit, all that Jesus has done would be like a will that was never read, a gift that was never opened, an inheritance that was never enjoyed.

God's Disturber of the Peace

Jesus offers forgiveness of sin, righteousness from above, and deliverance from the judgment to come. But most people do not feel that they need what He offers. That is why the first work of the Holy Spirit is to disturb our peace. "When he [the Holy Spirit] comes, he will convict the world concerning sin and righteousness and judgment" (John 16:8).

Think about opening a can of paint. You would probably use a screwdriver or some other kind of lever to pry the lid open. Around the edge of the can there is a rim that functions as a pivot for the lever. If there were no rim, there would be nothing for the lever to pull on. A lever has to pull on a pivot.

The gospel is like a lever, and it depends on an awareness of sin as its pivot. If a person has no sense of sin, the gospel will have no "pull" in that person's life. The Holy Spirit shows us our sin, and this is the first step in finding peace with God.

God's Three Alarms

When the Holy Spirit reveals to us what's wrong, we can see our need and will be ready to hear the gospel. The Holy Spirit disturbs us, not because He is against us but because He sees the position we are in—and He loves us too much to leave us there. He convicts us of judgment (John 16:8). He awakens us to the danger that we are in because He does not want us to stay there.

Suppose a person finds it difficult to wake up in the morning. He sets an alarm that should wake him gently with music. But in case he sleeps through the music he sets a second alarm with a more jarring sound. As a last resort, he sets a third alarm that makes a horrendous noise, but he knows that his day will begin much better if he gets out of bed before its deafening blast.

God has three ways to intercept sin in a person's life. You could think of them as three alarms. The first is the gentle work of God's Spirit opening up your conscience and revealing what's wrong so that you can change it.

If you sleep through that, the Holy Spirit may speak more loudly and directly. That's what happened to David. God exposed his sin through the prophet Nathan in 2 Samuel 12. It became public knowledge, and at that point, David turned to God in repentance.

If a person ignores God's second alarm, his or her situation becomes perilous. That is what happened to Pharaoh. God sent Moses to him, but Pharaoh repeatedly refused to listen to God's command, even when he was confronted directly. He continued to harden his heart, and eventually Pharaoh came under the judgment of God.

Consider these three alarms: the quiet work of God's Spirit in opening the conscience, God exposing a secret sin, and the direct judgment of almighty God. Which of these three would you like God to use to wake you up?

Showing us our sin is the first work of the Spirit. Thank God it is not His last. He awakens us to our sins, but He never leaves us there.

Turning on the Floodlight

When a building is floodlit, you can see its beauty. But without the floodlight, its beauty would be hidden in the darkness.[10] The Holy Spirit is like a floodlight shining on Jesus. He illuminates the truth that without Him we would not see. He opens our understanding to see who Jesus is and what He has accomplished.

Jesus said, "When the Helper comes . . . he will bear witness about me" (John 15:26). "He [the Holy Spirit] will glorify me, for he will take what is mine and declare it to you" (John 16:14). Like the floodlight, the Holy Spirit does not focus on Himself; He directs our attention to Jesus.

The Holy Spirit has a beautiful ministry. He shows us our need of a Savior, and He shows us that Jesus is the Savior we need. Then He brings the two together. The Holy Spirit is heaven's matchmaker. He brings us to Christ and joins Christ to us, so that everything Jesus accomplished on the cross becomes ours.

The Holy Spirit Is a Person

Speaking about the Holy Spirit, Jesus said, "I will ask the Father, and he will give you another Helper [or Counselor], to be with you forever" (14:16). For three years, Jesus had been the disciples' counselor, and the Holy Spirit would continue to be all that Jesus had been to them.

---

10. I owe the illustration of the floodlight to Dr. J. I. Packer. See Packer, *Keep in Step with the Spirit* (Revell, 1984), 65ff.

Notice that Jesus does not say, "I will send you help." He says, "I will send you a *Helper*." The Holy Spirit is as much a person as the Father and the Son, so we should not think of Him simply as a power or force. The Bible speaks about lying to the Holy Spirit and grieving the Spirit (Acts 5:3; Ephesians 4:30). You cannot lie to a force, and you cannot grieve a power. A burst of energy could never be to the disciples everything that Jesus was.

Jesus told His disciples, "I am going to the Father" (John 14:12), but "I will ask the Father, and he will give you another Helper, to be with you forever, even the Spirit of truth" (14:16–17). But then Jesus said, "I will come to you" (14:18). The presence of the Spirit with the disciples would mean that Christ Himself was truly with them.

Then Jesus said something even more astonishing: "If anyone loves me, he will keep my word, and my Father will love him, and *we* will come to him and make *our* home with him" (14:23). So where the Spirit is, both the Father and the Son will make their home.

You cannot know the Father apart from the Son, or the Son apart from the Spirit. It is through the Son that the Father has made Himself known, and it is the Holy Spirit who brings us to Jesus.

"In" and "With"

Jesus used two words to describe our relationship with the Holy Spirit: "He dwells with you and will be in you" (14:17). The Holy Spirit is *with* us. Notice the distinction between us and the Holy Spirit. The Holy Spirit is not you, and you are not the Holy Spirit, so don't fall into the trap of confusing what you think and say with the mind of the Spirit. Wise Christians allow others to test what they say.

Jesus also said that the Spirit would be *in* the disciples. Notice the union between us and the Holy Spirit. The Spirit is more than a mentor who tells us what to do and then leaves us to do it. He dwells in us, His power works through us, and His presence makes the Christian life possible.

Jesus said, "It is to your advantage that I go away, for if I do not go away, the Helper will not come to you" (John 16:7). This clearly meant that the disciples, who had been with Jesus for three years, would be given more. Jesus had been "with" them, but now by the Spirit, He would be "in" them.

It is natural for us to think that we have less than the first disciples who followed Jesus. But Christian believers have more. The Holy Spirit—the Spirit of Jesus Himself—lives "in" you. That's more, not less!

TRAIL MARKERS

God the Holy Spirit is the third person of the Trinity, and His ministry is central to our salvation. We *could not* be saved without the work of the Son of God on the cross, and we *would not* be saved without the work of the Spirit of God in our hearts.

The Holy Spirit disturbs us so that we see our sin and grasp our need of the Savior. And as He disturbs, He also illuminates so that we can see the glory of Jesus. If you have come to faith in Jesus Christ, God's Spirit lives in you (1 Corinthians 6:19). So don't ever say that you can't change.

1. What role does the Holy Spirit play in our salvation?

2. What is the Holy Spirit's *first* work in a person's life? What has been your experience of this?

3. What are God's three ways of waking people up? Are you personally aware of God using any of these in your own life?

4. The Holy Spirit is like a floodlight, shining on Jesus. What is one thing about Jesus that you've come to see clearly through your study of the Bible?

5. Respond to the statement: "He [the Holy Spirit] dwells with you and will be in you."

To memorize:

"I will ask the Father, and he will give you another Helper, to be with you forever, even the Spirit of truth, whom the world cannot receive, because it neither sees him nor knows him. You know him, for he dwells with you and will be in you." (John 14:16–17)

The world is filled with many claims, and sometimes it is hard to tell truth from error. So how are we to assess the claims of Jesus? The Gospels give you the evidence that you need to believe that Jesus is the Christ, the Son of God. They invite you to come and see. And as you take an honest look at the life, death, and resurrection of Jesus, you will be able to respond to Him with faith.

39

CHRIST

JOHN 20

Suppose you are in an unfamiliar city and you have lost your cellphone. You need to get to a place you have never been before, and you don't know how to get there. Here are two ways in which you might proceed.

First, you could ask for directions. Someone might tell you that you need to catch the Number 29 bus, get off at the second stop past the old cement works, take the third street on the left, go over the bridge, across the field, through the underpass, and then your destination is on your right.

A second approach would be to take a taxi. You would ask the driver to take you to your destination, and you would get in.

Now suppose, in the first case, that just after you get on the bus, the man who had given you the instructions has a heart attack and dies. This sad event will not hinder your journey because you already have the instructions—the directions do not depend on the person giving them.

But suppose you are in the taxi, and just as you are going past the old cement works, the driver has a heart attack. The paramedics come and take him to the hospital, leaving you behind. Now you are completely stuck. You do not know the way to your destination, and the person you trusted is unable to take you there.

The heart of Christianity lies not in a set of instructions, but in the ability of Jesus to take us to heaven. It is not the teaching of the New Testament that will save you; it is Jesus Christ who will save you. Christianity stands or falls with the ability of Jesus to do what He promised.

Jesus tells us that He can bring us to the Father, and when, like the taxi driver, He invites us to "get in," we face a decision: Am I ready to stake my destiny on Him?

You Are the Jury

The gospel of John was written "so that you may believe that Jesus is the Christ, the Son of God, and that by believing you may have life in his name" (John 20:31).

Say you are sitting on a jury. The apostle John wants to present you with certain evidence, and when he is finished, he will be looking for you to give a verdict.

John is not trying to intimidate you, nor is he playing on your emotions. He is presenting you with the evidence that he has seen and heard as a direct witness of the life, death, and resurrection of Jesus. All he asks is that you hear the evidence. "Come and see" (John 1:46).

Jesus Is the Christ

If you were asked to summarize the core of the Christian faith in one sentence, what would you say? John boils the essence of the faith down to just four words: "Jesus is the Christ" (20:31). So it is important for us to know what the name *Christ* means. We know that our Lord was given the birth name of Jesus, so why do we call Him Jesus Christ?

Our English word *Christ* comes from the Greek word *Christos,* which means "Messiah" or "Anointed One." *Christ* is a title referring to the promised one, who would be anointed by God, and a quick review of the people who were anointed in the Old Testament will help us understand its significance.

Throughout the Bible story, God *reveals* Himself so that we may know Him, He *reconciles* us to Himself so that we come to Him, and He *rules* over the world so that His purposes may be fulfilled. In the Old Testament, certain people were "anointed" as a sign that God would use them in one of these ways—they were prophets, priests, and kings.

As the Old Testament story progressed, there was a growing expectation that one day God would send an anointed one par excellence into the world. But since God's anointed one could be a prophet, priest, or king, it is easy to understand how different expectations developed regarding the Messiah. Some thought He would be a prophet, calling people to righteousness. Others were looking for a priest who would restore authentic worship. And others were convinced that the Messiah would be a freedom fighter who would lead a political uprising and deliver God's people from the oppression of the Roman Empire.

But when Jesus Christ came into the world, He fulfilled not one, but all three of the Old Testament offices. God the Father said to His Son, "You go and be their prophet. You go and be their priest. You go and be their king." Jesus Christ is God's anointed one, and John lays out the evidence to show us that He is the one who reveals the truth of God, reconciles men and women to God, and triumphs over the enemies of God.

Examine the Evidence

John sets out the evidence that Jesus is the Christ: He is the prophet who knows the secrets of every heart and life. He is the priest who lays down His life as the sacrifice for our sins. And He is the king who delivers us from our enemies.

Jesus is the prophet who knows everything about us. He knew the hidden truth about a Samaritan woman. Having met with Jesus, she said to her friends, "Come, see a man who told me all that I ever did" (John 4:29). But He is more than a prophet. When the woman said, "I know that Messiah is coming (he who is called Christ)" (4:25), Jesus said to her, "I who speak to you am he" (4:26).

Jesus is the priest who reconciles us to God. John the Baptist identified Jesus as "the Lamb of God, who takes away the sin of the world!" (1:29). And Jesus said, "The Son of man came not to be served, but to serve, and to give his life as a ransom for many" (Mark 10:45).

Jesus is the king who will deliver us from the tyranny of death and hell. When Jesus came to the tomb of Lazarus, He said, "I am the resurrection and the life" (John 11:25). He asked Martha, the dead man's sister, if she believed this. "Yes, Lord," she said, "I believe that you are the Christ, the Son of God, who is coming into the world" (11:27). Then Jesus went to the tomb of Lazarus and "cried out with a loud voice, 'Lazarus, come out'" (11:43). To the amazement of everyone, Lazarus "who had died came out" (11:44).

When we know that Jesus is prophet, priest, and king, we will understand what it means to have faith in Him. So believing in Jesus means that we trust what He says as prophet and take His Word as truth. It means that we trust Him as priest to bring us into the presence of God. It means that we submit ourselves to Him as king, to live under His authority and rule.

Abundant Life

When you believe that Jesus is the Christ, you will have "life in his name" (20:31). Jesus spoke about an abundant life that He alone can give: "I came that they may have life and have it abundantly" (10:10). What does that mean?

At the beginning of the Bible story, Adam and Eve enjoyed a life free from fear and frustration. They pursued meaningful work in beautiful surroundings. But most of all, they enjoyed the presence and companionship of God who walked with them in the garden. They had abundant life, but they lost it. And we have never known what they enjoyed.

Jesus came to deliver us from this fallen world with all its disease, danger, disasters, and death, and to bring us into an abundant life that begins now and will continue forever. It is by believing in Jesus that we have this life in His name.

Something Magnificent

Some time ago, Karen and I had the opportunity of hearing the Chicago Symphony Orchestra with a guest violinist. They were playing Tchaikovsky, and it was magnificent.

The soloist played as if his bow would set his violin on fire, and at the end, the audience rose in a standing ovation. It was irresistible. The applause went on and on, and when it would not subside, the soloist raised his violin and treated us to an encore. That brought the house down.

When we went out for the intermission, our spirits were high, and the audience was buzzing with delight. But in the foyer one man seemed upset. As we walked by, I heard him say, "I've been coming here for thirty years, and I have never seen a soloist give an encore. I don't like it. I can't see any reason for it!"

I had to restrain myself. Here was a man who had been in the presence of something magnificent, which had lifted hundreds of other people around him, and he was offended by the encore! What was wrong with the man?

As we have journeyed through the Gospels, we have been in the presence of something truly magnificent. We have seen the breathtaking sweep of God's plan in which the Son of God took our flesh, faced our enemy, laid down His life as a sacrifice, rose from the dead, and ascended into heaven—so that we may be brought into everlasting life through faith in His name.

Nothing would be more tragic than for someone to be confronted with the claims of Christ and the offer of the gospel and to go away as if he or she had not heard anything out of the ordinary. The Gospels were written "so that you may believe that Jesus is the Christ, the Son of God, and that by believing you may have life in his name" (20:31).

TRAIL MARKERS

The name *Christ* means "Messiah," or "Anointed One." In the Old Testament, God anointed prophets, priests, and kings to advance His purposes in the world. They pointed forward to One who would fulfill what they could only illustrate.

The Gospels give us the evidence that Jesus is the Christ and show us how He uniquely fulfills the ancient roles of prophet, priest, and king. The centerpiece of history is that God took human flesh in the person of Jesus, and it is through Him that all the promises of God are fulfilled.

1. If you were on the jury, what evidence about Jesus would be most convincing to you?

2. What does the Bible mean when it says, "Jesus is the *Christ*"?

3. In your own words, what does it mean to believe in Jesus Christ?

4. If all you had was the teaching of Jesus, would that be enough to get you into heaven? Why or why not?

5. How is the abundant life that Jesus offers different from life as we normally experience it in this world?

To memorize:

These are written so that you may believe that Jesus is the Christ, the Son of God, and that by believing you may have life in his name. (John 20:31)

Before He ascended into heaven, Jesus told His disciples that in a few days they would be "baptized with the Holy Spirit" (Acts 1:5). Then, He said, "You will receive power . . . and you will be my witnesses in Jerusalem and in all Judea and Samaria, and to the end of the earth" (1:8). They did not have to wait long. Just ten days later, when Jerusalem was crammed with visitors from many countries, the promise of Jesus was fulfilled.

40

POWER

ACTS 2

The chairman reported that the church roll now stood at 120 members. There was a good spirit at the prayer meeting and a lot of discussion about how they should fill a vacant leadership position. But besides that, not a lot had happened.

The task of reaching their community seemed beyond them. There was very little money, very few people, and outside of their meeting place, a culture that had very little room for their message. That's how the church was at the beginning of the book of Acts.

But on the day of Pentecost, the Holy Spirit was poured out on the first believers. And after that, the church was completely different.

A Sound Like the Wind

"Suddenly there came from heaven a sound like a mighty rushing wind, and it filled the entire house where they were sitting" (2:2). Think about an Olympic sprinter. Great gulps of air pulsate through his chest as breath fills his lungs and energizes his body. That's what happened at Pentecost.

In the ancient world, many languages used the same word for "wind," "breath," and "spirit." The sound of the wind is similar to the sound of breath, only it is much louder and it lasts longer.

When you find something unusual in the Bible, it is helpful to ask, "Where have we come across something like this before?" And if we ask, "Where have we come across the sound of wind or breath before?" two answers might quickly come to mind.

At the beginning of the Bible story, we read about God breathing life into Adam. God shaped a lifeless being from the dust of the ground. Then God breathed into this skeletal frame. God gave Adam the kiss of life, and the first man became a living being.

Then, before Jesus ascended into heaven, He breathed on the disciples, and said, "Receive the Holy Spirit" (John 20:22). In doing this, Jesus was anticipating what would happen on the day of Pentecost. So when the disciples heard a sound like the rushing wind just a few days later, they would immediately associate it with the sound of Jesus breathing on them, and they would recognize that this was the fulfillment of what Jesus had promised.

Great Balls of Fire

Having heard the sound of the rushing wind, "divided tongues as of fire appeared to them and rested on each one of them" (Acts 2:3).

A great ball or pillar of fire appeared above the gathered believers. As the fire came nearer, it divided into individual flames or "tongues as of fire," so that a flame rested on every person in the room. The astonishing thing was that none of them were burned.

Again, the best way to understand this is to ask where in the Bible we have seen something like it before. In the Old Testament, God appeared to Moses in flames of fire that rested on a bush that did not burn and commissioned him to lead God's people out of their slavery in Egypt. Now God was coming in the fire to give a new commission to His church.

Try to see yourself among the 120 people when the fire fell. You look up and see the fire above you slowly descending over the middle of the room. You realize what is happening: God's presence is coming among His people. You are filled with a sense of awe. The God who appeared to Moses is making His presence known again, and you are there in the room.

You remember that when the fire came to Moses, he was commissioned to advance God's purpose. So you wonder, *Who will the flames rest on now?* Will it be Peter, James, John, or perhaps all three? Or maybe even all twelve of the apostles.

But as you look up, you realize that one of the flames is coming toward you. You look around the room, and a flame rests on every person! God is commissioning every believer to advance His purpose in the world.

In the Old Testament, prophets, priests, and kings were anointed by God for ministry. But in the New Testament, God's fire falls not only on Peter, James, and John, but also on unnamed believers who had never aspired to leadership positions. God's Spirit rests on all who love and follow Jesus, and each one has a part to play in advancing God's purpose for the world.

They Spoke in Other Tongues

Suddenly and spontaneously, each of the believers found that they were able to speak in languages they had never learned: "They were all filled with the Holy Spirit and began to speak in other tongues as the Spirit gave them utterance" (Acts 2:4).

This was a reversal of what had happened long before at the tower of Babel (Genesis 11:1–9). Early in the Bible story, as man's rebellion against God was gaining momentum, men built a city with a tower that would proclaim their greatness and provide their security.

God came down and broke the momentum of man's godless kingdom by introducing the confusion of multiple languages into the human race.

At Babel, the tongues were a sign of God's judgment on man's rebellion. People could no longer communicate, and so they were divided. But the day of Pentecost was exactly the opposite. People from every nation under heaven had gathered in Jerusalem (Acts 2:5). And when the Spirit of God came, the believers found themselves spontaneously speaking in languages they had never learned, so that people from all over the world could hear and understand the good news of Jesus Christ.

At Babel, the tongues were a judgment from God leading to confusion and people being scattered. At Pentecost, the tongues were a blessing from God leading to understanding and people being gathered. At Babel, God used the curse of language to slow the advance of man's city. At Pentecost, God used the gift of language to speed the advance of Christ's kingdom.

God's purpose was to communicate the good news of Jesus to people from every language group on the face of the earth. Language would be no barrier to the gospel.

The crowd was amazed to hear people declaring the mighty works of God in their own languages (2:11). They couldn't work out what was going on, so Peter called the crowd to order. He told them that Jesus, who had been crucified, had risen from the dead, was exalted at the right hand of the Father, and now had poured out the Holy Spirit on His people. This was the explanation of what the crowd was seeing and hearing.

When the people believed what Peter had said about Jesus, he told them the next step: "Repent and be baptized every one of you in the name of Jesus Christ for the forgiveness of your sins, and you will receive the gift of the Holy Spirit. For the promise is for you and for your children and for all who are far off, everyone whom the Lord our God calls to himself" (2:38–39).

Three thousand people responded to Peter's invitation. And in the days that followed, they returned to their homes and took the good news of Jesus to people whose language they already knew.

God's Purpose Today

At key moments in the Bible story, God made His presence known in a visible way. We call these occasions *theophanies,* and they are of great importance because in them we see that God does for some people in a visible way what He does for all His people in an invisible way.

On the day of Pentecost, God was teaching us through the wind, fire, and languages what He always wants to do among His people. God gives us His power and presence and sends us out to bring the gospel to all people.

God gives His Spirit, not only to leaders, but to all His people. The presence and the power of Almighty God rests upon every believer in the Lord Jesus Christ.

TRAIL MARKERS

Every Christian, and every church, has a part to play in God's great purpose of blessing people from every nation on earth. For some people, that will mean going to another culture and learning another language so that the good news of Jesus may be known. For others, God's call will be to find our voice in the language God has already given us.

God wonderfully puts groups of people around every believer so that we can communicate the good news of Jesus in their language. Maybe you can speak the language of high schoolers or of children. God has wired you in a way that makes it possible for you to communicate with a certain group of people. Find out who they are, get among them, and tell them about Jesus.

1. What transformed the first believers? What is the Bible's explanation of how so few people could have such a great impact on the world around them?

2. Why is the Holy Spirit given to every believer?

3. Why were believers given the ability to speak in other tongues when the Spirit was poured out on them on the day of Pentecost?

4. What difference has the presence of the Holy Spirit made in your life? Or what difference would the presence of the Holy Spirit make in your life?

5. What two things did Peter tell the people to do as a response to hearing the gospel message? What two things did he promise would happen to them as a result?

To memorize:

"You will receive power when the Holy Spirit has come upon you, and you will be my witnesses in Jerusalem and in all Judea and Samaria, and to the end of the earth." (Acts 1:8)

After the day of Pentecost, the Christian church grew rapidly in Jerusalem. But from the beginning, the apostles faced hostility. Stephen, a man full of faith and the Holy Spirit, was put to death by stoning, and "there arose on that day a great persecution against the church in Jerusalem" (Acts 8:1). At the center of it was a Pharisee named Saul.

41

CONVERSION

ACTS 9

God can turn His most bitter enemies into His closest friends. He is able to change even the hardest of hearts, and we see this in the story of how the greatest enemy of the church became its leading apostle.

Saul of Tarsus had made it his mission to destroy Christians, and he believed he was serving God (Acts 9:1–2). "As he went on his way, he approached Damascus, and suddenly a light from heaven shone around him. And falling to the ground, he heard a voice saying to him, 'Saul, Saul, why are you persecuting me?'" (Acts 9:3–4).

Saul saw a blinding light, and he heard an audible voice. Those who were traveling with him also heard the voice, so this was not a psychological experience. And the blinding light was not a hallucination. It burned Saul's retina and left him blind.

You may be thinking, "*Nothing like this could ever happen to me.*" And yet Paul says, "I received mercy for this reason, that in me . . . Jesus Christ might display his perfect patience as an example" (1 Timothy 1:16).

Clearly, Paul does not mean that in order to become a Christian, you have to hear an audible voice or be blinded by a heavenly light. Paul's conversion is an example or model for us because it shows that there are no limits to God's mercy. Nothing you have done puts you beyond the reach of God's grace.

A True Knowledge of Jesus Christ

Saul knew a great deal about Jesus. He was a brilliant scholar, and his focus was on the followers of Jesus. He knew the claim of Christians that Jesus was the promised Messiah and that He had risen from the dead.

But reflecting on his conversion, he says, "I received mercy because I had acted ignorantly" (1 Timothy 1:13). Saul knew what Christians believed, and he knew how Christians lived. What he didn't know was the Savior they worshiped. But that all changed when Saul was surrounded by a blinding light, and heard the Son of God calling him by name: "Saul, Saul . . ." (Acts 9:4).

You may think of Christianity as a set of beliefs for you to debate, or a way of life for you to consider. But Paul says, "Here is what I missed: We are dealing here with a *person*, the sovereign Lord, Jesus Christ, who lays claim to every life. Seeing who He is changes everything."

A True Knowledge of Yourself

Then Saul said, "Who are you, Lord?" The answer was: "I am Jesus" (Acts 9:5). Saul thought he was fighting a system, a belief, a religious movement, but he found, to his horror, that he had set himself against the Son of God.

"I am Jesus, whom you are persecuting" (9:5). Saul was persecuting Christians, but Jesus said to him, "Why are you persecuting *me*?" (9:4; 26:14). Every sin we commit is a personal offense against Jesus Christ. When we wound others, we wound Jesus. When we grieve others, we grieve Jesus. If we serve others, we serve Jesus.

Suddenly Saul had a completely different view of himself. He thought he was on the road to heaven, but he discovered that he was on the road to hell. He had sinned against the sovereign Lord of the universe and, far from being a righteous man who would be richly rewarded by God, he found he was a sinner who could only cast himself on the mercy of God.

Saul had been telling himself for years that he was a good person. He had regarded himself as "blameless" (Philippians 3:6), but when he saw himself as he really was—a bitter, angry person, filled with resentment toward others and toward God—he began to change.

When you come to know Jesus Christ, you will have a new understanding of yourself. Any swagger will be gone, and there will be a new humility about you.

When You Don't Know How to Stop

Submission to the Lord Jesus Christ will bring you enormous relief. Christ said to Saul, "It is hard for you to kick against the goads" (Acts 26:14). Goads were sharpened sticks used by shepherds to prod stubborn animals.

Imagine a row of metal spikes, like javelins, lying horizontal about two feet off the ground. An angry man comes up beside you, and with all the force he can muster, he kicks the spikes. A spike goes through the toe of his shoe, and the man recoils in pain.

But his pain makes him even more angry, so he lashes out again. This time the spike sinks deeper into his shoe and blood now flows freely from his foot. But the man cannot stop, and you wince as he steps up and kicks again and again until his foot is reduced to pulp.

"Saul, Saul, . . . it is hard for you to kick against the goads." You don't hurt the spikes when you kick against them; all that happens is that you injure yourself. And the more you do it, the worse it gets.

Is this a picture of what you are doing? Repeating time after time what has hurt you before? Driven by some inner compulsion, you keep doing what hurts you and you don't know how to stop. There's only one way to stop, and that is to submit yourself entirely to the Lord Jesus Christ: "What shall I do, Lord?" (Acts 22:10).

When you submit yourself to Jesus, you will experience enormous relief. Metal spikes were hammered into the hands and feet of Jesus so that you could receive mercy. Kicking against the spikes need not be the end for you.

God Works Through People

When Jesus shows you that you are a sinner and that your only hope is to cast yourself on His mercy, His purpose is not to leave you groveling in the dust. He will lift you up and send you out to fulfill His purpose in the world.

Jesus said to Saul, "Rise and enter the city, and you will be told what you are to do" (Acts 9:6). Saul went into Damascus, and for three days, he gave himself to prayer and fasting (Acts 9:9, 11): *Lord, have mercy on me. Lord, show me what You want me to do.*

Saul came to know Jesus through a direct encounter with the risen Lord. God broke through the pride and prejudice of this man's heart by a direct intervention.

No one shared the gospel with him. No one else was involved in his conversion.

But when Saul asked, "What shall I do, Lord?" the Lord said, "Rise and enter the city and you will be told what you are to do." God uses means. His normal way is to work through His people, and the answer to Saul's prayer came through Ananias.

"Now there was a disciple at Damascus named Ananias" (9:10). The Lord spoke to this man in a vision and told him to go to the house where Saul was praying. Ananias did not want to go, and you can hardly blame him. God was calling him to pray for a man who three days earlier would gladly have killed him. "Lord, I have heard from many about this man, how much evil he has done to your saints in Jerusalem" (9:13). But the Lord said to Ananias, "Go . . ." (9:15).

Helping a New Believer

Saul was blind, and for three days he had been sitting in complete darkness. His entire campaign against Christians was based on the conviction that God is a God of vengeance, and now he had discovered that he deserved the vengeance of God.

Saul has been killing disciples of Jesus, and now a disciple of Jesus arrived and placed his hands on the blind man's head. It must have been a terrifying moment—*What is he going to do to me?* But the first words Saul heard were: "Brother Saul . . ." (9:17). Saul, my brother! Ananias surrounded Saul with love, forgiveness, and grace.

When a person comes to faith in Jesus, our first responsibility is to surround them with love. Then we must help ground them in the gospel. This is what Ananias did for Saul.

Saul's blindness was a sign of the judgment of God, and when Ananias prayed for his sight to be restored, it was a sign to Saul that God's judgment had been taken away. It was an assurance that Christ had shown him mercy, and that he had been brought into an entirely new relationship with God.

Ananias commissioned Saul, whom we know better as the apostle Paul, for ministry. You will "carry my name before the Gentiles and kings and the children of Israel" (9:15).

When Saul was awakened to his need for Christ, the first Christian he met loved him, forgave him, prayed for him, baptized him, fed him, guided him, and prepared him. God works through people: Paul prayed, and the answer came through Ananias.

The principle of God working through people is foundational to the ministry and to the mission of the church. God can transform a human life without any other person being involved, but He chooses to work through us. "We are God's fellow workers" (1 Corinthians 3:9).

TRAIL MARKERS

Jesus Christ is able to transform the life of any person, even a person who has been openly hostile to Him. This transformation is a work of God that begins at conversion, in which we discover our need for mercy and submit ourselves to Christ. When you are converted, God has work for you to do. And as you commit yourself to a local church, other believers will help you discover that work.

1. In what sense is the experience of Paul on the road to Damascus, an example, a model, or a pattern for us?

2. Was there a time in your life when you thought you understood Christianity, but later realized you didn't? What was missing?

3. Respond to the statement: "When you come to know Jesus Christ, you will come to a new understanding of yourself."

4. Who in your life needs to be surrounded with love, brought to a clearer knowledge of the gospel, or encouraged to serve?

5. How do you respond to God's Word that says, "We are God's fellow workers" (1 Corinthians 3:9)?

To memorize:

> The saying is trustworthy and deserving of full acceptance, that Christ Jesus came into the world to save sinners, of whom I am the foremost. But I received mercy for this reason, that in me, as the foremost, Jesus Christ might display his perfect patience as an example to those who were to believe in him for eternal life. (1 Timothy 1:15–16)

The conversion of Saul of Tarsus led to the gospel being proclaimed to all nations. Of the twenty-one letters in the New Testament, thirteen were written by the apostle Paul. The clearest explanation of the gospel in the entire Bible is given to us in the book of Romans, and over these next five chapters we will discover more of what God has done for us in Jesus Christ.

42

WRATH

ROMANS 1

In our journey through the Bible, we have seen repeatedly that God is love, and this means that God is absolutely committed to seek the good of all that He has made.

The Bible also tells us that God is holy. This means that God is absolutely opposed to anything that would destroy the objects of His love. You cannot love a person without, at the same time, hating that which would destroy him or her.

I will never forget being with a couple when they were caring for their son who was dying of cancer. One evening, the little boy's mother said to me, "I hate this cancer." She said it with venom, and understandably so. The cancer was destroying her son, and she hated what was destroying the object of her love.

Love and hate are often found together as natural partners in the Bible: "Let love be genuine. Abhor what is evil; hold fast to what is good" (Romans 12:9). These are two sides of the same coin. If we do not hate what is evil, we do not love what is good.

God is love and He is holy. He is also sovereign. This means that He is absolutely in control of all things. There is no place where He is not present, no task that He cannot accomplish, and no permission that He needs to seek.

The mother whose son was dying from cancer was relentless in her opposition to what was destroying him, but she did not have the power to overcome it.

God is relentless in His opposition to evil, and He is able to overcome its destructive power. He can rescue the people He loves from the sin that destroys, and His love will never be frustrated.

What Makes God Angry?

God's wrath is His settled resolve that evil will not stand, and we should thank God for it. What hope would we have of peace in a world stalked by terror if God merely looked on with a weak smile or a disapproving frown? Hope for a world whose history is strewn with evil and violence lies in a God who is relentlessly opposed to all evil and has the will and the power to destroy it.

God is love, and anger is not in His nature. If there were no sin in the world, there would be no wrath in God. So the Bible never says that God is wrath. It tells us that He is slow to anger (Psalm 103:8), and the Bible story demonstrates His great patience toward an evil world.

The wrath of God is not a random rage, and we should never think of God losing control or lashing out in acts of frustration. But God can be provoked to anger, and His anger is provoked by godlessness and unrighteousness.

"The wrath of God is revealed from heaven against all ungodliness and unrighteousness of men, who by their unrighteousness suppress the truth" (Romans 1:18). A godless person is one who doesn't want anything to do with God, and an unrighteous person is one who refuses to obey God. The godless and unrighteous person is someone who says to God, "I don't want to know You, and I will not obey You."

In order to sustain this response to God, a person must "suppress the truth" that God has revealed about Himself in the beauty and grandeur of creation. Imagine pressing down on a powerful spring. You have to put your whole weight on the spring to keep it compressed, and it takes energy to do that. If you let up for a moment, the spring will recoil.

In the same way, it takes energy to keep resisting God. Those who want nothing to do with God have to work hard at avoiding Him because His revelation is all around us. He has made His divine power and His glory known in the splendors of creation (Romans 1:20).

God Lets People Go

God's wrath is expressed in giving people up to what they choose:

> *God gave them up in the lusts of their hearts to impurity.* (1:24)
>
> *God gave them up to dishonorable passions.* (1:26)
>
> *God gave them up to a debased mind.* (1:28)

When an individual or a community says, "We do not want God, and we will not obey God," God expresses His wrath by standing back and allowing them to live with the full reality of their own choice.

Suppose a woman is holding a crystal vase. If she "gives it up," it will become subject to the pull of gravity. It will fall like a stone, and it will shatter. That is what happens when God "gives up" the godless and the unrighteous.

If you see impurity or dishonorable passions in your heart, you may wonder: "Has God given me up? And if God has given me up, does that mean that there is no hope for me?"

No one is beyond hope. That is why Paul says, "I am not ashamed of the gospel" (Romans 1:16). The gospel is the way God saves people who have been overwhelmed by the power of their own sins.

Storing Up Wrath

God's wrath is already being revealed, but only in part. History is riddled with evils that have never been brought to justice and lies that were never brought to light. But it will not always be so. God shows great patience toward us, and the purpose of His kindness is that we should come to Him in repentance.

"Do you presume on the riches of his kindness and forbearance and patience, not knowing that God's kindness is meant to lead you to repentance? But because of your hard and impenitent heart you are storing up wrath for yourself on the day of wrath when God's righteous judgment will be revealed" (Romans 2:4–5).

God's wrath is being revealed in part today, and it is being stored up for the day when His righteous judgment will be revealed toward those who refuse to repent. But the Bible speaks about a third occasion when the wrath of God was revealed.

God's Wrath at the Cross

God presented Jesus as the One on whom His wrath was poured out. As we will see in the next chapter, this is the meaning of the word "propitiation." Paul speaks of "the redemption that is in Christ Jesus, whom God put forward as a propitiation by his blood" (Romans 3:24–25). God's relentless opposition to all that destroys us was poured out on Jesus when He died on the cross.

When the wrath of God toward sin was poured out on Jesus, it was drained and exhausted for all who trust in Him. God says, "I will soon pour out my wrath upon you, and spend my anger against you" (Ezekiel 7:8). *Spent* means *gone*, and this takes us to the heart of what happened at the cross. God's wrath toward sin was poured out or spent on Jesus when He became the propitiation for our sins.

God found a way of separating the sins He hates from the people He loves by laying these sins on Jesus. "For our sake he made him to be sin who knew no sin, so that in him we might become righteous of God" (2 Corinthians 5:21).

God "did not spare his own Son but gave him up for us all" (Romans 8:32). This is why Jesus cried out, "My God, my God, why have you forsaken me?" (Matthew 27:46). Christ, the object of the Father's love, became the object of His wrath because we, the objects of His wrath, were also the objects of His love.

Remember the woman holding the crystal vase. When she gives it up with her right hand, it seems certain that the vase will be smashed. But if she catches it with her left hand, the vase will be saved. That's what God does for us in Jesus Christ. He saves us from the sins that would otherwise lead to our destruction.

To be under God's judgment and dismissed from His presence forever would be the ultimate disaster. No other suffering could ever compare with this. So why would you live with wrath stored up for you when it was spent on Jesus? Why would you trust your own feeble attempt at righteousness when God is ready to count the righteousness of Jesus as yours? Believe in the Lord Jesus Christ. Ask Him to have mercy on you and make you a new and different person.

TRAIL MARKERS

God's wrath is the response of His holiness and His love to evil. It is not in God's nature to be angry, but His anger is provoked by the godlessness and unrighteousness of men and women who suppress the truth that God has clearly revealed. God expresses His wrath by giving people up to their own choice with the result that they become bound by the power of sinful lusts, dishonorable passions, and a debased mind.

But God has sent His Son to deliver us from His wrath. When Jesus died on the cross, He endured the wrath of God for us. "There is therefore now no condemnation for those who are in Christ Jesus" (Romans 8:1).

1. When have you experienced in your own life loving someone and, at the same time, hating what destroys them?

2. Do you find it difficult to believe that God can be angry? Why or why not?

3. How is God's wrath expressed in the world today, according to the Bible?

4. How would you answer a person who says, "God has given up on me"?

5. Why is there "no condemnation for those who are in Christ Jesus"? (Romans 8:1).

To memorize:

You turned to God from idols to serve the living and true God, and to wait for his Son from heaven, whom he raised from the dead, Jesus who delivers us from the wrath to come. (1 Thessalonians 1:9–10)

We have seen that the wrath of God is revealed against sin and that Christ rescues us through the gospel. What did this mean for Jesus? And what does it mean for us? In this chapter, we will focus on four words that are found together in Romans 3: propitiation, redemption, justified, and faith. If this feels daunting to you, hang in there. What you are about to discover is life-giving.

43

JUSTIFICATION

ROMANS 3

The first time I visited America, I was taken by a friend to see a game of baseball. My friend started talking about sliders, splitters, curveballs, and changeups. I didn't have the faintest idea of what he was talking about.

Sports have their own distinctive vocabulary. People who love baseball learn the baseball words. People who love cricket learn the cricket words. And people who love Jesus learn the Bible words. In this chapter, we will learn four Bible words that will bring us great joy.

> For all have sinned and fall short of the glory of God, and are justified by his grace as a gift, through the redemption that is in Christ Jesus, whom God put forward as a propitiation by his blood, to be received by faith. (Romans 3:23–25)

Propitiation

Let me introduce you to Neil and Sally. Neil was in his early twenties when he began dating Sally, a woman he met at work. He had a reputation for being "a bit on the wild side," and there were times when Sally was uncomfortable with him.

One night, Neil took Sally to a party where things got a little out of hand. Neil began drinking, and by the time they drove home in the early hours of the morning, he was scarcely able to control the car. Neil drove in a blurry haze until the unthinkable happened. The car hit a bank, sped out of control, and rolled over several times. When the vehicle came to rest, both Neil and Sally were unconscious.

Several hours later, Neil came around in the hospital. His head was thumping, and his body ached as he tried to remember what happened.

"How is Sally?" he asked.

"It's bad news," the doctor said. "She's paralyzed. She won't ever walk again."

"Can I see her?"

"No, she will not talk to you."

It wasn't long before Neil received a letter from Sally's lawyer. In the light of her permanent disability, Sally was bringing legal action.

Neil lay in the hospital wondering how he could have been such a fool, and how one simple action could have landed him in a situation with such desperate long-term consequences. It was just one night, but it changed everything. Neil wondered how he could live with himself, and he had no idea what to do about Sally.

There are three factors in this situation: *First,* there is an offense. Neil acted recklessly and irresponsibly when he decided to drive home after drinking. *Second,* someone has been offended. Sally is angry, and rightly so. *Third,* there is an offender. Neil knows he is to blame. He is deeply sorry for what he has done, but that won't change the fact that Sally is paralyzed and that her lawyers are preparing to take legal action against him.

Neil hires a lawyer, and his lawyer talks to Sally's lawyer about what it would take to settle the case. Their discussion centers on one issue: What will it take to satisfy Sally? The issue is not what Neil thinks is appropriate. It's all about Sally, because she is the offended party.

Suppose that the lawyers identify a sum of money that would be acceptable to Sally. The payment of that money would be "a propitiation." A propitiation is a payment offered to placate the anger of the offended party and to satisfy the need for justice so that the case is settled and cannot be raised in a court of law again.

Since our sin is an offense against God, it follows that God is the one who determines what the propitiation should be. The question is, "What will satisfy God?"

The Bible gives us the answer: "Christ Jesus, whom God put forward as a propitiation by his blood, to be received by faith" (Romans 3:24–25). God presents

His Son, Jesus Christ, as the propitiation. His death on the cross satisfies God and placates His anger toward our sin.

The God whose holiness we have offended, whose world we have spoiled, and whose wrath we have incurred, sent His one and only Son. God became a man in Jesus Christ and bore His own wrath.

Redemption

Paul says we are "justified . . . through the redemption that is in Christ Jesus, whom God put forward as a propitiation by his blood" (Romans 3:24–25). What is redemption?

To redeem is to purchase by the payment of a price. I learned this Bible word as a child through a simple story that has stayed with me. It's the story of a boy who liked to make things.

One day the boy's father said to him, "Why don't you make a boat?" The boy loved that idea, so he worked with his father to make a beautiful sailing boat. He painted it blue and red, and it had a tall white sail. When it was finished, the boy put a special mark on the boat so that he would always know that it was his.

The boy loved his boat, and he had great joy when he took it out to sail on the lake. But one day the boat was caught in a great wind that took it away. The boy was heartbroken.

Sometime later, the boy was walking past a toy shop in the town when he saw a beautiful boat in the window. It was blue and red, and it had a tall white sail. And when the boy looked closer, he could see the special mark he had put on it so he would always know it was his.

The boy went home, gathered all the money he had saved, and went back to the shop and bought the boat. On the way home, he hugged the boat and he said, "You are twice mine! You are mine because I made you, and you're mine because I bought you!"

That is what Jesus Christ can say to you and me! "You're twice mine. You're mine because I made you, and you're mine because I bought you." That is what it means to be redeemed. You are bought by Jesus Christ through the shedding of His blood (1 Peter 1:18–19).

Justification

What comes of our redemption? Paul says we are "justified . . . through the redemption that is in Christ Jesus" (Romans 3:24).

Justification is a verdict passed by a judge in which a person is declared righteous. Every person will one day stand trial before almighty God, and in every case He will pronounce one of two outcomes: justified or condemned.

Justified is a word that belongs to the last day, but the Bible speaks here about justification in the present tense: "All have sinned and fall short of the glory of God and are justified by his grace" (Romans 3:23–24). God is saying to us, "Your case can be dealt with now! You don't need to spend your whole life wondering what God's final judgment about you will be. You can be justified, pronounced not guilty, today!"

The basis on which you can be justified is what Jesus has done for you when He died on the cross. He bore the wrath (propitiation), and He paid the price (redemption).

When God justifies us, He does two things: First, God charges our sins to Jesus, counting them against Him. And second, God credits the righteousness of Jesus to us.

When Karen and I got married, my parents paid for our honeymoon at a classy hotel in the Lake District of England. There were no charges for us because the cost was absorbed by someone else. God justifies us freely by charging our sins to His Son. This gift is ours because the charges we have incurred have been assumed and paid by Jesus.

Then God credits the righteousness of Jesus to us: "You are in Christ Jesus, who became to us . . . righteousness" (1 Corinthians 1:30). Our righteous standing before God does not lie in us. This is why Paul said that he wants to be "found in him, not having a righteousness of my own that comes from the law, but that which comes through faith in Christ, the righteousness from God that depends on faith" (Philippians 3:9).

What is the difference between a righteousness of our own and a righteousness that comes through faith? Our righteousness will never be complete in this life. Christ calls us to hunger and thirst for righteousness (Matthew 5:6). We hunger and thirst because our righteousness is always lacking. But Jesus lived the perfect life. His righteousness is complete and when, by faith, His perfect righteousness is counted as ours, we have peace with God.

Faith

Since the only basis for justification is what Jesus accomplished in His death and resurrection, it follows that God will justify those who belong to Jesus, and faith is the means by which Jesus becomes yours.

> All have sinned and fall short of the glory of God, and are justified by his grace as a gift, through the redemption that is in Christ Jesus, whom God put forward as a propitiation by his blood, to be received by faith. (Romans 3:23–25)

Faith is like a marriage in which you are united with Jesus Christ. For Jesus, being joined to you meant taking your sin as if it was His own. For you, being joined to Jesus means receiving His righteousness as if it were your own.

When you come to faith in the Lord Jesus Christ, all that He accomplished on the cross becomes yours. God justifies you because your sins have been paid for by Jesus and God credits the righteousness of Jesus to you.

TRAIL MARKERS

God justifies sinners on the basis of the propitiation that was offered by Jesus on the cross. He does this for all who will come to Jesus in faith. Faith unites a person with Christ who redeems us by paying our debt and crediting us with His righteousness. Justification does not depend on your performance in the Christian life but on Jesus, and all that He accomplished, being yours.

1. In your own words, what is a "propitiation"?

2. Can you think of a time when someone made a sacrifice in order to help you?

3. What does "redemption" tell you about Jesus' love for you?

4. What difference would it make to your life now if you knew what God's final judgment about you would be?

5. Faith involves a commitment to Jesus Christ. Why would you be drawn to this commitment? What might hold you back?

To memorize:

All have sinned and fall short of the glory of God, and are justified by his grace as a gift, through the redemption that is in Christ Jesus, whom God put forward as a propitiation by his blood, to be received by faith. (Romans 3:23–25)

We are justified by faith because of what Jesus accomplished on the cross. But how can we be sure that we are justified? Does God want us to be sure? And if so, how is that possible? Our passage today begins with "since we have been justified by faith" (Romans 5:1), and it ends with "more than that, we also rejoice in God" (Romans 5:11). These verses chart the course from having faith to having joy.

44

ASSURANCE

ROMANS 5

Imagine a business partnership in which you constantly had to call your partner and ask if he or she still wanted to work with you. Or imagine a marriage in which you didn't know for sure that your spouse loved you. Either relationship may be endured; neither could be enjoyed.

God wants you to enjoy your relationship with Him, and that means that He wants you to be secure in it. In this chapter we will look at three joy-killing questions that often arise in the minds of Christians, and how to answer them.

1. Why Is This Happening to Me?

The Bible tells me that I have peace with God, but if that is true, why am I often troubled? When you face a health issue, a family problem, or some other disappointment in life, you may wonder why God would allow such a thing to happen to you.

God uses our troubles in life to make us more like Jesus. "We rejoice in our sufferings, knowing that suffering produces endurance, and endurance produces character, and character produces hope" (Romans 5:3–4).

Jesus never promised us a trouble-free life. He said, "In the world you will have tribulation [trouble]. But take heart; I have overcome the world" (John 16:33). Trouble is part of our life on earth and having problems does not mean God is against you. He is for us! After all, "He who did not spare his own Son but gave him up for us all, how will he not also graciously give us all things?" (Romans 8:32).

Grasping this will help you persevere. There will be times when you look up to God through tears, but when you know that He is for you, you will have hope.

2. Does God Really Care?

Paul tells us that "God shows his love for us in that while we were still sinners, Christ died for us" (Romans 5:8). But how does the death of Jesus show the love of God?

A couple is sitting in a car on a moonlit night near Niagara Falls. He puts his arm around her shoulder and whispers in her ear, "I love you."

She looks at him suspiciously. "Do you really? I sometimes wonder."

"All right," he says, "I'll prove it." And with that, he gets out of the car, walks to the edge, and with one huge leap, throws himself over the side. As he falls into the abyss, he screams out, "I love you . . ." This may be an unforgettable experience, but it is not a demonstration of love. The man's death achieves nothing for the woman.

The death of Jesus is an expression of love because it achieves something of infinite value for us: Through His death, Jesus paid the debt of our sin, propitiated the wrath of God, and purchased the gift of eternal life for all who believe in Him.

God has demonstrated His love for us in giving the greatest gift at the point of our greatest need. So when you are tempted to wonder if God really loves you, don't look at the circumstances of your life—look at the cross and take in what Jesus has accomplished for you.

3. How Can I Be Sure I Will Make It to Heaven?

You have planned the trip of a lifetime. The tickets are booked, your passport is current, and the reservations have been made. All you need to do is get to the airport, but there are many things that could still go wrong! You could get sick the night before you leave. You could break your leg as you come down the stairs. It doesn't take much imagination to multiply the scenarios that could occur.

When we are justified, we have peace with God. But what if we mess up? Perhaps you know what it's like to say to yourself: "I'm not sure if I can keep this Christian life up! What if the temptations I face are too strong for me? What if something blows my faith out of the water?"

The answer to these questions is that "we have now been justified by his blood" (Romans 5:9). God justifies us through the blood of Jesus shed on the cross. Peace with God is not based on your performance in the Christian life. It is grounded in something entirely outside of you—the blood of Jesus. This is the basis of your security, and if you can grasp its meaning, it will help you to rejoice in God.

Confidence in the Right Place

If you were asked how you know that you will be in heaven, how would you answer? Here are three common but inadequate answers.

Question: *How do you know that you will be in heaven on the last day?*

Answer: *I love Jesus.*

That's great. But the test of loving Jesus is that we keep His commandments (John 14:15), and the fact that we don't obey His commandments fully shows that we don't fully love Him either. Our love for Christ is real, but it is mixed up with a great deal of love for ourselves. While it is true that we love Christ, our love for Him is hardly a ground for confidence when we stand in His presence on the last day!

Answer: *I have made a commitment.*

That's wonderful. But what happens if your commitment to serving Christ wavers? What happens if in ten years' time your enthusiasm wanes? Does that mean that your chances of entering heaven will diminish too?

People who think that their activity or enthusiasm for Christ is the basis for entering heaven soon find themselves under a great burden. Whatever you do, your level of commitment could always be higher, and believers who depend on their own commitment are on a path to spiritual burnout.

Answer: *I have faith.*

That's marvelous. But how strong is your faith? Are there not times when you struggle with doubt? Don't fall into the error of putting faith in your own faith, rather than faith in Christ. No one's faith is free from questions, anxieties, doubts, or fears. If you are trusting in your faith, you will never be sure that your faith is enough.

Did you notice the one common factor in these three inadequate answers?

They all begin with the fatal little word *I. I love Jesus. I am committed. I have faith.* And the problem with anything that begins with *I* is that it is never complete, never what it might be, and never what it should be.

God's work in us is begun, but it is not yet complete. So while it is wonderfully true that we love Jesus, are committed to serve Jesus, and have faith in Jesus, none of these things is what they might be or what, one day, they will be. Our faith, service, and love for Christ are still a work in progress.

After our first Christmas in America, our family took a trip to Wisconsin. We found our way up to Fond du Lac, where we stopped by the lake to look around. We had never been so cold.

Our boys, who were just ten and eight at the time, said, "Dad, can we go on the ice?" Parents know that when you are not thinking you give your default answer. In Britain, it gets cold but not that cold, and so where there is ice, it is often thin. So, I said, "Yes, but go carefully."

You can picture the scene, can't you? There we were, venturing out onto the ice, feeling our way, nervously inching forward, when suddenly there was the roar of an engine, and a vehicle carrying at least six high school students came screaming out over the lake. I don't think I have ever felt so foolish.

Inching out onto the ice, we had very little confidence, but we were completely safe. The ice on which we stood was rock solid. And our safety rested not on the strength of our "faith," but on the strength of the ice on which we were standing.

We are not saved by the strength of our faith, but by the strength of our Savior.

TRAIL MARKERS

If you want to cultivate assurance and joy in God, the question you should be asking is not "How strong is my faith?" but "How strong is my Savior?" Is the blood of Jesus Christ rich enough and strong enough to wash away my every sin and to cover my every weakness, failure, and inadequacy from this point until the day I arrive in the presence of God? The answer to that question is "Yes. Absolutely. Without question."

1. Which of the following questions is most difficult for you right now: *Does God really care? Why is this happening to me? How can I be sure I will make it to heaven?*

2. Why do you think God wants you to be confident about your relationship with Him?

3. On a scale of 1 (none) to 10 (absolutely) how confident are you that when you die you will go to heaven? Where does your confidence or lack of confidence come from?

4. What would be the effect of trusting in your own faith?

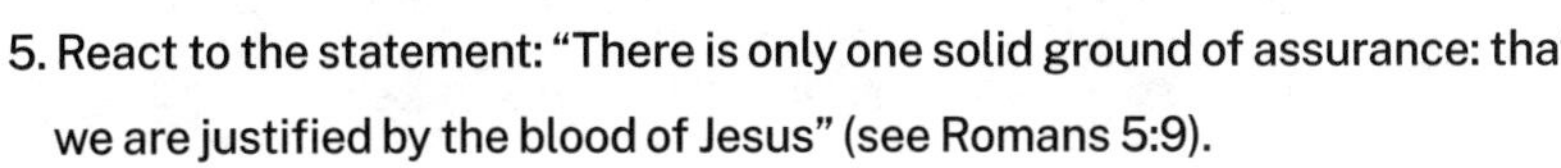

5. React to the statement: "There is only one solid ground of assurance: that we are justified by the blood of Jesus" (see Romans 5:9).

To memorize:

Since, therefore, we have now been justified by his blood, much more shall we be saved by him from the wrath of God. For if while we were enemies we were reconciled to God by the death of his Son, much more, now that we are reconciled, shall we be saved by his life. (Romans 5:9–10)

In Romans 5, we learned that when we are justified by faith we have peace with God and that God's grace covers all our sins. If that's the case, why not carry on and sin some more? Paul answers this question in Romans 6: "What shall we say then? Are we to continue in sin that grace may abound?" (6:1). The answer to that question is "By no means" (6:2). And the reason is union with Christ.

45

UNION

ROMANS 6

Some time ago, I was issued a traffic ticket. The officer explained that the offense would be on my driving record, but then told me that the state of Illinois had provided a way in which the offense could be removed. "You can take the class," he said. "And it will be as if this had never happened."

Now think about the way in which this system works. We can reasonably assume that one day a rather tired administrator yawned as he or she scrolled through a long list of all the Smiths driving in Illinois to find the wretched one against whose name an offense should be recorded.

Then, a few weeks later, another administrator would have the laborious task of scrolling through the same list for the purpose of pressing the delete button and erasing all record of the offense. The process is legal, but it is profoundly impersonal. No relationship is involved.

It is a wonderful truth that Jesus died to erase the record of our sins. But if that is all we grasp, our love for God will be as weak as the affection I have for the computer operator who erased my offense.

Christ died not only to clear your record of sin, but also to bring you into a loving relationship with God. Salvation is not an arm's length transaction performed by an unknown heavenly administrator. It is God reaching out to bring us into an intimate union with Him.

United with Christ

When you come to faith in Jesus, the Holy Spirit makes a connection between the death and resurrection of Jesus and your life today. "If we have been united with him in a death like his, we shall certainly be united with him in a resurrection like his" (Romans 6:5).

What does it mean to be "united" to Jesus Christ in His death and resurrection?

Think of it like this: Certain things were once true of you—you were under the reign of sin, you were alienated from God, and you were powerless to do anything about it (Romans 5:21; Ephesians 2:12; 2:1). But when you came to faith in Jesus, the person you were ceased to exist (Romans 8:1). He or she died with Jesus at the cross. That's what Paul means when he says, "We have died with Christ" (Romans 6:8).

But it doesn't end there. Paul also wrote about us being "united with [Christ] in a resurrection like his" (Romans 6:5). When the Holy Spirit plunged you into Christ, He brought a new person into being. Now you are under the reign of grace, you are a child of God, and your destiny is everlasting life (Romans 5:21; Galatians 4:4–7; Romans 6:22–23). You still fail in many ways, but no matter how often you fail you cannot ever revert to the person you once were. That person is dead and gone forever. He or she has ceased to exist.

Union with Christ is so much more than turning over a new leaf or making a decision; it is the life of Christ flowing into you by the power of the Holy Spirit.

Jesus spoke about this union when He said, "I am the vine; you are the branches" (John 15:5). Just as sap rises from the vine and flows into the branches, so the life of Christ will flow from Him into His people. This is much more than a legal transaction in which your sins are forgiven and your passport is stamped for heaven. This is the life of God entering into you. It's hard to imagine a more intimate picture.

When the Holy Spirit unites us with Christ, He invades our lives with His love. A good marriage is both legal and relational. It is both a binding agreement and an intimate union. It promotes deep security and deep affection. God wants to bring us into a relationship of love that is both secure and intimate. It is secure because God makes a covenant with us, and it is intimate because it involves union with Jesus Christ.

Blessed in Christ

Consider the difference between a pair of socks and a pair of pants. You know what happens when you put a pair of socks in the wash? One of them gets lost. The problem, of course, is that there is nothing that unites them together. The pants are different. I have never known a pair of pants to come out of the wash with one leg missing.

God does not throw out blessings from heaven like socks: "Would anyone like forgiveness? Any takers for everlasting life?" God gives us one blessing, Jesus Christ. He has "blessed us in Christ with every spiritual blessing" (Ephesians 1:3). All of God's blessings come to us in Jesus, and none of them come to us apart from Him.

Forgiveness, eternal life, holiness, and strength are all found in Jesus. God has made Him our "wisdom . . . righteousness and sanctification and redemption" (1 Corinthians 1:30). These gifts are all joined together inseparably in Him, and if you are in Christ, all of these blessings are yours.

Set Free by Christ

Being in Christ equips you for your battle against sin. Once you were destined for defeat in the battle, but now in Christ, you are positioned for victory. "Sin will have no dominion over you, since you are not under law but under grace" (Romans 6:14).

Picture yourself on a field of battle. Your unit comes under heavy fire, and you are taken captive. You surrender your weapons, and you are carted off to what looks like a massive cage. The man in charge of the cage looks quite terrifying. When he shouts orders, the people inside do what he commands. You value your life, and so you decide to do the same.

For the next year, your whole life is in the cage. You sleep, you are fed, and you exercise, but all the time you are under the power of your enemy. And as long as you are in the cage, there is absolutely nothing you can do about it.

Then one night, you hear the roar of an engine and the sound of gunfire. Your captain has come with all his forces to set you free. As you climb into his jeep, he hands you a gun: "Take this," he says, "you're back in the battle now."

The next day the man who runs the cage comes looking for you. He shouts orders, but you no longer have to do what he says. You are not in the cage.[11] When you are in Christ, you are in an entirely new position. You are free, and you are in a position to fight. Sin will always be your enemy, but it is no longer your master.

"Let not sin therefore reign in your mortal body, to make you obey its passions . . . but present yourselves to God as those who have been brought from death to life, and your members to God as instruments for righteousness" (Romans 6:12–13).

Secure in Christ

Faith puts you in Christ, where you are completely safe—even if you are often afraid. A friend of mine tells the story of the first time he flew on a plane. He was seated in a row of three. On one side was a person who looked quite nervous. On the other side was a businessman who was busy on his laptop. My friend in the middle was up for the journey, but a little apprehensive.

When the plane took off, the man continued working on his laptop, my friend held on to the armrests of his seat, and the person on the other side reached for the barf bag.

When the snack was served, the businessman ate the lot, my friend ate half of his, but the nervous traveler didn't even touch it.

The conclusion to the story is that all three of these passengers arrived at the same place at the same time! They were all equally safe, though they had very different experiences of the journey.

Your eternal safety does not rest on how well you do in the Christian life; it rests on you being in Christ.

TRAIL MARKERS

A Christian is a person who has been united with Christ in His death and resurrection. When you were united with Christ by faith, the person you were before

11. I found the image of the cage in the field in Martyn Lloyd-Jones, *Romans 6, The New Man* (Banner of Truth Trust, 1992).

ceased to exist, and a new person came into being. You still have many struggles, you will fail in many ways, but since Christ has set you free, you are in an entirely new position.

Discovering your new position in Christ is one of the most important keys to living the Christian life. Sin will always be your enemy, but it is no longer your master. You are now in a position to put up a fight.

1. How would you describe the kind of relationship God wants to have with you?

2. How would you answer the person who says, "Now that I'm saved, I'll live however I want to"?

3. In your own words, what does the illustration of the socks and the trousers tell us about how God's blessings come to us?

4. How do you respond to this statement? "Sin will always be your enemy, but it is no longer your master."

5. How would knowing that you are secure in Christ, impact your experience of the Christian life?

To memorize:

"I am the vine; you are the branches. Whoever abides in me and I in him, he it is that bears much fruit, for apart from me you can do nothing." (John 15:5)

When Adam and Eve committed the first sin, there were two long-term consequences: Sin brought a penalty against them, and it became a power within them. We need saving from both, and this chapter is about how we can overcome the power of sin. We are going to meet three characters: Hostile, Helpless, and Hopeful. Try to decide which of them you identify with most. Then we will see what God has to say to each of them and to us.

46

PROGRESS

ROMANS 7–8

Some years had passed since John first used drugs at a party. He said he wouldn't do it again, but he found that he couldn't stop. He had a hard time admitting that he was hooked, but his friends knew that was the truth.

Then one day, John was caught in possession. The police pressed charges, and the court set a heavy fine. There was a penalty to pay, and John had no money.

After a lot of soul searching, John's mother paid the fine on his behalf, but afterward she wondered if she had done the right thing. "I'm afraid that by paying the fine, I'm just enabling him to continue his habit," she said.

She's right. John is an addict. The drugs are exercising a power in his life. He is trapped and he cannot make progress.

If John is to overcome the power of his addiction, he will need both the desire and the ability to say no. But John doesn't seem to have the desire. And even if he did, does he have the ability?

Hostile: No Desire and No Ability

In Romans 8, Paul describes a person who is hostile to God: "The mind that is set on the flesh is hostile to God, for it does not submit to God's law; indeed, it cannot" (Romans 8:7). Hostile has neither the desire nor the ability to obey God's law.

At one time, Paul himself was hostile. He led a furious persecution of Christian believers, "breathing threats and murder against the disciples of the Lord" (Acts 9:1). That's hostile!

But while Paul was traveling on the road to Damascus, the risen Lord Jesus Christ appeared to him, and said, "Why are you persecuting me?" (Acts 9:4). Paul's violent anger against Christians was actually a reflection of a deeper rage in his heart against Christ.

You don't have to look too far to meet Hostile in our society today. He gets angry about the public mention of God, and he is offended by the suggestion that there is a God to whom we are all accountable.

Kind and reasonable people can become hostile when it comes to the things of God. Have you noticed that a conversation can be quite civil until God's name is introduced? It is as if a switch is triggered and a deep hostility within the soul is exposed.

Helpless: Desire Without Ability

In Romans 7, we meet another character we'll call Helpless. The big difference between Helpless and Hostile is that while Hostile hates God's law, Helpless loves it: "I agree with the law, that it is good," he says (Romans 7:16). This is something that Hostile would never say; he hated God's law and wanted nothing to do with it. But Helpless loves God's law and he wants to keep it: "I delight in the law of God, in my inner being," he says (Romans 7:22).

The problem for Helpless is that while he loves God's law, he isn't able to obey it. Despite his best efforts and intentions, he does not make progress. He says, "I have the desire to do what is right, but not the ability to carry it out" (7:18).

Helpless is a prisoner. He describes himself as a "captive to the law of sin that dwells within my members" (7:23). For this reason, he does not do what he wants to do, and ends up doing what he never intended (7:15). His inability leaves him feeling absolutely miserable. "Wretched man that I am!" he says. "Who will deliver me from this body of death?" (7:24).

The problem for Helpless is that while he agrees with the law of God, he lacks the ability to do it.

Hopeful: Desire with Ability

In Romans 8, we meet a third character, Hopeful. Like Helpless, Hopeful wants to live in a way that is pleasing to God. The big difference between them lies in the area of ability.

Paul tells Hopeful to "put to death the deeds of the body" (Romans 8:13), and that is precisely what Helpless could not do. But Hopeful is in an entirely different position. He has the *desire* to fight against sin in his life, and he has the *ability* to prevail because the Spirit of God lives in Him.

Helpless and Hopeful face the same struggles. They feel the pull of the same temptations. The difference between them lies not in the battle but in the outcome. Helpless faces inevitable defeat; Hopeful will enjoy ultimate victory.

The Proper Application of Overwhelming Force

When Pearl Harbor was attacked on December 7, 1941, Winston Churchill was at Chequers, the British Prime Minister's country retreat. On hearing the news, he called President Roosevelt, who said, "We are all in the same boat now."

Churchill recorded his thoughts as he went to bed that night. "No American will think it wrong of me if I proclaim that to have the United States at our side was to me the greatest joy. . . . We had won after all. Yes, after Dunkirk; after the fall of France . . . after seventeen months of lonely fighting and nineteen months of my responsibility in dire stress. We had won the war. England would live; Britain would live. . . .

"How long the war would last or in what fashion it would end no man could tell, nor did I at this moment care. . . . All the rest was merely the proper application of overwhelming force. . . . Many disasters, immeasurable cost and tribulation lay ahead, but there was no doubt about the end. . . . I went to bed and slept the sleep of the saved and the thankful."[12]

The war would drag on for another four years. It would continue to be a bitter struggle, but even in December 1941, Churchill could say, "We had won the war." The outcome was certain. Churchill had been helpless. But now he was hopeful.

---

12. Winston Churchill, *The Second World War* (Mariner, 1986), 3.475–477.

The difference lay in the involvement of an "overwhelming force."

The problem with Helpless is that he is limited to the range of his own ability. That's why he finds the Christian life impossible. In Romans 7, Helpless says nothing about Christ or about the Spirit. He only talks about himself and his own limited abilities, which are insufficient to fulfill the law of God.

But when you belong to Christ, the Holy Spirit lives in you. You are not helpless, so don't talk as if you were. God has placed you in an entirely new position in Christ. You will face the same battles as you did before, but there will be a different outcome.

Identify Your Position

Maybe you feel there is a sin that is too strong for you. You are tired of fighting it, and you feel defeated.

I've often had a conversation with someone who comes to speak with me about a temptation that is overwhelming to him. "It's too strong for me," he says. "I'm helpless to overcome it."

So I say to him, "Let me lead you to Christ."

Then he will say to me, "Oh no, pastor, I've been a Christian for many years!"

"Well now, wait a minute. If you are a Christian, the Holy Spirit lives in you. How can you say that you are helpless?"

For a Christian to say "I am helpless" is to repeat the lie of the devil. If you are helpless, come to Christ. But if you have come to Christ, the Holy Spirit lives in you. So stop telling yourself that you are helpless.

With which of our three friends do you most closely identify: Hostile, Helpless, or Hopeful? It's important to answer this question, so that you can hear what God has to say to you.

God's Word to Hostile

If you're hostile, God offers an amnesty to you. He invites you to lay down your arms, and He calls you to repent (Romans 2:4). Repentance is giving up your resistance to God. Jesus Christ came into the world and went to the cross, so that those who were once God's enemies could become His friends.

God showed His love for us while we were still hostile toward Him (5:8). He has loved you through all your struggling, all your resisting, and all your fighting against Him. He loves you still, even in your hostility. You have nothing to lose and everything to gain by turning to Him in repentance.

God's Word to Helpless

God's word to Helpless is quite different. Telling Helpless to repent won't help him. He already wants to do what is right. His problem is that he doesn't have the power.

When Helpless cries out in despair, "Who will deliver me from this body of death?" God's answer is "Jesus Christ" (7:25).

Come to Christ in faith. Tell Him that you cannot live this life on your own. Tell Him that you need the power of His Holy Spirit, so that you will have the ability as well as the desire to live a new life. Ask and you will receive. God will give you a new name. You will no longer be Helpless; you will be Hopeful.

God's Word to Hopeful

God's Word to Hopeful is to put to death the misdeeds of the body by the power of the Spirit (8:13). Start an intentional battle against the sins that remain in you. Learn to fight, and don't ever say that you are helpless. The Spirit of God is within you. Christ has put you in a position to fight and to win.

Are you making a proper application of overwhelming force? Can you identify specific sins on which you are launching an intentional assault at this point in your life? Have you formed a strategy for change, knowing that the power of the Spirit has been given to you to make this possible?

Remember that the enemy will try to confuse you about your position. He loves to tell Hopeful that he is really Helpless. Many of his greatest successes come from that kind of propaganda. So identify your position, and then follow God's instructions. If you are hostile, repent—God's love reaches out to you. If you are helpless, come—Christ will deliver you. If you are hopeful, fight—the Holy Spirit is within you.

TRAIL MARKERS

The power that you have depends entirely on your spiritual position. Without Christ, the Christian life is beyond your power. But when you come to Christ in faith, He gives you His Spirit. And that puts you in an entirely different position.

You will face many struggles, and you will have many defeats as well as victories. But you are not alone in this battle. The Spirit of God is within you, and He makes the Christian life possible. The Christian life is all about the proper application of overwhelming force. Never say you are helpless when the Spirit of God lives in you.

1. Is there an area of your life in which you have often felt defeated?

2. How do you think the Holy Spirit might be able to help you in that area?

3. Do you identify most with Hostile, Helpless, or Hopeful? Why?

4. What difference do you think it would make to your daily life if you knew that an "overwhelming force" was helping you?

5. Do you think you have the ability to live the Christian life? Why or why not? Do you have the desire?

To memorize:

If you live according to the flesh you will die, but if by the Spirit you put to death the deeds of the body, you will live. For all who are led by the Spirit of God are sons of God. (Romans 8:13–14)

God's great purpose is to display His glory by reconciling people to Himself and to each other. The church is central to this purpose. When we believe in Christ, we become part of His church that comprises all believers in every time and place. And God's purpose is fulfilled when we worship and serve Him in a local congregation. Christ loves the church, and if we are His friends, we will love her too.

47

CHURCH

EPHESIANS 3

What is the first thing that comes to your mind when you hear the word *church*? Stained glass windows? Organ music? Drums and guitars? Robes? Candles? Traditions? Hypocrisy? Christmas? Appeals for money?

I sometimes talk to people who are drawn to Jesus Christ but don't think much of the church. We live in a highly individualistic society, and it is not always easy to see where the church fits in. What is the point of the church?

Some people say that the church exists for worship, but you can worship on your own or with a few friends. Others say that the church exists for evangelism. But evangelism flows out of relationships, so if you bear witness to Christ where He has placed you, why do you need the church? Others believe that we need the church for fellowship. But if you have deep relationships with a small group of friends, you will find a level of personal fellowship that you are unlikely to find in a larger congregation. So why do we need the church?

The problem goes deeper than the question of relevance. Some people say that their faith has been wounded by the church. A pastor or priest failed them, a congregation divided, or someone offended them, and it has been a barrier ever since.

It is important to face these questions honestly. The New Testament does. The apostles never suggested that the early churches were little colonies of heaven on earth. The New Testament letters speak about problems of sexual misconduct, legal wrangling, doctrinal errors, division over personalities, exaggerated claims about spiritual experiences, selfishness, lack of compassion, legalism, authoritarianism, pride, manipulative leaders, abuses of power, and misappropriation of funds. The list is depressing, but the honesty is refreshing.

Churches are communities of sinners in the process of being restored. And not everyone who claims that Jesus is their Lord will enter the kingdom of heaven. On the last day some preachers, ministry leaders, and church members will find themselves outside of God's kingdom. Christ will say to them, "I never knew you" (Matthew 7:23).

God's Eternal Purpose

Along with the rigorous honesty that confesses and addresses our sins, the Scriptures give us a vision of the church that we desperately need to recover. God's purpose is "that through the church the manifold wisdom of God might now be made known to the rulers and authorities in the heavenly places" (Ephesians 3:10).

God's purpose has always been to display His wisdom to a vast audience in heaven, and the way He does this is through the church.

God is drawing people from every nation of the world to Jesus, and gathering them into a new community—the church—that crosses the barriers of race, language, and culture. In God's new community, "there is neither Jew nor Greek, there is neither slave nor free, there is no male and female, for you are all one in Christ Jesus" (Galatians 3:28).

Think about it! Jew and Gentile, young and old, men and women, rich and poor, all brought together in a new community. The world dreams of this. In Christ, we have a profound unity that transcends everything that makes us different.

Let's get specific. A Christian professor of astrophysics has more in common with an illiterate believer than with a fellow academic who does not know the Lord. A multimillionaire who knows Christ has more in common with the poorest believer than with friends in the yachting club who know nothing of Christ. A refined Christian woman who enjoys classical music has more in common with a high school rapper who loves Jesus than she does with her friends at the symphony who have never seen their need of a Savior!

The distinctions of education, income, and culture exist only for a time. But the unity of God's people is eternal, and angels gasp when they see God's wisdom on display through the church (Ephesians 3:10).

What Is the Church?

What exactly is the church? If three Christians meet at a bus stop every morning, are they a church? What if they talk about the Bible at Starbucks? Is your small group a church? Is a Christian family a church? And if not, why not?

A growing number of Christians have the idea that "church" is simply the plural of "Christian," and that any group of Christians meeting at any time or place is a church. Are they right?

What did Jesus mean when He spoke about the church? Jesus used the word "church" twice and what He said defines the church for us. The first time was when Peter confessed that Jesus is the Christ. Jesus said to him: "I tell you, you are Peter, and on this rock I will build my church, and the gates of hell shall not prevail against it" (Matthew 16:18).

Jesus was not speaking here about a local church or a denomination, but about all believers at every time and in every place. There is one church, composed of all believers, and Christ builds it.

The "gates of hell shall not prevail against" this church (16:18). You can't say that about any local church or denomination. All over the world there are sad stories of churches and denominations that have lost their way and closed. But the church that Jesus is building is alive and well. It encompasses all believers at every time and in every place.

The second time Jesus spoke about the church, He said, "If your brother sins against you, go and tell him his fault, between you and him alone. . . . But if he does not listen, take one or two others along with you. . . . If he refuses to listen to them, tell it to the church" (Matthew 18:15–17).

The word "church" here clearly has a different meaning. It cannot mean: "Tell it to all believers in every time and place." No one could do that. Jesus was clearly speaking here about a local congregation of believers.

So, our Lord used the word *church* in two ways: First, to describe all believers in every time and place. Second, to describe a local congregation of believers.

The church is not a self-selecting group of people. It's never just you, me, and a few friends chosen by us. Christ builds His church as He brings people to faith in Himself and gathers them together in local congregations.

Cinderella Will Go to the Ball

There is a big difference between what the church is now and what the church will one day be: "Christ loved the church and gave himself up for her, that he might sanctify her, having cleansed her by the washing of water with the word, so that he might present the church to himself in splendor, without spot or wrinkle or any such thing, that she might be holy and without blemish" (Ephesians 5:25–27).

Once upon a time, there was a girl who had a wicked stepmother and two cruel stepsisters. She was made to work in the kitchen and used to sit in her ragged clothes among the cinders, so they called her Cinderella.

One day the king invited all the maidens in the land to a grand ball in his palace. He wanted his son, the prince, to fall in love and to marry. The stepsisters were taken to the ball, but Cinderella had no dress to wear—and she was left at home.

Then the fairy godmother touched her with the wand, and Cinderella's rags were turned into a beautiful dress—but only until midnight.

When Cinderella arrived at the ball, she captivated the prince's heart. And they danced until midnight, when she had to leave. But as Cinderella ran from the ballroom, one of her glass slippers fell off.

The prince was determined to find the woman he loved. He ordered that the slipper be tried on the foot of every maiden in the land, and that the one to whom it belonged should be brought to the palace.

Picture Cinderella sitting at home. She is dressed in rags, despised by the stepsisters and oppressed by the wicked stepmother. But her destiny is a life of love and joy in the palace.

That's a wonderful picture of the church. She sometimes looks a bit ragged. Some people despise her and count her as of little value. There are parts of the world where a wicked stepmother persecutes her and imprisons her. But Christ loves the church, and He will bring her home.

When Christ presents the church to Himself, we will not be in rags and tatters. The church will be "without spot or wrinkle or any such thing . . . holy and without blemish" (Ephesians 5:27). The church will be radiant. She will be glorious. And she will share Christ's joy forever.

Always remember that *the church* is the bride that Christ will present to Himself. Christian schools, seminaries, radio ministries, missionary societies, and evangelistic organizations are like bridesmaids who assist the bride as she gets ready for the bridegroom. The bride needs her bridesmaids, but it's a great mistake to make more of the bridesmaids than you do of the bride.

At the end of the Bible, John the apostle hears the voice of a great multitude crying out from heaven, "Hallelujah! For the Lord our God the Almighty reigns. Let us rejoice and exult and give him the glory, for the marriage of the Lamb has come, and his Bride has made herself ready. . . . Blessed are those who are invited to the marriage supper of the Lamb" (Revelation 19:6–9).

TRAIL MARKERS

The church is a work in progress. She is not yet all that God calls her to be, and she is not yet what one day she will be. But the church is the bride of Christ. He laid down His life for her, and she is central to the purpose of God.

The Heidelberg Catechism answers the question: "What do you believe about the church?" with these words: "I believe that the Son of God, through His Spirit and Word, out of the entire human race, from the beginning of the world to its end, gathers, protects, and preserves for Himself, a community chosen for eternal life and united in true faith. And of this community I am and always will be a living member." I cannot conceive of a greater privilege than that.

1. What are some of the first things that come to your mind when you think of the church?

2. According to the Bible, what is God doing through the church?

3. In your own words, what are the two different ways Jesus used the word *church*?

4. What is most striking to you about the Cinderella illustration?

5. Where would you put yourself on a scale of 1 (I want nothing to do with the church); 5 (I am neutral toward the church); to 10 (I love the church)? Why?

To memorize:

> Christ loved the church and gave himself up for her, that he might sanctify her, having cleansed her by the washing of water with the word, so that he might present the church to himself in splendor, without spot or wrinkle or any such thing, that she might be holy and without blemish. (Ephesians 5:25–27)

When you became a Christian, four things happened. First, you were brought into a new relationship with God in which your sins were forgiven and your condemnation was removed. Second, you became a new creation as God's Holy Spirit invaded your life. Third, being a child of God, you became part of His family, the church. And fourth, you provoked the attention of an enemy, whose set purpose is to oppose and destroy the work of God. So to become a Christian is to engage in a battle.

48

BATTLE

EPHESIANS 6

The more you progress in the Christian life, the harder your battles will be. The more you resist the enemy, the more he will throw at you. So, if your battles are becoming more intense, it may be a sign that you are making progress.

Who are we fighting against?

Paul says, "We do not wrestle against flesh and blood" (Ephesians 6:12). There may be people who bring pain in your life, but they are not the enemy. You may have suffered wounds, defeats, or injustice, but they are not your primary battle. Your battle is with the unseen enemy who wants to destroy you.

Your first objective is to stand against this enemy. Paul uses the word *stand* four times:

> Put on the whole armor of God, that you may be able to *stand* against the schemes of the devil. (Ephesians 6:11)

> Take up the whole armor of God, that you may be able to *withstand* in the evil day, and having done all, to *stand* firm. (6:13)

> *Stand* therefore, having fastened on the belt of truth. (6:14)

When the day of evil comes—when the battle is most intense—God calls you to one thing: It is not to have the most marvelous testimony or to make phenomenal progress. It is simply that when you face the heat of the battle at its most intense, you will stand.

So make this your goal: aim simply to maintain your position and stand your ground. Be steadfast, unmovable. And do not quit!

How are we to stand in the battle? We must put on the whole armor of God (6:11).

1. Stand in Truth

Stand therefore, having fastened on the belt of truth. (Ephesians 6:14)

> Paul is not talking about the truth of the Bible here. That comes later, when he speaks about "the sword of the Spirit, which is the word of God" (6:17). Here he is speaking about candor, honesty, facing the reality or the truth of the situation you are in. The belt of truth is what David spoke about when he said, "Behold, you delight in truth in the inward being" (Psalm 51:6).

When you find yourself in the heat of battle, your starting point must always be to establish what is true. God will bring the truth to your attention through the Scriptures, so use the Bible as a mirror. Learn to listen to close friends and wise counselors who will speak the truth into your life. Allow those who know your situation to contribute what is true that you may have missed.

If you want to help someone in the heat of battle, this is where you must begin. What is the truth of this situation? What is the reality here? What you can contribute may often be something that you can see, which the person has not yet been able to perceive.

Wise counsel begins with a proper understanding of the truth of a situation, which is why James says that we must be quick to listen and "slow to speak" (James 1:19).

We need to put on the belt of truth because the fastest way to become an ineffective Christian is to live in the shallowness of an unexamined life.

2. Stand in Righteousness

Stand therefore, having fastened on the belt of truth, and having put on the breastplate of righteousness. (Ephesians 6:14)

The breastplate of righteousness does not refer to the righteousness of Christ that is counted as ours when we come to Him in faith. Paul is writing to those who are in Christ. His righteousness is already theirs. When the righteousness of Christ is counted as yours and you are clothed with it, you do not have to put it on every day.

What Paul speaks of here is our daily choice to do what is right. The only way to stand in the battle is to determine what is right before God and to do it—irrespective of the cost.

The belt of truth and the breastplate of righteousness are at the top of the list because the first questions to ask in any conflict are "What is true?" and "What is right?" A father tells his daughter that she must be home by midnight. When she arrives at 2:00 a.m., he is ready to unload. But first he must find out what is true. It may be that she has flouted his curfew, but it could also be that her car has broken down. If he takes time to discover what is true, he will be able to discern what is right. That principle holds true in any situation of conflict.

3. *Stand in the Gospel*

As shoes for your feet, having put on the readiness given by the gospel of peace. (Ephesians 6:15)

Notice that the gospel is described as the gospel of peace. Here's how you can endure when everything is raging around you: The good news of Jesus is that He has made peace by shedding His blood on the cross; that in Him, you have peace with God, even though your sins are many and your life is far from what you would want it to be. So stand firm in the knowledge that through Christ you have peace with God.

When you have this peace, you will want to share it with others. Shoes are for movement and putting on these shoes means that you become intentional about sharing the gospel with others.

4. *Stand in Faith*

In all circumstances take up the shield of faith, with which you can extinguish all the flaming darts of the evil one. (Ephesians 6:16)

Have you ever had the disturbing experience of destructive thoughts, hate-filled thoughts, or even blasphemous thoughts coming into your mind? When they come, you feel ashamed, and you say, "I cannot believe that I have been thinking these things."

In a very real sense, it is not you who is thinking these things. These are the flaming darts of the evil one. They come from outside, not from within, and you know that these thoughts come from outside because you hate them when they come.

How are you to stand against these darts? Take up the shield of faith. Faith believes that God is for you and that He is greater than all that is arrayed against you.

Roman soldiers protected themselves with two different shields. A small, round shield worn on the forearm was used in hand-to-hand combat, but it did not offer protection against a volley of flaming arrows.

The picture here is of a larger, rectangular shield, four feet high and two feet wide, like a police riot shield. The Romans developed the idea of a phalanx, in which a small group of soldiers would stand together, arranging their shields to form a protective cover around the whole group, rather like the shell of a tortoise.

Satan wants you isolated in the battle. He would love to have you fighting alone against attacks in your mind and in your home that nobody else knows about. But God never intended you to fight alone, so share your struggle with someone you trust who will stand with you.

Take the shield of faith and bind yourself together with other believers under its protective cover.

5. *Stand in Hope*

And take the helmet of salvation. (Ephesians 6:17)

If you are to sustain a lifetime of useful service to Jesus Christ, you will need to overcome discouragement. There will be times when the results of your work will be disappointing. Prayers won't seem to be answered as you hoped, and you will find yourself facing problems to which there is no obvious answer. Tiredness will cloud your judgment, and you may begin to despair.

The Bible speaks about salvation in the past, present, and future tense. We have been saved from the penalty of sin. We are being saved from the power of sin. We will be saved from the presence of sin. And when Paul writes about the helmet of salvation, he is referring to the hope of future salvation (1 Thessalonians 5:8).

Paul placed his sufferings alongside the glory that would ultimately be revealed, and concluded that it was well worth the cost of staying in the battle. "For this light momentary affliction is preparing for us an eternal weight of glory beyond all comparison, as we look not to the things that are seen but to the things that are unseen. For the things that are seen are transient, but the things that are unseen are eternal" (2 Corinthians 4:17–18).

If you are tired of the battle, keep your eyes focused on the hope that lies ahead of you.

6. Stand in the Word of God

Take the helmet of salvation, and the sword of the Spirit, which is the word of God. (Ephesians 6:17)

The Bible is described here as the sword of the Spirit. In other words, the Scripture is the means that the Holy Spirit uses to accomplish His work. Drip feed God's Word into your life, and in the power of the Holy Spirit, you will be able to stand your ground.

And remember that the armor you wear is the armor *of God*. He gives this armor to you. The truth that holds you is the truth that He reveals. The righteousness that covers you is the righteousness He gives. The gospel on which you stand is His gospel. The faith that shields you is confidence in Him. The hope that sustains you is the anticipation of His deliverance. The strength that He gives you comes through the power of His Word.

Thank God there is more here than a call to greater effort. The Lord is with you in the battle. You can prevail because your Savior is with you! So, "be strong in the Lord and in the strength of his might" (Ephesians 6:10).

TRAIL MARKERS

How do you stand when the battle is raging all around you? Face the truth. Do what is right. Rest in the peace of the gospel. Exercise faith alongside other believers. Anticipate the joy of your future deliverance. Move forward in the power of the Spirit, mediated through the Word of God.

1. Where is the battle most intense for you right now?

2. Who are the people who have stood with you in the battles of your life? How have they helped you?

3. What one step could you take in order to stand more firmly in your battle?

4. "The first questions to ask in any conflict are 'What is true?' and 'What is right?'" How might this help you in a conflict you are facing?

5. What in this chapter has encouraged you to keep fighting your battle?

To memorize:

Finally, be strong in the Lord and in the strength of his might. Put on the whole armor of God, that you may be able to stand against the schemes of the devil. (Ephesians 6:10–11)

The work of Jesus for us is completed, continuing, and still to come. The completed work of Jesus is that He laid down His life as a sacrifice for our sins. He did this "once for all" (Hebrews 7:27). The coming work of Jesus revolves around His glorious return. In this session we will explore the continuing work of Jesus.

49

INTERCESSION

HEBREWS 7

Motherhood involves both an initial and painful event in which a woman gives birth to a child and an ongoing process in which she cares for the child.

If you have given birth, you know what this is like. After hours of exhausting labor, the nurse thrusts a tiny bundle of life into your arms and says, "This little one needs feeding!" The care of a child involves both the initial and painful event of the physical birth and the ongoing nurture of supplying the child's needs. The labor and delivery has been completed upon the birth, but childcare is also a continuing work, and goes on far longer than the process of the physical birth. As many have said, a mother's work is never done!

The ministry of Jesus also involves both a completed act and a continuing work. The completed act was the painful event in which He offered Himself as the sacrifice for our sins when He suffered and died on the cross.

The continuing work is the ministry in which He applies to us what He has accomplished on the cross and supplies all that we need to bring us safely home to heaven. The continuing work is Christ's ministry of care, protection, and nurture that the Bible calls His intercession.

Many Priests, Many Sacrifices

The Bible speaks of Jesus as our "great high priest" (Hebrews 4:14). Aaron was the first high priest, and when he was about to die, he climbed the mountain of Hor with his brother, Moses, and his son Eleazer. Moses removed Aaron's robes and put them on his son, indicating that Eleazer would assume the role of high priest (Numbers 20:22–29).

Throughout the Old Testament, there was one high priest after another. They all served for a time, but death prevented them from continuing in office (Hebrews 7:23). Sooner or later, they all had to take off the robes.

There were also many sacrifices in the Old Testament. Hebrews tells us that the Old Testament priests had to "offer sacrifices daily," first for their own sins, and then for the sins of others (7:27). Every time a new sin was committed, there had to be a new sacrifice. So, the priest's work was never done.

This point was illustrated by the design of the tabernacle where the priests exercised their ministry. In the first room there was a lamp, a table, and bread, but no chair (Hebrews 9:2). The priests could never sit down because their work was never done. There was always another sin to be dealt with, another sacrifice to be offered.

That was the story all the way through the Old Testament—many priests and many sacrifices. Sin was a problem that always needed to be dealt with, and making sacrifices was a job never done.

One Priest, One Sacrifice

But now God has given us one High Priest who lives forever. Jesus "holds his priesthood permanently, because he continues forever" (Hebrews 7:24).

Jesus went through death and triumphed over it. He lives in the power of an endless life. There will never be a time when the high priest's robes are taken from Jesus! He is our High Priest forever.

Jesus is unlike any other high priest: "He has no need, like those high priests, to offer sacrifices daily, first for his own sins and then for those of the people, since he did this once for all when he offered up himself" (7:27).

In contrast to the Old Testament priests, whose work was never done, Jesus offered Himself once for all on the cross, and when He ascended into heaven, He sat down. "We have such a high priest, one who is seated at the right hand of the throne of the Majesty in heaven" (Hebrews 8:1).

Jesus is seated because His work of offering Himself as the sacrifice for sin is done: "It is finished" (John 19:30). He made full atonement for our sin. No other sacrifice for sin will ever be needed.

Think of your sins as being like large rocks that you carry in a bag on your back. In the Old Testament, every time you felt the weight of a rock in your bag, you would go to the priest, who offered a sacrifice for that particular sin. Every time you committed another sin, you had to go back to the priest, and you needed another sacrifice.

The Old Testament priests took rocks out of the bag. Jesus takes the bag off your back! He deals with all your sin by separating it from you. He bore our sins on the cross and carried them for us (1 Peter 2:24).

The Bible tells us that if we claim to be without sin, we are deceiving ourselves (1 John 1:8). Your bag is never free from rocks, and God calls you to deal with the sin in your life. But your salvation does not depend on you merely emptying the bag. It depends on Christ removing the bag from your back.

Christians sometimes live as if we were still in the Old Testament era. When we sin, we feel as if we come under condemnation. But Jesus has dealt with our sins—past, present, and future—by nailing them to the cross (Colossians 2:14).

The reason there is no condemnation for you is not that there are no rocks in your bag, but that, in Christ Jesus, the bag itself has been lifted from your back. Jesus took it from you. He dealt with it fully and finally on the cross.

Jesus Lives to Save You

How would you complete this sentence: Jesus is able to save those who draw near to God through Him, because ________________________________?

If you said, "Because He died on the cross for our sins," you would be right. But Hebrews says something else. Jesus "is able to save to the uttermost those who draw near to God through him, since he always lives to make intercession for them" (Hebrews 7:25).

Intercession is the continuing ministry of Jesus. What Jesus is doing now is saving those who draw near to God through Him. He is doing everything that is needed to bring you through whatever you will face until you arrive safely in His presence in heaven.

Suppose that after Jesus died on the cross and rose from the dead, He retired in heaven and simply watched to see how we would get on. If He had only opened a way of salvation, and then left it up to us to pursue it, how many people would make it to heaven? None! Salvation would remain a theoretical possibility, and no one would actually be saved.

But Jesus lives to intercede for us, and when you draw near to God through faith in Him, Jesus will bestow on you everything He purchased through the shedding of His blood on the cross. Forgiveness, justification, reconciliation with God, adoption into His family, a new heart, the gift of His Holy Spirit—every blessing you enjoy and every gift of grace you receive comes through the intercessory ministry of the Lord Jesus Christ.

Jesus always lives to intercede for us. He never takes a day off! He is never distracted by something else! The continuing ministry of Jesus is to supply everything we need, and to make sure all His children are brought safely home. Jesus died to save you, He lives to keep you, and He will never let you go.

What Makes the Christian Life Possible

Throughout your Christian life, you will face all kinds of trials, challenges, temptations, sorrows, and conflicts. How will your faith survive? Christ always lives to make intercession for you. He brings your needs to the Father, so that everything you need will be supplied.

There is a beautiful illustration of this in the Gospels. Jesus knew that Peter would come under great pressure and told him, "Before the rooster crows, you will deny me three times" (Matthew 26:34).

Peter felt sure that he was up to the challenge of following Jesus, but Jesus knew that Peter would fail. He said to Peter, "Satan demanded to have you, that he might sift you like wheat, but I have prayed for you that your faith may not fail" (Luke 22:31–32).

Peter failed big time when he denied Jesus, and that might have been the end of his story. But Jesus prayed that his faith would not fail. Jesus' prayers were answered and Peter was restored.

What Jesus did for Peter is a wonderful picture of what He continues to do for us. Christ intercedes for you. This does not mean that Jesus is on His knees in heaven agonizing in prayer as He did in the garden of Gethsemane. No, He is seated at the right hand of the Father, and what He asks, the Father gives.

The intercession of Jesus is what makes the Christian life possible. Christ speaks with authority in the presence of the Father, and His Word releases the resources of heaven for the pressures and temptations you are facing today.

Christ gives strength to match the particular burdens you carry in any season or circumstance of your life. When He doubles your load, He can also double your strength.

Help When You Pray

Knowing that Jesus intercedes for you will give you a new incentive to pray. When we feel that our prayers are feeble and that our faith is weak, we may prefer to have a pastor or priest pray for us than to pray ourselves. But what we are being told here is that we already have a priest who prays for us.

Jesus is your great High Priest and He intercedes for you. He stands in the gap between you and the Father, and He brings your stumbling requests to the Father on your behalf. Every time you pray, Jesus is praying with you and for you.

Jesus said, "Whatever you ask of the Father in my name, he will give it to you" (John 16:23). To ask in Christ's name means to ask according to His will. The promise is that every time you pray something that aligns with the will of Jesus, He presents your request to the Father. With Christ as your intercessor, nothing you ask in His name will be denied to you, because nothing that He asks of the Father will ever be denied to Him.

TRAIL MARKERS

Jesus Christ has completed the work of offering Himself as the sacrifice for our sins. He now engages in His continuing work for us in heaven. He saves us, applying what He accomplished on the cross. He intercedes for us, releasing all that we need for the Christian life. And He presents our prayers to the Father, giving us confidence that our prayers will be heard and answered.

1. Which part of Jesus' work as our High Priest is most encouraging to you?

2. What difference would it make if Jesus removed the rocks of sin from your bag or if He removed the whole bag from your back?

3. Reflect on your own journey. What means did Jesus use to bring you to faith?

4. Where in your life this week do you need to remember that Jesus is praying for you?

5. Where do you feel that your prayers are weak and/or feeble? How will what you have learned about the intercession of Jesus help you?

To memorize:

> He is able to save to the uttermost those who draw near to God through him, since he always lives to make intercession for them. (Hebrews 7:25)

The whole Bible is one story. It begins in a garden, ends in a city, and all the way through it points to Jesus Christ. In Genesis, one couple enjoyed the blessing of God, but through sin they were plunged into a world scarred by pain, sorrow, and death. In Revelation, a vast company of people are brought into a world of joy and peace, where sin and death shall be no more, and God Himself will wipe all tears from our eyes.

50

CITY

REVELATION 22

The Bible begins with God creating the heavens and the earth. It ends with God creating a new heaven and a new earth, where everything Adam lost will be restored and much more besides.

> *Then I saw a new heaven and a new earth, for the first heaven and the first earth had passed away.* (Revelation 21:1)

John saw a "new earth." "New" means that it will be wonderfully different; "earth" means that it will be strangely familiar. The destiny of the Christian believer is not a dreamlike existence in an imaginary world. God will re-create, replenish, and renew this planet. "The creation itself will be set free from its bondage to corruption and obtain the freedom of the glory of the children of God" (Romans 8:21).

The joys of the new heaven and earth are beyond anything that we can imagine, but God uses two pictures to give us a taste of what lies ahead. They are the city and the garden.

The City

At this point in John's vision, history as we know it has been brought to a close. New York, London, Jerusalem, Beijing, and Moscow are all gone! The earth has been laid bare in the fervent heat of God's judgment (2 Peter 3:10).

But now John sees a new city coming down from heaven, and immediately he recognizes its skyline: "I saw the holy city, new Jerusalem, coming down out of heaven from God" (Revelation 21:2). Jerusalem is full of significance in the Bible story. This was the place where God came down to meet with His people when the cloud of His presence filled the temple.

The new Jerusalem was vast! An angel "measured the city with his rod, 12,000 stadia" (21:16). That's about 1,400 miles! Remember that the book of Revelation is using pictures to help us grasp something of the glory that lies ahead. God's redeemed people are more than anyone could number (Revelation 7:9), and God is telling us that He has a place for every one of us.

The measurements of the city are given in three dimensions. "Its length and width and height are equal" (Revelation 21:16). In other words, it is a perfect cube. John would have seen the significance of this immediately. The Most Holy Place in the temple, where God met with His people, was also a perfect cube—thirty feet long, thirty feet wide, and thirty feet high (1 Kings 6:20).

The old Jerusalem *had* a holy place. The new Jerusalem *is* a holy place. In the old Jerusalem, one little room was filled with God's glory. In the new Jerusalem, the whole city will be filled with His glory. In the old Jerusalem, only one person could enter the presence of God. In the new Jerusalem, all God's people will enjoy Him forever.

God knew what He was doing when He created a world in which we would rebel and find ourselves hopelessly lost. A redeemed creation will display His glory infinitely more than an innocent one ever could. In the new creation, reflections of God's glory will burst out everywhere—in us and all around us.

People who have been forgiven much will love much, and God's redeemed children will sing, "Worthy is the lamb who was slain" (Revelation 5:12). "Worthy are you . . . for you were slain, and by your blood you ransomed people for God, from every tribe and language and people and nation" (Revelation 5:9).

The Garden

Up to this point in the vision, John has viewed the new Jerusalem from the outside. But now, he is invited to come inside. As he enters, the picture changes, and no doubt to his astonishment, John sees a beautiful garden: "The angel showed me the river of the water of life . . . also, on either side of the river, the tree of life with its twelve kinds of fruit, yielding its fruit each month" (Revelation 22:1–2).

The Bible story began in a garden, where God blessed Adam and Eve with four marvelous gifts: a home, work, relationship, and God's visible presence. Each of these gifts was marred when sin came into the world. Adam and Eve were driven out from the garden and had to make their home in a world scarred by sin, pain, and death. Work that had been blessed was marked by frustration. The world's first family was divided, and Adam and Eve had to walk with God by faith, rather than sight.

Paradise was lost when sin came into the world. But at the end of the Bible story, the gifts that were lost are not only are restored, they are surpassed in God's new garden city.

Better Home

> On either side of the river, *the tree of life* with its twelve kinds of fruit, yielding its fruit each month. The leaves of the tree were for the healing of the nations. (Revelation 22:2)

One striking difference between the old Eden and the new garden is that there is no tree of the knowledge of good and evil in God's new garden city. Evil cannot be known there. This garden is free not only from its presence but even from its possibility.

In the old Eden, the man and the woman were not permitted to eat from the tree of life. But now they have free access, and the tree bears twelve different crops of fruit. The variety of fruit speaks of the richness of life continually replenished in the presence of God. Eternity will never be dull.

The greatest joys of life in this world are like pointers to the greater delights of God's new creation. The pleasures of God's new garden city will surpass anything Adam knew in the garden of Eden. We will savor fruits that Adam never tasted and enjoy pleasures Eve never knew.

Better Work

> No longer will there be anything a ccursed, but the throne of God and of the Lamb will be in it, and his *servants* will *worship* him. (Revelation 22:3)

> The Lord God will be their light, and they will *reign* forever and ever. (Revelation 22:5)

In the new creation, you will serve, you will worship, and you will reign. In Eden, Adam served by working and keeping the garden. His calling was to exercise dominion over all that God had made (Genesis 1:26). He was to fill the earth and subdue it (Genesis 1:28). When the serpent came, Adam did not maintain his rule. But now, God's people are restored to a position of serving and reigning.

When God speaks about us reigning, He is telling us that life will be ordered and brought under your control. Your work will be free from frustration. You will no longer be subject to the tyranny of time, tedious tasks, contentious colleagues, or meddling managers. You will no longer be swept away by unpredictable tides of emotion or impulses of the will. And you will no longer be subject to danger or death.

Better Company

> It had a great, high wall, with *twelve gates*, and at the gates *twelve angels*, and on the gates the names of the twelve tribes of the sons of Israel were inscribed — on the east three gates, on the north three gates, on the south three gates, and on the west three gates. (Revelation 21:12–13)

The old Eden was enjoyed by just one man and one woman, but now a vast crowd is streaming in through the gates. God has redeemed these people out of the pain of human history, and He has brought them into greater joy than they had ever known.

John sees twelve entrances to the new garden city. People are coming into the city from every direction—China in the East, Russia in the North, Africa in the South, and America in the West. Every nation is represented in God's redeemed and reconciled new community.

An angel stands at each gate in John's vision, and all the gates are open (Revelation 21:12, 25). At the beginning of the Bible story, the cherubim guarded the entrance to the tree of life with a flaming sword. But now, Christ has broken the sword of judgment, and the angels are at the gates to welcome all who belong to Him.

Better Knowledge of the Lord

And I heard a loud voice from the throne saying, "Behold, the dwelling place of God is with man. He will dwell with them, and they will be his people, and God himself will be with them as their God." (Revelation 21:3)

God's presence in this garden city is its greatest blessing. In the garden of Eden, God would come down and make Himself known at certain times. He walked with the man and the woman in the cool of the day. God came into the garden as a visitor. He did not impose Himself on the man and the woman, but gave them the opportunity to choose a relationship with Him. So He came and walked with them, cultivating that relationship.

But now God has gathered a vast community of people whose minds have been illuminated by His truth and whose hearts have been melted at the cross of Jesus. Their wills have been directed by the power of the Holy Spirit, and they have come to love God freely. So God is no longer a visitor. God's throne comes down into the garden city so that His people may live in His presence and enjoy Him forever. The Lord announces this with a note of triumph: "Behold, the dwelling place of God is with man" (Revelation 21:3).

TRAIL MARKERS

When you don't feel at home, remember that a day is coming when you will be more at home than you have ever felt at any time or place in this world.

When you find your work frustrating, remember that a day is coming when you will find joy and fulfillment in all that God gives you to do.

When you experience the joy of love, remember that this is a small taste of what you will experience in the presence of the Lord.

When you have questions or struggle with your faith, remember that one day you will see God's face. And when you see Him, you will be like Him.

 1. How has this glimpse of the city changed your thinking about the new heaven and new earth?

 2. Which of the four joys of the garden city are most attractive to you right now? Why?

 3. How does knowing about God's new creation help you live today?

 4. Do you think God wants *you* to enjoy the new heaven and earth that He has prepared? Why or why not?

 5. Looking back on your journey through the Bible story, what has been most helpful to you?

To memorize:

> "Behold, the dwelling place of God is with man. He will dwell with them, and they will be his people, and God himself will be with them as their God. He will wipe away every tear from their eyes, and death shall be no more, neither shall there be mourning, nor crying, nor pain anymore, for the former things have passed away." And he who was seated on the throne said, "Behold, I am making all things new." (Revelation 21:3–5)

Congratulations! You've completed *the Hike.*

So where do you go from here? Keep feeding on Christ through His Word.

Jesus said, "Whoever feeds on me . . . will live because of me" (John 6:57). Spiritual life is sustained as we draw strength, faith, hope, love, peace, and joy from Jesus. And we do this as Jesus feeds us through His Word.

Feeding is more than reading. It involves taking something good into yourself and absorbing it, so that it becomes part of you and is life-giving to you. The Bible is food—milk, meat, and bread that sustain your life. As you eat and are nourished, you will develop an appetite for more of the Word of God.

Years ago, my pastor taught me to feed on Christ through the Word by reading a passage of the Bible and identifying a verse to carry with me throughout the day. Over the years, I have found this really helpful.

When you read a passage of the Bible, try to find a verse that grabs your attention, and camp on it for a while. Your aim will be to turn that one verse into prayer and carry it with you for yourself and for others.

When you have found your verse, ask some questions:

What does this say? Is there a promise to believe, a command to obey, a warning to heed, an example to follow? What do I learn here about God, about myself, about God's people, and about the world? How does this lead me to Jesus?

Remember, as you read, that Scripture is the Word of God. What the Bible says, God says, so when you open the Bible, you hear the voice of God. And since God never changes, what He has said in the Bible, rightly understood and applied, is what He says to you today.

As you spend time in God's Word, your faith in Christ will be stronger, your love for Christ will be deeper, and your hope in Christ will shine brighter.

ACKNOWLEDGMENTS

The sharp eyes, skilled hands, and wise counsel of many people have contributed greatly to this book.

I would like to thank my friend and colleague Tim Augustyn who labored with me in editing the manuscript. Working with Tim is truly a joy for me.

I am grateful for our Open the Bible team. John Aiello, John Martin, Stephanie Close, and Gina O'Brien have all contributed in significant ways to this project.

It has been a joy to work with the team at Moody Publishers. Drew Dyck, Pam Pugh, Tammy Adelhardt, and Brittany Schrock have all done a fine job in overseeing, editing, typesetting, proofreading, and cover design.

Andrew Wolgemuth has guided this project from the beginning, and I am grateful for his wise counsel.

And heartfelt thanks to my wife, Karen, whose love and partnership in ministry are incomparable gifts to me.

Finally, I am grateful to you for the time you have invested in reading this book. May its fruit be a stronger faith in Christ, a deeper love for Christ, and a brighter hope in Christ as you press forward in following and serving Him.